Growing
Your Church
Through
Evangelism
and Outreach

Growing
Your Church
Through
Evangelism
and Outreach

MOORINGS
Nashville, Tennessee
A Division of The Ballantine Publishing Group,
Random House, Inc.

Library of Christian Leadership
GROWING YOUR CHURCH THROUGH EVANGELISM AND OUT-
REACH

Copyright © 1996 by Christianity Today, Inc./*Leadership*

All rights reserved under International and Pan-American Copyright Conventions. Published in the United States by Moorings, a division of the Ballantine Publishing Group, Random House, Inc., New York, and simultaneously in Canada by Random House of Canada Limited, Toronto.

The material in this book was previously published in *Leadership*, by Christianity Today, Inc.

Scripture taken from the HOLY BIBLE, NEW INTERNATIONAL VERSION®. NIV®. Copyright © 1973, 1978, 1984 by International Bible Society. Used by permission of Zondervan Publishing House. All rights reserved.

Library of Congress Cataloging-in-Publication Data

Growing your church through evangelism and outreach : 30 strategies to
    transform your ministry / Marshall Shelley, general editor.
        p.   cm. — (Library of Christian leadership)
        ISBN 0-345-39598-0
        1. Church growth.   2. Evangelistic work.   I. Shelley, Marshall.
    II. Series.
    BV652.25.G735   1996
    254'.5—dc20   95-51544
                                                                        CIP

First Edition: February 1996

10   9   8   7   6   5   4   3   2   1

Contents

Introduction

As with most of church ministry, leading your church to reach out is more art than science.

—David L. Goetz

Finding Christians who think evangelism and outreach are important is about as hard as finding a lawyer in Washington, D.C. The real trick is trying to locate someone who *isn't* one. In an evangelism survey conducted by *Leadership* and Church Growth Institute of Lynchburg, Virginia, 97 percent of laypeople indicated that *every Christian has the responsibility to share his/her faith with the lost.*

And who can disagree?

Fresh out of seminary, I would have quickly concurred: *Yes, evangelism is important, and lay leaders should be doing more of it. Don't they care about the Great Commission?*

I lost my smugness, though, when I met Craig. I don't remember how we met. Or how we ended up as roommates. But he and I wound up renting a dream home in the foothills west of Denver for next to nothing. The house had been on the market for more than a year, and the out-of-town owner was relieved to rent it to two guys he could trust. We lived in the lap of luxury for three hundred dollars a month.

It must have seemed odd: a twenty-something Protestant pastor and a middle-aged agnostic Catholic as roommates. I was single, and Craig was divorced. But Craig didn't seem to mind, and the early lesson I learned was that non-Christians make good friends, even for pastors.

I'm not evangelistically gifted, so I felt uncomfortable trying to convert every conversation into a spiritual moment. But I didn't have to. The subject of Christianity surfaced naturally. In 1990, I returned home after serving at a Christmas Eve service. I felt a little lonely; I had no family in the area. While church attenders went home to unwrap presents, I went home to a sparsely decorated bachelor pad (without much Christmas color and no presents)—and Craig, lying on the couch watching the TV set. I think he felt a little lonely, too: his ex-wife had their two kids for the holidays.

Several hours later, Craig flipped the channel to midnight Mass at the Vatican being celebrated by the Pope himself and asked, "Where did Protestants come from?" I began to draw on my seminary knowledge of church history.

"All three branches of Christianity—Orthodox, Catholic, and Protestant," I said, "make Christ the center of their beliefs. Christians have always said salvation comes through faith in Jesus Christ."

No response. Craig stared blankly into the TV screen.

"I've got a book you can read," I offered, and promised to give him an easy-to-read book on church history. The conversation moved on. Surprisingly, Craig plowed through the book. On several occasions, he even asked questions about it, but our conversations never dipped below the head to the heart. Six months later I moved out in order to marry my wife, and a few months after that I moved to Chicago. I wondered if I would ever have the chance to share Christ with him.

Two summers after I moved to Chicago, Craig called and said he was in town and he'd like to meet me for lunch. When we met, he told me of dealing with his angry teenage son and coming to terms with his divorce. He had been seeing a psychologist.

The moment seemed right.

"Let me tell you the difference Christ has made in my life,"

I began. My mouth felt parched; I felt as nervous as when I asked my wife to marry me. But I plunged ahead and weakly told him how Christ's story had intersected with mine. I rambled for a few minutes, and then Craig said, "You mean to tell me that you believe Christ and God are the same person?"

"Why, yes," I mumbled.

"But Catholics say . . ." Craig replied, and the conversation deteriorated into an unfortunate discussion on the Trinity. Craig left lunch looking confused. I left feeling incompetent. As far as I know, Craig is still searching.

Experience taught me that evangelism is work, and there's no substitute for, well, experience. That's why I think you'll benefit from *Growing Your Church Through Evangelism and Outreach*. It's written by doers—men and women who are spending their lives looking outward and helping others do the same.

As with most of church ministry, leading your church to reach out to the world is more art than science. Yes, this book offers the science—the proven principles and practical help. But it also offers the art, the stories of God igniting hearts and changing lives. My hope is that *Growing Your Church Through Evangelism and Outreach* first changes your heart and then changes your ministry.

—David L. Goetz
associate editor, *Leadership*

Contributors

Jim Abrahamson is teaching pastor of Chapel Hill Bible Church in Chapel Hill, North Carolina. He is the author of *Put Your Best Foot Forward.*

Greg Asimakoupoulos is pastor of the Evangelical Covenant Church of Naperville (Illinois). Before that he pastored Crossroads Covenant Church in Concord, California. He is coauthor of *The Time Crunch.*

Myron Augsburger is president of InterChurch, Inc., and professor of theology at Eastern Mennonite Seminary in Harrisonburg, Virginia. He is coauthor of *Mastering Outreach & Evangelism.*

Don Cousins is founder and director of T.D.I. (Team Development, Inc.), a nonprofit organization in Barrington, Illinois, that helps church leadership teams carry out their ministry. Before that he was associate pastor at Willow Creek Community Church in South Barrington, Illinois. He is coauthor of *Walking with God, Networking,* and *Mastering Church Management.*

Ed Dobson is pastor of Calvary Church in Grand Rapids, Michigan. Before that he served as vice president for student life at Liberty University in Lynchburg, Virginia. With Jerry Falwell and others, he wrote *The Fundamentalist Phenomenon,* and with Ed Hinson, *The Seduction of Power.* He is also the author of *Starting a Seeker Sensitive Service.*

Ronald J. Fowler has been senior pastor of the Arlington Church of God in Akron, Ohio, since 1969. During his tenure there, he has led the church in developing an independent living facility for seniors, a preschool, and a Christian academy for kindergartners through sixth graders.

David Galloway is an Episcopal rector at Christ Church in Tyler, Texas, and consults with churches on evangelism and change management.

Joel Hempel is director of pastoral care and clinical pastoral education at Laclede Groves Retirement Community in St. Louis, Missouri. He served as an inner-city pastor in Cincinnati, Ohio, for almost twenty years.

Josh Hunt is minister of education at Calvary Baptist Church in Las Cruces, New Mexico. He is the author of *Let It Grow.*

Bill Hybels is senior pastor of the interdenominational Willow Creek Community Church in South Barrington, Illinois. He has written *Descending into Greatness* and *Fit to Be Tied* and coauthored *Mastering Contemporary Preaching.*

Wayne Jacobsen is director of BodyLife Resources, a ministry to encourage spiritual intimacy and Christian community. He also serves on the leadership team of Living Water Christian Fellowship in Visalia, California. He has written *A Passion for God's Presence* and *The Vineyard.*

Marilyn Kunz founded Neighborhood Bible Studies, Inc., and was director of that ministry for thirty-one years until her retirement in 1991. She is coauthor of the Neighborhood Bible Studies series of adult discussion Bible study guides.

Greg Laurie is pastor of Harvest Christian Fellowship in Riverside, California. He is heard daily on his radio and TV program, *A New Beginning*. He is also the crusade evangelist for Harvest Ministries. His books include *The Great Compromise, The New Believers Growthbook,* and *Life: Any Questions?*

John MacArthur Jr. is president of The Master's College and Seminary, pastor-teacher of Grace Community Church in Sun Valley, California, and speaker on the *Grace to You* radio broadcast. His books include *Ashamed of the Gospel, The Vanishing Conscience,* and *Reckless Faith.*

Mark Matheson has been pastor of First Baptist Church of Windermere, Florida, since 1985. Before that, he served as an associate pastor at Cliff Temple Baptist Church in Dallas, Texas.

Donald McCullough is president of San Francisco Theological Seminary. Before that he pastored Solana Beach (California) Presbyterian Church. He has earned a Ph.D. from the University of Edinburgh, Scotland, and has written *Waking from the American Dream, Finding Happiness in the Most Unlikely Places,* and *The Trivialization of God.*

Stephen McMullin is pastor of United Baptist Church in Woodstock, New Brunswick, Canada. Before that, he served for eight years as pastor of the Waterville and Victoria United Baptist Churches in rural New Brunswick. He serves as a member of the evangelism commission of the Atlantic Baptist Convention.

Mike Meeks is senior executive pastor at Eastside Foursquare Church in Kirkland, Washington. He was part of the pioneer team at Eastside and has served on staff for thirteen years.

Calvin Miller is professor of communications and ministry studies, and writer-in-residence at Southwestern Baptist Theological Seminary in Fort Worth, Texas. Before that he served as pastor of Westside Church in Omaha, Nebraska, for more than twenty-five years. His many books include *Spirit, Word,* *and Story; The Singer; A Requiem for Love;* and *Empowered Communicator.*

Doug Murren is founding pastor of Eastside Foursquare Church in Kirkland, Washington. He hosts a daily radio program, *Growing Together,* and is the author of *Baby Boomerang* and *Leadershift.*

Earl Palmer is senior pastor of University Presbyterian Church in Seattle, Washington. His books include *Communicator's Commentary, Vol. 12: 1, 2, 3 John & Revelation;* and he cowrote *Mastering Teaching.*

Calvin Ratz is pastor of Brightmoor Tabernacle in Southfield, Michigan. Before that, he pastored Abbotsford Pentecostal Assembly in Abbotsford, British Columbia, Canada. He has been a speaker at the Billy Graham School of Evangelism and is coauthor of *Mastering Outreach & Evangelism.*

John Savage is president of L.E.A.D. Consultants, Inc., which provides training in caring ministries for churches. He also is a consultant in conflict management and problem-solving strategies for parish life.

Doug Scott is rector of Saint Martin's Church in Radnor, Pennsylvania. Before that, he served as rector of the Church of Saint Thomas of Canterbury in Smithtown, New York. He is coauthor of *Mastering Transitions.*

Stephen W. Sorenson is an assignment writer/editor and operates Sorenson Communications in Colorado Springs, Colorado. His books include *Time with God* and *Living Smart, Spending Less Workbook.*

D. Elton Trueblood was a Quaker theologian whose writings and teachings had a lasting impact on Christians throughout the world. He founded the Yokefellow movement in 1952 after he became a philosophy professor at Earlham College, a Quaker school in Richmond, Indiana. He also served as chaplain at Stanford University. He died in 1994.

Virginia Vagt lives in Wayne, Pennsylvania, and enjoys anecdotal writing. She and her husband, Peter, teach a high school Sunday school class.

Stu Weber is pastor of Good Shepherd Community Church in Boring, Oregon. He has a special passion to see men enjoy God's intentions for their masculinity. He is the author of *Tender Warrior* and *Locking Arms.*

Ravi Zacharias is president of Ravi Zacharias International Ministries in Atlanta, Georgia. He has spoken in more than fifty countries and in many major universities, including Harvard and Princeton. He is the author of *A Shattered Visage: The Real Face of Atheism* and *Can Man Live without God?* His radio program, *Let My People Think,* is broadcast on 150 stations nationwide.

Dieter Zander is teaching pastor at Willow Creek Community Church in South Barrington, Illinois, where he is also developing a ministry to Generation Xers. Before coming to Willow Creek, he founded New Song Church, a San Dimas, California, fellowship designed for Generation Xers.

Section 1:
Growing Your Church Through Evangelism

I used to ask God to help me. Then I asked if I might help him. I ended up asking him to do his work through me.

—HUDSON TAYLOR

PART 1

Understand

1

Preparing Your Church to Evangelize

Getting a big crowd to a special event is one thing;
getting them to church is another.

—DOUG MURREN AND MIKE MEEKS

I asked one woman who was about to be baptized, "How long have you been coming here to church?"

"Two years," she said.

"When did you meet the Lord?"

"Two weeks ago."

I was intrigued. After the service I looked for her and asked, "You have to tell me: Were you here every week for two years, or once a year, or what?"

"I came almost every week."

"And you just received Christ last week?"

"Yes."

"I don't want to make you feel bad," I said, "but why did you wait so long?"

"My family started out Christian and kind of broke up. I've had three abortions and drug problems. I attended one of the church musicals with a friend, and she brought me to the worship services. I had heard this was a place where I would be loved for who I am. But it took me a while to believe it."

In 1990s America, unchurched people who come to Christ usually go through a long "preconversion phase." We find most visitors attend at least four outreach events before they come to one regular service. This preconversion phase may last a year to two and be marked by sporadic attendance.

Why? When unchurched people walk into our building, they're at a different starting point than the unchurched of fifty years ago. The truly unchurched are thoroughgoing relativists, having taken pluralism to its absurd limit, and cannot perceive how Scripture could be authoritative in their lives.

They need a safe and often long preconversion stage, in which they build confidence in the church, establish the authority of Scripture, and cement relationships. We have to honor that phase. Unchurched people today distrust the church, and they need to come and just watch for a while.

The biggest difference between a church successful in outreach and one that is not is willingness to begin with people, and patience with them during the preconversion phase.

Over the years we have put much prayer, research, and trial and error into helping people overcome the high hurdles between them and the Christian faith.

Focus on bringers-and-includers

Getting unchurched people to an outreach event isn't all that hard. But getting them to regularly attend a worship service—that's hard.

At Eastside Church, we sponsor support groups and twelve-step programs, hold a Christian arts and jazz festival, and put on musicals and seasonal events at Christmas and Easter. We have always been able to muster a crowd for such outreach events. But getting someone to a special event is one thing; getting him or her to a church service is another.

The secret is not more paid staff.

A church will fail if it tries to assimilate today's unchurched person only through events and programs. The effective glue is relationships—friends bringing friends and including them in church life. Research has shown that of ten people who visit a church and stay, nine were brought by a friend.

We invest the bulk of our time and money not in advertising but in helping our people bring and include their friends (rather than *evangelism* we use the phrase *bringing and including*). At least four times a year, we hand out a bringing-and-including packet. It includes training tapes on how to include your friend in a small group or an outreach event (which we call bringer-and-includer services). The packet includes cards to give to friends; each card lists service times and shows a map to church.

We also survey our people: "What would your friends be most disposed to come hear?" Several times a year we use those results to create messages geared toward people without church experience. One sermon series on the family, for example, targeted the unchurched. We assumed hearers were unconvinced about God's plan for the family, so we explained and illustrated why God's plan works. In such an outreach sermon, we begin with our culture—the songs of John Lennon or a film of Woody Allen—and work toward the Bible, ending with exposition.

We follow up visitors based on the assumption they have been brought by friends. When visitors make a decision to receive Christ, we'll say something such as, "If you brought a guest today, and he or she would appreciate assistance in learning more about the Christian life, we encourage you to go together to the reception room. There you can pick up packets geared for those who have just made a decision for Christ. Please consider setting a time this week—perhaps over lunch—to go through the packet together.

"Then, you can do several good things for your friend. First, if you're not in a small group, join one with them. Our information booth will direct you to a good one. Second, get into our Church 101 class with your friend." (Often a friend's conversion becomes the bringer's first step in full-blown discipleship.)

In the weeks following an outreach event, we make one call to that visitor, but we make three phone calls to the bringer. We ask, "Are there specific issues we can help you with?"

Several years ago we thought about how to make our church less pastor-driven and more lay-driven. It struck us that we encouraged our people to minister, and, as a result, they would often bring a friend to Christ. But then we took the celebration away from them: the pastors, the paid people, did all the baptizing. So we made a decision: "From now on, no pastors baptize. If someone brings a friend to the Lord, he or she gets to baptize that friend."

Immediately we saw an explosion in the number baptized. Big burly guys would step into the baptistery tank and start crying. Joe the mechanic would tell how his buddy Bob came to one of our musicals and three months later received the Lord.

Other churches may have theological reasons for not doing that, but the point is this: We emphasize the convert's bond with the body of Christ, not with the professional. The strategic step is to invest in the layperson, viewing pastors as lending assistance and giving tools to the people who are really doing the ministry.

Create a safe place

One man had visited a few outreach events and started attending Saturday night meetings. He realized he was trapped in a homosexual lifestyle and was looking for a way out, but he feared he would be rejected by the church. One day he came up to me after a service and said, "I'm a homosexual. I've been attending for several months and been watching your demeanor. I'm persuaded this is a pretty safe place. I want to commit my life to Christ."

We prayed, and afterward I introduced him to the leaders of our ministry to homosexuals. He joined the program, and three months later he handed me a letter. "The deciding moment in my life for overcoming homosexual desires," he wrote, "was when I came up to you and told you where I was. After sitting in services for several months, I guessed I would be accepted. When I introduced myself to you, the look in your eye told me I was accepted. I knew you saw a person rather than a gay person. At that moment I knew I was free." The unchurched will come back to a church that feels safe. For them, this is the most important ingredient. If they don't feel safe with you, they will not stay around long enough to hear the truth.

You can do several things to make you and your church feel safe to the unchurched:

Explain what you mean. When we ask the unchurched why they don't come to church, the number one complaint is they can't understand what's going on or what preachers are saying. We try to make no assumptions about what visitors will understand, and we work hard to talk the language of those unfamiliar with church.

Explain why. Postmoderns resist directive-type communication. A sermon that starts off with an authoritative statement about how people ought to behave turns them off. I've found it works better to speak persuasively, sometimes taking twice as long to explain a point. "If you believe this, so-and-so occurs; if you believe that, such-and-such happens."

In other words, people today are more likely to return to a church that explains why. One of our most requested tapes is "How We Got the Bible and Why We Know It's the Word of God."

Don't rush people. I have a friend who is a rabbi. One time I said to him, "Don't you get nervous hanging around a guy like me—a confessed evangelist who'd love to see you converted?"

He's an expert on Romans 9–11 and teaches in seminaries. He said, "Oh, no. I'm a gift of God to you. According to my understanding of the New Testament, my job is to give you an opportunity to love. If I'm to be convinced, that's the Holy Spirit's job. You're to love, and the Holy Spirit is to convince."

That rabbi may understand this process better than we do!

People feel safe when we love them and don't try to force decisions for Christ too soon.

Don't be surprised by their problems. Unchurched people assume churches don't want people with sin problems. They assume those who come to church are perfect—or hypocritical enough to act like they are. When your jaw doesn't drop at their sins, they feel safe. When the pastor is transparent in sermons, it gives seekers permission to have problems.

Give nonthreatening invitations. We don't give altar calls at church, because many unchurched people have seen them on TV and don't like them. Still, we always give an invitation at outreach events. Usually we'll have everyone close his and her eyes and ask those who want to receive Christ to look up at the speaker. We look at all who do and ask a couple of questions, having them nod in response, to make sure they know what they're doing. We'll ask, "Were you brought by a friend?" If they nod yes, we ask them to let that person know the decision they made. We pray and then offer a free packet of tapes and Bible studies.

We gently encourage them to go with their friend to the reception room: "We realize many people don't want to do this right away. So do it next week, when you feel less stunned about everything. We're interested in your making decisions that are yours, not imposing our wishes on you."

Not long ago one man in our church brought about thirty-five people from his company to an outreach event and afterward threw a big party at his house. There they talked about what they experienced in an easy, nonthreatening environment. At night's end, he said, "Come back to church as soon as you can. I think you'll like it."

Many of his colleagues have; some have received Christ.

People trained to be bringers-and-includers can get their friends to a church they know is relevant and safe. And sooner or later, a good percentage of those friends will return.

Maybe we've been making this harder than it really is.

2

Giving People Time and Space

*Evangelism, like sanctification, takes time. Therefore, we must
take the time it takes.*

—Earl Palmer

A man who liked C. S. Lewis's *Screwtape Letters* went on to
read *Mere Christianity*—and was infuriated. He wrote the author a scathing letter. Lewis's response, in longhand, shows a
master evangelist at work:

> Yes, I'm not surprised that a man who agreed with me in
> *Screwtape* . . . might disagree with me when I wrote about
> religion. We can hardly discuss the whole matter by post, can
> we? I'll only make one shot. When people object, as you do,
> that if Jesus was God as well as man, then he had an unfair
> advantage which deprives him for them of all value, it seems
> to me as if a man struggling in the water should refuse a rope
> thrown to him by another who had one foot on the bank,
> saying, 'Oh, but you have an unfair advantage.' It is because of
> that advantage that he can help. But all good wishes. We must
> just differ; in charity I hope. You must not be angry with me
> for believing, you know; I'm not angry with you.

What impresses me about that exchange is the light touch.
Lewis acknowledges the man's complaint, gives him one
thing to think about, and stops. He steps back as if to say,
"Your move," which opens the way for the man to write again.

Evangelism, like sanctification, takes time; therefore, we must take the time it takes.

Journey evangelism

When we relate to people, we must remind ourselves that we are on a long journey together. The idea that *this is my only chance to talk to this person* is a great detriment. Even on an airplane, we should speak as if we're going to know that seatmate for the rest of our lives. After all, to use another line from C. S. Lewis, "Christians never say good-bye."

When we share the gospel, it is part of a larger whole. Let me illustrate with small-group Bible studies, which our church has found to be our most authentic and exciting evangelistic event. What is fascinating is that we don't try to be evangelistic. Our goal is to let the text make its own point, and then enable group members to express their feelings about what is being read together. We consciously try not to cover everything the first week, but only what the text says. Our approach is: "Read this book as you read anything else. When you start Mark, don't give him an inch. Make him win every point. Don't worry about whether this is supposed to be the holy Word of God; just read it with the same seriousness you apply to your own thoughts."

The amazing thing is that the text inevitably reveals its living center. Some weeks Mark (or Paul or John) wins, some weeks he loses. But over time, the text comes out ahead, and the Christ of the text wins respect.

Too many of us preachers try to say too much all at once. Especially at the end of sermons—we throw in the kitchen sink trying to get somebody to make some sort of decision. We rattle off the most precious facts of our faith—the blood of Christ, the cross, God loves you—and reduce them to hasty, unexplained sentences. It is far better to let the text make its own point.

I've found the same tendency in counseling. Somebody

comes into my office and begins sharing his life. I listen very closely, trying to hear with my heart as well as my head. My mind is soon flooded with impressions, statements, Bible verses that I can hardly wait to unleash as soon as my turn comes. "Look at this . . . let me tell you this story . . . read this book . . . what you need to do is . . ."

As I've grown older, I've been asking God in such situations to help me say one or two things—not twenty-three. The poor person is already troubled and highly emotional. What is he supposed to do with a flood of input? He can only nod and say, "Oh, yes, thank you, pastor," and before long he's nodding just to get out of the room.

In evangelism, people do not need admonishments as much as they need to be carefully heard. Once I'm listening, I sort through their arguments to find out where I can agree. Very often the "god" they're rejecting I would reject, too. Why not let them know that?

A Christian friend of mine was a high school principal in Los Angeles. One day a father came charging into his office, irate because of the F his son had received in a course. The man had dreams of his son's going to an Ivy League school, and now this teacher was destroying the plan. He wanted the grade changed.

My friend listened to the threats and demands for a while, and finally when there was a pause he said quietly, "I can see that you care a great deal about your son."

The man suddenly began to cry. The mask came off. He was strong but aloof, and the only way he knew to do anything for his son was by bullying. When the principal spoke about relationship, the point of deepest hurt was exposed. Now the father was ready to be helped.

My friend knew he wasn't going to ask the teacher to change the grade. So why be defensive? Instead, he listened with his heart until he got in touch with the man's underlying journey.

I remember going to a Navigators conference in Colorado Springs during my student days. As part of our training, we

were all going to go out and hit the city with a great witnessing blitz; Colorado Springs would never be the same. Jim
Rayburn of Young Life had been invited to talk to us, and he
said, "Well, I know what you're headed out to do. . . you're
going to go out there and say to people, 'Brother, are you
saved?' and you've got to say it real fast, because you may
never see that person again. . . ." He paused a moment before continuing.

"And you won't. You won't."

Then he shared his philosophy of evangelism, which was to
take the time it takes to share the good news of Jesus Christ
with people.

I'm not saying we should not be zealous. But the gospel has
its own urgent edge and does its own convicting of sin. Isn't it
good that the Holy Spirit takes care of that as we simply
witness to the truth?

A crusty engineering professor in our city was shattered
when his Christian wife died unexpectedly of a heart attack
just as they reached retirement age. After the funeral, he came
to see me. I steered him toward the Gospel of Mark and some
additional reading. After several weeks, I could see the New
Testament was gradually making sense to him. My closing
comment in our times together was usually, "Let me know
when you're ready to become a Christian." (I rarely say, "*Are
you ready?*" Instead, I ask people to let me know when they
have enough information to trust Jesus Christ. I believe the
most central evangelistic question is "Are you able, on the
basis of what you've discovered about Jesus Christ, to trust
your life to his faithfulness and love?" This combines repen-
tance of sin and response to his love.)

One Sunday after church, with a lot of people milling
around, the engineer stood in the back waiting for me. He's
not the kind of man who likes standing around. Finally he
got my attention so he could call out, "Hey, Earl . . . I'm
letting you know." That was it; he became a Christian at age
sixty-five.

We have to make room for people to struggle because the

stakes are so big. We should not be too pleased if someone comes to Christ with little struggle—it may mean this is simply a compliant person, and the same compliance that eases them into Christianity may also ease them toward the next thing that calls for their obedience.

The next-to-the-last word

The more sensitive we are to journey evangelism, the more we will recognize pre-evangelistic preparation. So many things in our culture are pre-evangelistic. I don't know whether Robert Frost was a Christian, but his "Mending Wall" is most definitely a pre-Christian poem. It raises all the right questions. Joseph Conrad's *Heart of Darkness* and Francis Ford Coppola's movie *Apocalypse Now* both raise huge questions that the gospel addresses.

As Dietrich Bonhoeffer said, "You cannot hear the last word until you've heard the next-to-the-last word." The next-to-the-last word is the law; it makes us feel guilty, trapped, judged. Only then are we ready for the good news.

Evangelists who ignore the person's journey are missing something important. Or, we make the mistake of listening once, and then freezing people in that state of rebellion. They may have spoken more outrageously than they believe; they may have only been trying to shock us; or they may have moved on from their first rejection of Christ. We must keep hearing the clues and moving along as they move.

G. K. Chesterton wrote in *Orthodoxy* about five steps in his journey as a young man:

> One, I felt in my bones; first that this world does not explain itself. It may be a miracle with a supernatural explanation, it may be a conjuring trick, with a natural explanation. But the explanation of the conjuring trick, if it is to satisfy me, will have to be better than the natural explanation I have heard. The thing is magic, true or false.

Second, I came to feel as if magic must have a meaning, and
meaning must have someone to mean it . . .

Third, I thought this purpose beautiful in its old design, in
spite of its defects, such as dragons.

Fourth, the proper form of thanks to it is some form of
humility and restraint. We should thank God for beer and
burgundy by not drinking too much of them.

And last, and strangest of all, there came into my mind a
vague and vast impression that in some way all good was a
remnant to be stored and held sacred out of some primordial
ruin. Man had saved his good as Crusoe had saved his goods.
He had saved them from a wreck, and all this I felt, and my
age gave me no encouragement to feel it.

And all this time I had not even thought of Christian theology.

What a slow but elegant orbit he makes toward the living
center.

Our part in the mystery

In the San Francisco Bay Area where I lived, I sometimes
made jokes at the expense of a small town called Milpitas.
Once while speaking on radio, I said, "You know, Beethoven
is not on trial when the Milpitas Junior High Orchestra plays
the *Ninth Symphony*. And Jesus Christ is not on trial when
you or I or even C. S. Lewis tries to express the faith in a
conversation or a sermon."

Then about a year later it occurred to me: *But were it not for
the Milpitas Junior High Orchestra, who would hear Beethoven?*
Playing badly is better than no playing at all. Who plays Beethoven perfectly?

Some people trudge from church to church looking for the
perfect rendition. They'll never find it. W. H. Auden once
observed that even though the line is smudged, we can read
the line. That is the mystery of evangelism: Even though we
smudge the line, it can still be read. You can whistle the tune
of the *Ninth Symphony* even after listening in the Milpitas
gymnasium.

Evangelism is far greater than any of us. That is why it takes time. But without us, it would take an eternity. And human beings do not have that long to make up their minds.

3

Reaching the "Happy-Thinking Pagan"

Every generation will try to get us to change the message.

—RAVI ZACHARIAS

At Ohio State University, I participated in an open forum on a radio talk show. The host was an atheist.

From the start, callers were antagonistic. I could feel the tension as soon as the lines lit up. One angry woman, referring to abortion, said, "All you people have is an agenda you're trying to promote. You want to take away our rights and invade our private lives."

Abortion had not even been brought up.

"Just a minute," I replied. "We didn't even raise the subject."

"What is your position on abortion, then?"

I said, "Can I ask you a question? On every university campus I visit, somebody stands up and says that God is an evil God to allow all this evil into our world. This person typically says, 'A plane crashes: Thirty people die, and twenty people live. What kind of a God would arbitrarily choose some to live and some to die?'

"But when we play God and determine whether a child within a mother's womb should live, we argue for that as a moral right. So when human beings are given the privilege of playing God, it's called a moral right. When God plays God, we call it an immoral act. Can you justify this for me?"

That was the end of the conversation.

I feel called to minister to people such as this woman, whom I affectionately call a "happy-thinking pagan."

Such a person believes this world and the success it affords are the greatest pursuit in life. He or she feels no need for anything transcendent. Life has been reduced to temporal pursuits disconnected from all the other disciplines necessary for life to be meaningfully engaged.

Some are completely unreflective; they don't think enough to know they have no right to be happy. They borrow on capital they don't have. Many of these people, though, are sophisticated thinkers in their field—scientists, mathematicians, computer engineers. They are specialists with a glaring weakness: They do not ask the questions of life itself.

What does the gospel sound like to the ears of the happy-thinking pagan? How can church leaders reach the people in today's postmodern world?

Postmodern pathology

One characteristic of postmodern thinking is extreme relativism. At universities I visit, the exclusivity of Christ is raised in every forum: "How can you possibly talk about one God or one way when there are so many good options?"

Today, sensitivities are at an all-time high, and rightfully so. Tolerance of different races and religions had been lacking in previous years. But pluralism has given way to relativism. Most of the intellectual elite of this country completely disavow the idea of absolute truth.

At a Harvard forum, I established the law of noncontradiction (no statement can be true and false at the same time and in the same relationship). This law is a simple principle of logic you expect most students would have learned in Philosophy 101. But as in virtually every other setting, it stirred up quite a debate. Even though the law of noncontradiction is fundamental to rational discourse, the audience grew silent for several minutes after I described it. That the laws of logic apply to reality floors people, even though they use logic to attack Christian truths.

Here's the rub: While the average secular person will believe something without subjecting it to rational critique, he disbelieves things on the basis that, he or she says, they are rationally inadmissible. So he critically attacks Christian assumptions using principles of logic that he doesn't even hold.

Engaging someone who doesn't believe in truth is difficult. But if the purveyors of postmodernism talk long enough, you will hear that the reason they disavow Christianity is because they do not see it as *true*. I call this their "smuggled-in epistemology": They use the principles of logic to criticize our system but refuse to apply them to their beliefs.

When I was asked to do a lectureship in England, the inviting body wrote, "We have received one criticism of this seminar: "Will you be focusing too much on reason and logic and not deal with the postmodernist mind-set?' "

I smiled at that. English newspapers are filled with astrology, the occult, New Age thought—what years ago would have fallen under the general category of the bizarre. At the same time, Islam has made great inroads in England; Prince Charles is now patron of the Center for Islamic Studies at Oxford. Islam knows how damaging postmodern thinking is: It creates a huge vacuum often filled with something else.

Postmodernism is dangerous not only because of what it has done to the secular person, but also because it destroys our apologetic, our methods for determining truth. What's happening in the West with the emergence of postmodernism is only what has been in much of Asia for centuries but under different banners. For many years, the Indian would say, "All roads lead to God because truth is never absolute." (That assumption was not in keeping with classical Hinduism, but became popular.)

So, too, with the way postmodernism works. The point of engagement must come through the common ground that even the postmodernist assumes in disbelieving something.

As Chesterton said, "In truth, there are only two kinds of people: those who accept dogma and know it, and those who accept dogma and don't know it."

At every university at which I've lectured, the intellectual questions eventually turn into questions of meaning. Often behind a difficult or angry question is a hurting heart; the intellect is intertwined with the heart. Nothing is as offensive as answers perceived to be mere words, uncaring of a human situation.

Once a couple walked up to me after a church service and began asking questions about the problem of evil. As I began answering their questions, I happened to glance at their baby, who had Down's syndrome. Seeing their child, I had a whole new appreciation for their questions and the context behind them.

Postmodern aggression

In our postmodern culture, attacks against Christianity have principally come on two fronts. First, the academic world has made great gains in its philosophical and scientific exploits. It extrapolates those advances as giving credence to an agnostic or an atheistic worldview.

Unfortunately, the questions of today's young person, who is the product of America's intellectual bastions, have been left virtually unaddressed by the church. There is a danger when we give young people only a catalog of do's and don'ts. So in these young minds, the gospel is not intellectually credible.

Second, while our country's intellectual skeptics attack us rationally, the arts attack us by appealing to the passions. Today there is no force greater in the molding of the North American mind than the invasion of the imagination by the medium of the visual.

Malcolm Muggeridge, quoting Simone Weil, said that in reality nothing is so beautiful as the good and nothing so monotonous and boring as evil. In our imagination, however, it's reversed: Fictional good is boring and flat; fictional evil is varied, intriguing, attractive, full of charm.

Between intellectual attacks that pummel the mind and arts that provide immeasurable allurements, the idea of God in a pleasure-mad society is a hindrance. And so Christianity is increasingly relegated to the margins of society.

At the same time, Christianity seems to bear the brunt of society's anger toward religion. The secular historian William Edward Hartpole Lecky said Christ was the supreme personality in history who motivated humanity to the best of ethical thinking. There has been none like him. Society itself recognizes this and hence expects of the Christian a higher standard.

But as understandable as that is, American culture, or at least the cultural elite, has become particularly vicious in its anti-Christian attacks. The whole episode of the film *The Last Temptation of Christ* said more about us as a culture in North America than anything in recent memory.

All of the Middle East banned the film, as did India. We are long past talking about whether an unbeliever should be punished for being irreverent. Chesterton said now a person is considered irreverent for being a *believer*. In the West, Islam and Hinduism could never be so mocked with impunity. So the media will never engage in it because they see those religions as culturally protected. But Christianity, being transcultural, is open to such criticism.

Secularism has bred irreverence, which has come on the heels of so much pleasure, so much indulgence. This is not a sign merely of arrogance; this is a sign of emptiness. Chesterton said that meaninglessness ultimately comes not from being weary of pain but from being weary of pleasure.

Postmodern evangelism

We do our universities a disservice when we brand them as lost causes. In spite of the advances of postmodernism, the gospel is gaining a hearing among our thinking elite. We see this in all arenas—politics, business, academics, the arts. There are some frightfully honest students out there. When their questions are respectfully dealt with, many admit their vulnerability.

Even though the search for meaning is debunked today, it is still rigorously pursued. The postmodern world is still a world where technology and means play a greater role than people and relationships. But the cries of the human heart can be smothered only so long. And in these yearnings, the search for significance and fulfillment continues.

At universities, much of the hostility toward me is mitigated because of my racial background; audiences seem to have more acceptance for someone who is not Caucasian. I have felt more antagonism from faculty than from students.

Other religious groups are not so much hostile as suspicious; they want to see what I'm going to say about them. But when there is tension at the beginning of a lectureship, I've never sensed it at the end. In every setting the response has been overwhelmingly gratifying.

The temptation when speaking to the happy-thinking pagan is to become angry. It can be frustrating seeing how society has desacralized everything. But Jesus resisted the temptation of outrage and the quick-fix of condemnation. He spent most of his time preparing the wineskins before pouring new wine into them. Our tendency is to start pouring the wine into skins that will only burst.

At a university in Thailand, I was speaking about existentialism, Marxism, pantheism, and Christianity. A Muslim stood up and said, "You have just insulted your God by mentioning Karl Marx and Jean Paul Sartre in the same sentence that you mentioned Christ."

I could feel the irritation welling up inside me. I wanted to retort, "I have done nowhere near what the Muslim world has done in stripping Christ of his deity." Instead, I paused, took a drink of water, and said, "I deeply appreciate your sensitivity. I know where you are coming from. But don't forget you also used all three names in the sentence as you raised the question for me."

I continued, "Did you mean to equate them by naming the three of them?"

"No," he said.

"Neither did I. Mentioning two names in the same sentence is hardly suggesting they are equal. But I want to commend you for your sensitivity because in many cultures we have lost reverence for the name of God."

We must critique alternative beliefs to Christianity in a way that encourages people to listen. If you can make any religion look idiotic, chances are you haven't understood that religion. You can't take treasured beliefs from the past and mock them.

After I spoke at Brigham Young University, a well-groomed student came to me and said, "Dr. Zacharias, you didn't directly attack Mormonism. Was there a reason?"

"Of course," I said. "I was assigned a subject on which to speak, and the subject was getting to the truth: Who is Jesus? I lectured on that.

"If I had been asked to deal with the differences between Mormonism and orthodox Christianity, I would have done so. But I still would have done so graciously."

"I just want to thank you for that approach," he said. "Two weeks ago there was a man on campus who came on his own invitation and started crying down hellfire and brimstone. He was escorted off campus."

The old Indian proverb holds true: Once you've cut off a person's nose, there's no point giving him a rose to smell. We tend to think being kind and listening to the opposition implies we have sacrificed the message. But we need to learn how to handle critique, how to address an antagonist. Even while you wrestle with the ideas of an opponent, you must keep the dignity of the opponent intact.

We cannot go to a university with the attitude, "I'm here to deal with your tough questions." I always begin by telling them a little bit about my life. I often tell about my struggles as a teenager when I nearly committed suicide in a New Delhi hospital. My stated vulnerability gives me an entry point. But even with a hard-edged question, I answer with graciousness. I have to earn the right to be heard every time I get up to speak.

"I'm going to defend why Jesus Christ is the only way to God," I might say. "You may disagree with that, but if you do, make sure your arguments counter the arguments I'm now presenting to you."

One key is the willingness to say, "I'm not sure how well I will deal with what you're going to say, but give me a chance. I have struggled with these issues."

I also plead with my audience: "Let's both agree these matters are important. And if we both agree they are important, let's get more light then heat. Let's try to find some answers, because hiding behind words is not going to solve the problem."

Whether it is a business or academic setting, their heartwarming response is an indicator that people are hungry for answers.

Postmodern common ground

Although it is difficult to reach someone whose framework doesn't allow any common ground, opportunities are unprecedented. Here are several:

Being present in pain. The church still meets people in the transition points. Marriages break down. Children commit suicide and leave parents helpless. Death and suffering are everywhere.

Christ's teaching is restorative; it is therapeutic in the sense that it provides answers to our needs. Life's difficulties make the questioner more reachable. God often enters our lives through our brokenness to show that we're not as autonomous as we think. But Christ's teaching is therapeutic because it is *true*. That truth has greater implications for life than just being therapeutic. It is not just a "feel better" but a "know better" situation. Truth demands a commitment. The question of truth has to emerge; everything else hangs on it.

Somebody who responds to a watered-down gospel will only make more work for someone else down the road; the hard work of discipleship has to be done. That is one danger of reaching nonbelievers solely through the medium of art. What the arts should do is create legitimate hungers that only God is big enough to fill. But at some point, art has to give way to reason. The visual has to be anchored beyond itself.

Preaching engagingly.   Our preaching can and should anchor the imagination. We need to give our audiences more credit. They want to think. We assume sometimes they don't. It is fatal to assume that everything we preach should be on the bottom shelf, where people don't have to reach for it. We wind up talking down to people and perpetuating the fallacious idea that spiritual pursuit is handed to you. It isn't. You reach out; you seek; you knock; you search; you find.

Jesus spoke in parables not only to reveal truth but also to disclose the heart of the listener, to see how much that listener wanted to pursue the truth. Having to reach is indispensable to spiritual maturity.

When you preach engaging the mind—keeping the idea within reach—you are complimenting your audience; they recognize they need to reach for that slightly higher level, that they need to stand on their toes to grasp what you're saying. (In reaching the heart, we can't forget the mind. *Balance* is the key word.)

Helping people make connections.   In a fragmented society, the role of the preacher is undoubtedly one of the most difficult. Many people in the pews see Christianity as disjointed from day-to-day life. They see it as one aspect of their lives, something they do in addition to everything else. Nothing is connected for them. There is no unity in the diversity of their roles. One of the important roles of the preacher is to be a connector. The pastor is the only person who can help them make sense of it all.

What has helped me in making the connection for others is to see a sermon as incorporating three components: the argument (or proclamation), the illustration, and the application. The Scriptures provide the truth; the arts, poetry, literature, or current events provide the illustrations; and the application should go right to daily living. This approach helps connect ideas with concrete reality.

But a pastor must work hard to connect fragmented lives. Most professions afford the luxury of one line of thinking. If I am a biology teacher, for example, biology is my discipline and all I need to still study. But a pastor or Christian teacher today has to keep up with so many fields because the audience is so diverse, and the pastor is looked up to for wisdom in trying to connect it all. This demands much study and is a tall order. With knowledge growing exponentially, it's easy to wind up sounding ignorant.

A. W. Tozer said that we are all ignorant, only in different subjects. Some pastors might not be given to philosophical thinking, but all of us wrestle with these issues at some level. We need to rise to the level we can.

I recommend that pastors formulate a book list representing five of the major worldviews. Take three-by-five cards and write down the fundamental beliefs of each. What are the basic doctrines of this worldview? Who are the leading thinkers advocating it?

Preachers must work hard at being familiar with the leading thinkers of our day. The ideas of Jacques Derrida and Paul de Man, for example, give firsthand insight into deconstruction, a worldview that trumpets the meaninglessness of meaning. The reading is difficult, but you'll get a feel for our times. If one is not given to this type of content, then it is still important to know where to direct the inquirer who struggles with these issues.

One of the names being resurrected on university campuses today is Ayn Rand, an egocentric humanist popular twenty years ago. I gained an awareness of that in my latest couple of open forums, so I hurried back to reread *We the Living* and her other works. Our listeners respect firsthand knowledge.

Staying faithful to our calling. If our preaching leads people to genuine worship, we will help meet the deepest longing of the heart and mind; the secular worldviews have left them bankrupt.

Every generation will try to get us to change the message, but wisdom is justified by her children. We are called to be faithful to our calling in the Word. And God has promised to honor those who honor him.

4

Opening the Closed American Mind

In a relativistic culture hostile toward notions of unchanging, ultimate truth, the gospel can be an offense, no matter how positive my presentation. Sometimes that can't be avoided. But sometimes it can.

—ED DOBSON

The audience at our Saturday night outreach service is one-third unchurched individuals, one-third church dropouts, and one-third church adherents, so the majority come from a secular viewpoint. At the end of the service, I respond to their written questions; I have no idea beforehand what they will be. Questions range from predestination to masturbation, from abortion to suicide, and my answers aren't always what people want to hear.

One evening someone wrote, "I'm gay, and I've always been gay. Is that okay?"

"What you're really asking," I responded, "is 'What does the Bible say about human sexuality?' The Bible teaches that sexuality is a gift from God to be experienced within the commitment of heterosexual marriage. My understanding of the Bible is that all expressions of our sexuality outside of those boundaries are not within God's creative intent.

"Are you asking me if it's okay to have homosexual feelings? Yes, it is. But Scripture does not permit you to follow through with those feelings as a legitimate expression of sexuality. If you try to ignore that fact, there are consequences, one of which is displeasing God."

Answers like that can irritate people who don't accept an absolute standard of truth. One man said to me, "I really like Saturday night, but when you answer those questions, I wish you would quit referring to the Bible and tell me what you really think."

I congratulated the man on being so perceptive. The point of our seeker-sensitive service is not to tell people what I think but to help connect them with biblical truth. In a culture committed to relativism, hostile toward notions of unchanging, ultimate truth, the gospel can be an offense, no matter how positive my presentation. Sometimes that can't be avoided.

But sometimes it can. I've found that I can gain a hearing for the truth of the gospel, even in a relativistic culture. As I've conducted seeker-sensitive services and befriended non-Christians, I've gathered several principles for reaching skeptics with the truth.

Explain why

The spirit of individualism, rather than community, dominates our culture, giving relativism a strong appeal. "You believe what you want, and I'll believe what I want" is the spirit of the times.

If a couple on *Donahue* says, "We've been married sixty years, and we're still happy," the audience applauds. But if they say, "We believe everyone should remain married for a lifetime," they'll get booed off the set.

Pervasive individualism has a positive side. People want what enhances their lifestyles, so I can reach them if I demonstrate that the values I teach are truths beneficial to anyone. I must show the modern skeptic the practical wisdom of biblical principles, particularly those principles that appear rigid or intolerant.

Appeal to curiosity about the Bible

While many secular people reject the notion of absolute values, they are curious to know what the Bible says. And if they have come to church, I assume they have at least some interest in biblical teachings or they wouldn't be there in the first place.

When answering the questions of seekers and skeptics, I nearly always preface my remarks with, "If you're asking me what the Bible says, here is the answer." If I dodge and weave around the Bible, my audience won't respect me. Sometimes I must frankly say, "I may not like the Bible's answer, you may not like it, but this is what it says."

One Saturday evening a questioner wrote, "I'm a Christian. My brother was not a believer when he committed suicide. I still believe he'll be in heaven. What do you think?"

"What you're asking is whether the Bible gives several options on how to get to heaven," I responded. "I have to be honest with you. Scripture says Christ is the only way to heaven, and there are no other options. You are probably thinking, *So what does that mean for my brother?* Since you are a Christian, you undoubtedly had some influence on him; perhaps before he made this horrible choice he did turn and commit his life to Christ."

I would have loved to assure him that his brother was waiting for him in heaven, but I couldn't. I concluded, "If you're asking whether people can go to heaven without accepting Christ, no, they cannot. I'd like to tell you it doesn't matter, but if I did, I would be dishonest about the Bible." People respect that level of integrity.

Sometimes people are surprised by what the Scriptures say. People often ask me, "Will I go to heaven if I'm gay?"

"Whether you're gay or not has nothing to do with whether you will go to heaven," I say. "The relevant issue is the nature of your relationship with Jesus Christ. Have you placed your faith in him as your Savior? That's the sole criteria by which God will judge every human being."

I try to satisfy natural curiosity about the Bible in two ways. I preach verse by verse on Sunday mornings, and on Saturday nights I use the Bible to answer topical questions. By going through a book one verse at a time, I'm eventually going to bump into the issue that concerns an individual. The questions on Saturday night force me to deal with listeners' urgent concerns.

Know your essentials

We gain a hearing with a secular audience when we don't confuse essentials with nonessentials.

One summer night, we held our Saturday service downtown, outdoors. We had just started when a ruckus broke out at the back of the crowd. It turned out to be a group of angry Christians staging a protest; they hoisted signs proclaiming that Christian rock music was of the devil. They became so disruptive that police patrolling the event arrested them.

Meanwhile eighty punk rockers, attracted by the music in our service, were sitting on a wall nearby, listening to my message.

No doubt the protesters were sincere in their beliefs about rock music, but they failed to see their preferences about music were not on the same level of truth as biblical absolutes. (No one has yet shown me where Scripture explicitly condemns rock music.) I believe that will prevent them from effectively reaching unbelievers.

This not only affects how we go about evangelizing but what and how we preach and teach. When preaching or answering questions on Saturday night, I periodically make a distinction: What someone believes about Christ and the nature of salvation is far more important than what he or she believes, let's say, about women's ordination. I lose respect with outsiders if I treat both topics with the same level of authority.

Actually, I try to distinguish between three types of truth:

absolutes are truths essential to the faith, truths that never change; convictions are beliefs about which orthodox Christians may differ; preferences are traditions or customs, like musical tastes, that may be compatible with the Bible but aren't biblically based, and they may change with the culture and over time.

Naturally, sometimes people will differ about which category a subject belongs to, but most issues seem to fall into one or another.

Don't skip the tough topics

I was flying back from California one day, sitting in an aisle seat across from some businessmen. One of them happened to notice I was reading my Greek New Testament and asked, "What language is that?"

"Greek," I replied.

"What kind of Greek?"

"New Testament Greek."

"That's amazing," he said. "I studied Greek when I attended a religious college in the Midwest. Why are you studying it?"

"I'm preparing for my sermon on Sunday."

"Really? What are you speaking on?"

I paused at that point. I looked at his buddies sitting next to him who were half-listening to our conversation. Did I really want to break the news to him in front of all his friends? But I knew I had to be honest with him.

"Well, Sunday morning my subject is hell," I said.

That was the end of the conversation for the rest of the flight.

When you're trying to gain a hearing from a secular audience, it's tempting to water down demanding Scriptures or avoid them altogether. We're afraid people will tune out the sermon.

But I've discovered that's a mistake. Just when I think I know what the culture wants to hear and what it doesn't, I'm surprised all over again. Our most popular Saturday night series was, "What Does It Mean to Be a Christian?" By any measure—attendance, audience response, or follow-up—it was the most successful four evenings in our Saturday history. Until then, I had dealt with subjects such as depression, bitterness, and forgiving your parents. The last thing I expected was an overwhelming response to such a simple, straightforward topic.

I learned a valuable lesson: I don't need to trade away forthright, biblical messages for something faddish or trendy. People have a basic spiritual hunger that only faithful biblical preaching can satisfy.

I've found that I can preach even about the most sticky subject, as long as I balance it with good news. We did a two-part Saturday night series, one on heaven and the other on hell.

We introduced the subject of the afterlife by relating near-death experiences from popular literature. I wasn't prepared to say these experiences were real, but I pointed out they often paralleled the biblical teachings on death and the afterlife. The evening on heaven was well received.

But the next week, I said, "What I didn't tell you last week was there are other near-death experiences described in the literature that are not so pleasant. In fact, it's incredible how much these experiences parallel what the Scriptures say about hell."

I could tell people were uncomfortable in that second session, but they listened intently.

Establish authority

I suppose in earlier generations most preachers could assume their listeners conferred to them a certain level of authority. Many preachers could also assume their congregations had a minimal level of biblical knowledge.

Today I take nothing for granted. I assume virtually everyone will question virtually everything I say. Furthermore, I assume most listeners know little if anything about the Bible.

But how do you establish authority with a group that grew up on the maxim, "Question authority"? I've discovered such people will view me as credible if I do the following:

Let the people do some talking. On Saturday evenings, we always take five to eight minutes to let someone share what God has done in his or her life. Listeners will accept my message if they see that it makes a difference for someone who doesn't get paid to spread religion.

I recently renewed the vows of a couple who had been on the brink of divorce. The husband had been living with another woman for more than a year. The divorce decree was about to be granted when they started attending Saturday night services independently. They both ended up committing their lives to Christ.

The husband soon broke up with the woman with whom he had been living. The estranged couple began talking again. They eventually decided, "Hey, if God can forgive us, we can forgive each other. Let's start over again."

So in front of their unbelieving friends, they renewed their vows. I went to the reception afterward. It was fascinating to hear their unsaved friends try to figure out what had happened to this couple. Out of that experience, several of them began attending our Saturday night service. They couldn't deny the difference Christ had made in the lives of these two people.

Practice what you preach. The Scriptures say we can silence the foolishness of ignorant people by our good behavior. That involves going places Christ would and spending time with people he would. I've said from our pulpit that if Christ were in my city today, he probably wouldn't attend my church. He would be down among the poor and dispossessed.

That's one reason we've gotten involved helping people dying of AIDS. When the AIDS resource center of Grand Rapids hosts its annual Christmas party downtown, some of us from our church attend. Such events are a great opportunity for ministry. At one of those parties, I met a woman dying of AIDS who had two children also diagnosed with the virus. I was able to talk with her about Christ's love.

Our church donates money to cover burial costs for those who die of the disease without funds. In addition, each Christmas the AIDS resource center gives us a list of names of people suffering from the disease (first names only, because they wish to remain anonymous) and a wish list that we distribute to our people. We gather the gifts, and when we give them, the recipients know it's Calvary Church that donates the presents.

Our involvement with AIDS sufferers has built credibility. It's not uncommon for our Saturday night services to attract large numbers of seekers from the gay community. Women have stood and said, "I'm a former lesbian. Christ changed my life through this church."

Accept people as they are. One Sunday morning a man walked into our morning service with the F-word printed on his T-shirt. That wasn't easy for many to tolerate. As I heard later, when people stood to sing the first hymn, many couldn't get their minds off his shirt.

But as inappropriate as wearing that shirt was, it was important that we accepted that man in that condition. When the church requires that people clean up their lives, dress, and act a certain way before we will love them, we lose the respect of our culture.

So I remind our congregation that Jesus showed compassion to a maniac living naked among the tombs. Christ cared about him just as he was. So anything above nakedness ought to be acceptable dress code in our midst.

One evening I presented a man to the board who was wearing his hair in a long rat tail. He had contracted AIDS through years of intravenous drug use. He began attending our Saturday night service shortly after accepting the Lord.

"I don't know how much time I have left," he told board members, "but what time I do have I want to live for the Lord." By the time he finished, all board members were weeping. They gathered around him, laid hands on him, and prayed for his future.

Any church that practices that type of Christianity will win the respect of outsiders and gain a platform to be heard.

Keep the playing field level. Someone once complained that our church was soon going to be overrun with homosexuals. I responded, "That would be terrific. They could take a seat next to the gossips, the envious, the greedy, and all the rest of us sinners."

I try to communicate that same attitude in my preaching: We all stand under God's judgment, and we all are in desperate need of his grace. Letting people know that I'm not speaking down to them from some lofty moral position helps them listen to what I have to say.

Don't pretend to play God. I have to be honest with people when I don't know the answers to their questions. A woman once asked, "Where was God when my father was molesting me?"

"I wish I knew where he was during your ordeal," I answered. "I just don't know. But I do know this: God loves you and wants to heal the wounds of your past." It's ironic, but not having all the answers helps people better trust the answers I do have.

Use the culture to introduce good news. Secular people know popular music, entertainment, and news media. So I've used such worlds to help make the Christian case. In my messages on Saturday nights, I cite secular studies, read from news sources, and quote from popular music to bridge the listeners' world to the Scriptures.

On the night I addressed the theme "Is there something in this world to believe in?" I showed the music video, *Give Me Something to Believe In* by the rock group Poison.

On another night, I used John Lennon's famous song "Imagine." I asked the audience to imagine a world with no competing religions, no wars, no fights, where complete peace and harmony reigned. "Will there ever be such a place?" I asked. "Such a world is possible only through Jesus

Christ, who gives us personal peace and changes hatred into love."

One evening we showed a film clip (with the unsavory language edited out) from a Burt Reynolds film, *The End*. It's about a man with terminal cancer who is afraid to die. He keeps trying to commit suicide but chickens out at the last moment. His prayers of desperation resonate with the fears most people carry of death.

Explode stereotypes. People in our culture hold many misperceptions about Christians. When I explode those negative stereotypes, primarily with humor, and perhaps satirize now and then the real foibles of Christians, I gain credibility.

One Easter morning, knowing many unchurched people would be in the audience, I wore my doctoral robes to the pulpit. Standing in this long, flowing black robe, I began my message, "In case you're watching by television this morning, I'm not Robert Schuller. This is Calvary Church." Once the laughter died down, I pointed to the various parts of this beautiful robe—the colors, the hood, the sleeves— and explained what each symbolized. Then I unzipped the robe and stepped out in a T-shirt and blue jeans. People gasped.

"On Easter Sunday, we all put on our robes," I said. "By that I mean we all get dressed up. We all put on our best image. But underneath all the hype, at the blue-jeans level, we often are very different people. We need to ask, 'Does Easter make a difference?' "

On another Sunday, I tied my hair, which I had let grow, in a pony tail. The idea that Christians ought to look and dress a certain way was another stereotype on my hit list. In a community as conservative as ours, that was pushing the envelope.

I finished my sermon, "I'm sure some of you are outraged that I wore my hair in a pony tail. But are you just as upset that your neighbors don't know the Lord? We get bent out of shape over things that have no eternal significance. But can we get equally agitated over people dying of starvation and millions who have never heard the gospel?

"I'm going to cut off my pony tail this week. My question to you is 'What are you going to do to show compassion to this world?' "

When I was a young pastor of a Baptist church in the mountains of Virginia, we started with only thirty-three people. *Seeker sensitive* wasn't even a term then. Instead we used gimmicks such as "Water Gun Sunday." But the leading moonshine bootlegger in that area came to know Christ. Soon his wife and children became believers. One Sunday, I counted fifty people he had brought with him.

Reaching out to committed unbelievers is a great challenge requiring creativity and dedication. Sometimes the results are slow in coming; sometimes we have to endure a lot of misunderstanding and hostility. But sometimes the results are remarkable.

5

Making Worship Visitor Friendly

Visitors can be made to feel welcome without name tags,
official greeters, or special recognition.

—DON COUSINS

If you visit Willow Creek Community Church, don't be surprised if no one asks your name. You won't be given a name tag, and you won't be asked to stand or raise your hand as a new person. No one will even give you a form to fill out for a follow-up contact.

Don't we care about visitors? Of course we do. Don't we want them to come back? Sure! In fact, it's because we want them to return that we try not to pressure them on their first visit.

Let me explain with a personal example. I grew up in a nondenominational church. When I went away to college, I visited churches of various denominations. I soon learned that my home church was similar to most Baptist, Presbyterian, Lutheran, and other denominational churches. Even as a visitor, I knew pretty much what to expect—how I should dress, what information would be in the bulletins, and how to respond to the greeters. I fit right in.

Then a friend invited me to a Catholic Mass, a first for me. I felt anxious about attending, and the reasons soon bore themselves out. As the service unfolded, people were standing up, sitting down, and singing (similar to other churches I had attended), but this time I was completely lost. At one point, the priest came down the aisle, waving what looked to be a large saltshaker. As he swung it in my direction, three or four drops of water hit my face. I had no idea what was happening.

Of course, all of this was perfectly normal for my Catholic friend. But to me, it was not normal. What was expected of me? Was I doing anything improper? My insecurity multiplied when I couldn't anticipate or understand the order of events.

I'd been a comfortable visitor at the other churches. At this service, I was an outsider.

That distinction makes a huge difference in the way people feel when they attend church, and it has shaped the way we've tried to approach those who visit our church.

Ins and outs

We think of visitors in two major categories. First, we expect a lot of insiders, people who understand traditional church subculture. They know what to expect before they walk through the door.

The second group I'll refer to as outsiders. They have no idea what takes place during a church service. Many don't know the basic beliefs of the Christian faith. It's easy for this group to feel anxious about their first visit. It's the fear of the unknown.

Some churches regularly receive visitors from both groups, insiders and outsiders. Our church, for example, has visitors each week who are Jewish, Catholic, Hindu, or completely unchurched. Many of these first-timers are uncomfortable with even our basic songs and prayers, not to mention the suspicion that they might be asked to speak or to find a Bible verse.

Conversely, traditional methods of greeting are acceptable to insiders. These people expect to stand and be recognized, to meet several of the regular members, and to respond to other church customs.

Potential problems surface when the service regularly tries to accommodate both insiders and outsiders. Should the church risk subjecting outsiders to discomfort in order to make visiting insiders feel welcome? Or is it better to do everything possible to reduce the anxiety of visiting outsiders, even though insiders may tend to feel overlooked?

As we faced this dilemma, we finally decided to place more consideration on the feelings of the outsiders, without writing off the insiders. Experience shows us that visitors can be made to feel welcome without the name tags, official greeters, or special recognition. The objective of making a visitor feel welcome has been one of our driving goals. Let me take you through what we hope is a first-timer's experience at Willow Creek.

Anxiety reduction

Our attempt to make people feel comfortable by reducing anxiety begins in the parking lot. Friendly attendants show visitors where to park. We try to prevent confusing hassles, whether they involve searching for parking places or wondering which door to enter.

Inside each entrance of the church are two or three greeters. They offer a "Good morning" or "Hello," and try to spot people who look disoriented. They give directions when needed, help newcomers guide their children to the appropriate locations, and generally direct incoming people toward the auditorium.

As people enter the auditorium, they receive a program. (Our references to auditorium/program rather than sanctuary/bulletin are intentional; they reflect the language of our nonchurched visitors.) The program clearly outlines the order of the events, and it includes only announcements that might be of interest to outsiders. (Insiders also attend a

church service on Wednesday nights, where they receive a
program geared to reach regular church attenders.) Ushers
guide people to open sections rather than specific seats, so
they are free to sit where they wish and claim their own
space. Our auditorium has theater-type seats rather than
pews. (First-timers don't have to worry that some stranger
will slide up against them.)

We also strive to keep anxiety to a minimum with the
service itself. The first thirty minutes of our service are allot-
ted for programming such as a short Scripture reading to
introduce the topic of the day, a drama, and a short, easy
song or chorus that even first-timers can learn effortlessly.
After the chorus, during which people are standing, we say
something such as, "As you're seated, turn and greet some of
the people around you." We don't distinguish members and
visitors. It's just a time for a brief and friendly interchange.

Only after these attempts to reduce the anxiety of our visitors do we formally acknowledge them. During the announcements (about twenty minutes into the service), we tell
them we consider visitors our welcome guests we want to
serve. If they want to find out more about our church, we
give them the options of: (1) stopping by a counter in the
lobby for more information as they leave; (2) being contacted
later, which they can arrange by filling in a section of the
program and dropping into the offering plate; or (3) calling
the church at the number listed in their program. Our program also includes an invitation to our Wednesday night service if they want to take the next step in their spiritual life.

We don't pressure visitors any further. We try to take the
first step in their direction. Then, when they're ready to take a
step toward us, we'll take another step. Our goal is for visitors
to think, *That wasn't so bad!*

Intangible overtures

Instead of focusing on the tangible overtures to visitors—name tags, address forms, the firm handshake of a greeter—we strive to achieve two important intangibles.

The first is warmth. When you enter someone's home for the first time, you can tell within fifteen seconds whether the living room creates warm or cold impressions. You may not be able to explain how you know, but you do.

The same is true for churches. It's possible to be name-tagged, greeted numerous times, and asked to stand—all in the name of friendliness—only to go home with the impression that the church you visited left you cold. So here are a few things we do to try to warm the atmosphere.

Greeters.   We train our greeters and ushers in how to make people feel comfortable, and to be comfortable themselves. I've seen churches where some of the volunteers were willing servants but made curiously inappropriate greeters (people with perpetual scowls, arrogant attitudes, or overbearing dispositions). And I've come to believe it's better to do without than to have greeters who overwhelm, alienate, or intimidate newcomers.

The building.   Most congregations have a person or two with interior decorating talent. We sought these people and asked them to suggest ways to warm up the church through interior appointments, plants, auditorium banners, and so forth. This is one area where smaller churches can be particularly effective, because many larger church buildings often have more of a corporate feel.

People also appreciate a clean, well-maintained building. Research shows that cleanliness outscored the thrill of the attractions and friendliness of employees as the number-one draw at Walt Disney World. It means a lot to church visitors, too. Problems such as cracked paint, litter, dirt, ugly trash cans, and other unkempt items can destroy a warm image.

Music.   Most church music leaders plan their preludes, hymns, offertories, and choral selections. They also include long, reverential pauses for prayer and brief silences during transitions. But what some don't realize is that almost any length of silence can be uncomfortable for visitors. So we try to utilize pleasant background music prior to the service, during transitions, and anywhere else it might reduce anxiety.

Prayer.   The way people pray communicates how they relate to God. When congregational prayers are simple, basic, and conversational, God may not seem so foreign to visitors.

Miscellaneous elements.   Several other components can help create warmth: (1) Humor is effective in bringing down defenses, though it is important to select appropriate times and people to make it work naturally. (2) Visitors can feel uncomfortable when leaders seem anxious. But if an inexperienced speaker or singer admits nervousness, those in the congregation won't be so likely to feel uneasy when his voice quivers or her hands shake. (3) When an unexpected event takes place (such as a loud sneeze), a spontaneous response from the pulpit (perhaps a "God bless you") demonstrates warmth. (4) While clothing, in itself, may not generate much warmth for your church, it can become a barrier if newcomers perceive your leaders as either too tailored or too tattered.

A second intangible is electricity. If you've ever walked into a football stadium full of excited people waiting for a game to begin, you've no doubt experienced that "special something" in the air. The power of anticipation surges through such a place, and you feel as if you belong, even though you may not know a soul. You sense a common bond of expectation.

Churches also can create that exciting sensation. While it's a little more difficult to generate electricity than to promote warmth, as we consider the possibilities in our church, we keep three things in mind:

The importance of creativity. If the order of events is much the same from one week to the next, people may not try too hard to attend regularly. The feeling is similar to watching a taped football game, knowing the final score ahead of time. The element of the unknown is lost. We want people to walk into our church with a sense of anticipation, wondering what's going to be different this week.

First impressions. The first fifteen minutes of a service are extremely important. If you traditionally start slowly or tend to get the announcements "out of the way" first, it's hard to pick up the momentum. We try to start strong, usually with music, and then vary the intensity level for the individual elements of the service.

The scope of the service. It's better to do a few things well than a lot of things poorly. Electricity is not the result of trying to do something more and bigger each week. A simple song with piano accompaniment likely will be more effective than an unrehearsed full ensemble.

The presence of warmth and electricity will speak volumes about a church and God. Even when omitting the traditional means of greeting, visitors can feel welcome and leave with a satisfied feeling that they would like to return.

System convert

Does our system work? Most people like it, although we occasionally get complaints from insiders who didn't feel as welcomed as expected. But outsider Lee Strobel endorsed our system.

Lee was an atheist when he first came to Willow Creek. He recalls, "I didn't like traditional church services, and my number-one desire was anonymity. I didn't want to be singled out, smothered with affection, or forced to sign anything. As the legal affairs editor of the *Chicago Tribune*, I even carried my reporter's notebook so I could brush off anyone who tried to get too personal with me."

But Lee became a Christian. The anonymity we provided gave him the time to investigate Christianity at his own pace. Knowing he wouldn't be embarrassed at a service, he kept coming back. And by coming, he learned. Lee says he liked having control over when he would take the next step.

How do I know so much about Lee? Because a few years after becoming a Christian, he wholeheartedly traded in his lifelong passion as a journalist to join our staff. He began as director of service activities, which put him in charge of making good first impressions on newcomers. Today he is director of communications, where he uses his experience as a journalist, and teaching pastor.

As leaders, we evaluate our church as a newcomer would. Where we find "traditions" that might cause anxiety or self-consciousness, we try to substitute new ways to yield warmth and electricity.

We want first-timers to leave our services not only with the spoken message that God cares, but also with the unspoken message that we care. If we're unsuccessful the first time, we may not have another opportunity.

PART 2

Engage

6

The Gospel for Generation X

*Busters don't want to talk; they want to respond. This is their
great strength.*

—DIETER ZANDER

Perhaps no other generation has needed the church so
much, yet sought it so little.

In *Life after God,* Douglas Coupland describes this generation: "Life was charmed but without politics or religion. It
was the life of the children of the pioneers—life after God. A
life of earthly salvation on the edge of heaven."

Coupland is writing about *baby busters,* those now in their
teens, twenties, and early thirties. The surge in births following World War II gave us the baby boom and the huge, well-
known generation dubbed baby boomers. From about 1965
through 1980, the number of births went bust, giving a name
to a new generation with a substantially different mind-set.
Sometimes called Generation X, this group has been much
maligned and badly stereotyped in the media.

I began working with busters while coaching the Pomona
(California) College soccer team. I invited the players to
church. They shook their heads. "I don't want to go 'cause it's
boring, irrelevant, and there's no one there like me," was a
typical response.

I'd say, "Well, they've got this great singles thing." But then
came the reply, "I'm not into a singles thing, either." That
puzzled me; when I was single, I would have been drawn to a

singles group. But this generation was saying, "Look, if it's not for me, I'm not interested." I learned that busters don't want to be a boomer subset, waiting to become "legitimate."

What came out of those conversations was a wild idea of starting a church, and in 1986, I helped launch New Song, a church for busters. When I left last year, to create a buster ministry at Willow Creek Community Church, the average age of New Song members was twenty-six. Seventy percent of the church was single. Of the fourteen staff members, ten were under age thirty.

I love with passion this generation, and one of my missions in life is to reach busters for Christ and to inspire others to do the same. Here is what I've discovered in trying to connect with busters.

Buster characteristics

Technically, everyone born between 1965 and 1980 is a baby buster. Being a buster, however, is more attitude than age. One important demarcation is whether you want to, or believe you can, achieve the traditional American dream. This dream includes a house in the 'burbs, corporate success, and financial rewards. As a whole, baby boomers pursued this dream, and many achieved it.

Most busters, though, believe that the traditional American dream is beyond their grasp. Plus, they have watched boomers destroy their families and relationships while climbing the corporate ladder. To busters, owning expensive cars and homes doesn't matter as much as the feeling of being loved and accepted.

Busters are fashioning a new American dream: to be whole, and to live in harmony with others and their surroundings. They would rather work to live than live to work. A career is a means to an end, a way to pursue the deeper things in life; it's not the end in itself.

It is all too easy to generalize about busters, but here are several additional parts of their story:

Pain.   On the surface, busters can seem positive, even bubbly. But below the surface often lies pain. Close to fifty percent come from divorced and blended families. Many were latchkey kids who came home from school each day to an empty house and fended for themselves. One effect is that many lacked role models necessary for success in life. Some busters I know still lack basic skills in communicating, resolving conflict, keeping a job, balancing a checkbook.

This pain in family life created an aloneness, which is different from just being lonely. Aloneness is an experience of the soul: you are surrounded by people but unable to connect with them. The search for intimacy is a driving force in their lives. As a result, many busters are searching for the family they never had.

For busters, family is more frequently defined as those who will love them, not those who produced them. Often, friends are more family than are parents or siblings. Thus, community—open, safe, inclusive relationships in which people help each other rather than compete—is the highest value of this generation.

Postmodern mind-set.   Busters don't believe in absolute truth. To them, everything is relative, and everything could be true. They are the first generation to reflect the postmodern ideas circulating in French and American universities since the 1970s. (For an explanation of the postmodern mind-set, see "Star Trek and the Next Generation: Postmodernism and the Future of Evangelical Theology" by Stanley Grenz, originally published in the March 1994 issue of *Crux,* the journal of Regent College. An expanded version will be published by Eerdmans in *A Postmodern Primer.*)

Busters can live with two contradictory ideas. They can be pro-choice in regard to abortion, for example, and pro-life in regard to whales and trees. They will also say they want a meaningful and lasting relationship with a lover, but if someone better comes along, they'd rather have him or her.

Fear.   Many busters fear the future. Everything out there seems broken. The economy seems beyond repair. The environment is ruined. Sex isn't fun anymore because of AIDS, and marriage is a risky venture likely to fail. Busters are angry because they know they'll have to pay for the national debt and the social security of the generation that handed it to them. The world holds little hope. Even the label *buster* reinforces this feeling. Boomer sounds positive, as if something is about to break out and happen. But buster sounds like something broken, something that needs to be thrown away.

Paradoxically, in the midst of this nearly hopeless outlook, busters are trying to create hope on a local scale. They want to put their lives into something that will make a difference.

Grassroots orientation.   As with the Dutch boy in the fable, busters want to plug the hole in the dam, even though it seems inevitable that the dam will break anyway. This feeling of inevitability comes from the belief that busters have never really had a chance to win big. Most of the soldiers who served in the Persian Gulf War, for example, were busters, but they weren't allowed to put Saddam Hussein out of business for good.

Busters graduated from college, only to find the tightest job market in two decades, because boomers were holding all the jobs.

Since they feel they can't win on a large scale, some busters look to win on a small scale—in relationships, or local causes, or personal contributions to global needs. *U.S. news & World Report* called them "the fix-it generation," a label with which many seem to resonate.

For example, recycling is not found on any spiritual-gifts list in the Bible, but at New Song we had a recycling ministry. There was a consensus that God created the earth and that he gave us the responsibility of taking care of it; therefore recycling is a legitimate ministry. We began to make sure we printed on recyclable paper and provided recycling bins. We even found recyclable plastic cups for Communion.

Spiritual hunger.   Finally, busters are looking for transcendent meaning, and in this sense they are a spiritual generation. Again, with their postmodern mind-set, they don't believe that science alone—the empirical method—can solve our problems. They believe that something is wrong with the world, and that there must be something beyond what they can see, feel, touch, taste, and smell.

This makes them as open to Christian revival as any generation, but it also opens them to cult activity. Many toy with various forms of New Age and Eastern religion, including the pantheistic idea of connecting with God through nature.

Buster evangelism

One young woman was still living with her single mother when she started attending our church. She participated for a long time. Then she became a Christian. The primary thing that drew her to Christ was the church as the family of God. She became a Christian because she found a place in which love was being expressed.

In years past, becoming a Christian preceded becoming a church attender. That sequence is no longer valid with busters. Incredibly, they may be part of a fellowship for months or years before taking that first step of faith. Churches effective at reaching busters for Christ encourage nonbelievers to participate in small groups or other ministries.

Obviously, we're not going to ask nonbelieving attenders to be leaders in the church, but to reach busters, we must increase their contact with Christians. Busters are attracted to Christ by being attracted to what's happening in the lives of Christians. We need to find ways to make nonbelieving busters feel welcome and participate, even before they provide evidence of commitment to Christ.

Large-group meetings can build credibility with busters, but if relationships aren't built outside those settings, busters will not respond. At New Song, evangelism efforts were never a big rally and a big-name speaker. A raise-your-hand, stand-up-and-come-forward presentation didn't work.

Nor will busters respond to a book that is handed to them. Many will read a book and say, "That's fine. That's true in that book, but I don't believe it's true for me." Busters process truth better relationally than propositionally. Evangelism at New Song happened through bicycle trips, hikes, and mountain climbs.

To reach busters means someone will need to spend time with them, someone who feels comfortable sharing why he or she became a Christian, someone willing to expose the work of Christ in his or her life. This approach is labor-intensive, so it's more important than ever for pastors to empower people on the front lines. It is the church members who will help their friends cross that line of commitment to Christ.

Of course, to win busters, we must overcome the negative caricature of Christianity that many of them hold. To the unbelieving buster, Christians are whacked-out extremists. In *Life after God,* Coupland writes that religious types "take things too literally and miss too many points because of this literalism. . . . Now the radio stations all seem to be talking about Jesus nonstop. And it seemed to be this crazy orgy of projection with everyone projecting onto Jesus the antidotes to the things that had gone wrong in their own lives. . . . I was cut off from their experience in a way that was never connectable."

To present a picture of Christ that busters can relate to, we need to rely on the power of story. Busters have never read the Bible, and unlike boomers, they don't care what *Time* magazine or other experts have to say. But they will listen to your story, especially if it honestly describes the difficult as well as the good aspects of following Christ. They will listen to the story of someone who hasn't necessarily been successful but has been faithful.

Storytelling is the most effective way to reach this generation, because busters won't argue with a person's story. In fact, it may be their only absolute: everyone's story is worth listening to and learning from. Here's what needs to be communicated: "God's story intersected with my story; now I can share it with you so that you can consider making it a part of your story."

Buster communication

Jay Leno's *Tonight Show* began boomer style—predictable, news-based, a sequence you can set your watch by. David Letterman's show, on the other hand, started as a stream of consciousness—radical, unpredictable, messy. It's buster style.

You may not be ready to retool your service to look like Letterman's show, but what's most important is the way we communicate to busters. Here are several principles I keep in mind when I'm "communicating" (a term I prefer to "preaching").

Be real.   I'm more boomer in age, and in trying to speak to busters, I tried to be busterish. Some close friends pulled me aside and said, "Dieter, what are you doing? This isn't you. You be you, and we'll be us. We love you the way you are." While busters want to be accepted as they are, they're also willing to accept you as you are, provided you're *real*. That's freeing.

You don't have to change the way you dress—just be willing to accept the way they dress. Real means being vulnerable and honest. Busters don't believe that in the course of an hour a problem can be solved with an acronym.

Periodically, I would say, "Folks, I don't want you to think that I've got this together, because we're all wrestling with this," or "You're probably sitting there thinking, *I could never do that.* Well, you can."

With so much in life image-based, the busters hunger for reality.

Be rousing.   The term *rousing* is a hunting term for flushing an animal out of hiding. To reach busters, fresh methods are needed: videos, music, drama, personal stories. But an axiom every baby-boomer pastor ought to note is that busters do not just want to be entertained. A slick presentation that avoids the tough, honest, and sometimes unanswerable questions will not impress.

When we addressed homosexuality, I talked about what the Bible said and also had an actor perform a soliloquy, reading a letter written by a buster who struggled with homosexuality. In the letter, this young man had written about what it felt like to come to church as a homosexual and about his fear of God. That was rousing for our people; it allowed me to clearly explain the Bible's guidelines on sexual activity and also emphasize compassion.

At New Song, our goal was not that people would say "Wow!" We wanted people to say "Hmmm"—to have a thoughtful experience.

Be relevant.   Busters are crying out for practical sermons. At New Song, we did a teaching series on sex, and I talked about the fact that God is the inventor of sex. While it may sound elementary, the concept was radical for our busters, who had viewed Christianity as a litany of don'ts.

In this series, we talked about why God doesn't want us to be involved sexually outside of marriage; we said God's rules were God's ways of protecting us. And we incorporated people's stories into the services. One young woman told about a sexual relationship in which she contracted AIDS; later, when she became pregnant, she unknowingly passed it to her daughter. Another couple talked about how when they became Christians, they made a concerted effort not to be sexually active until marriage, and how that had positively affected their relationship.

At New Song, we tried not to make sex a bigger issue than it is. For many busters, sex is the only language of love they know. We helped them to see that this is a knee-jerk reaction and then held them accountable to develop good habits to replace the old ones. But we tried to do it in a way that stressed grace: "Even if you've failed, there's hope. We're not going to judge you. We're here to help you. We're not doing this because we have a hidden agenda, but because you're valuable."

But does *relevance* mean talking only about sex, or other thinly disguised psychological topics? No, for busters what is most relevant is the core of the gospel—redemption and reconciliation. To be reclaimed and made beautiful again, and to be brought back into relationship with God and others, are two truths that penetrate busters' broken hearts. Busters have been trashed, so they feel like trash.

When we explain that God is saying, "You're not trash," they'll listen.

Be relational.   With busters, avoiding "us-versus-them" dichotomies is essential. We tried to emphasize "talking with" rather than "talking to" in an environment akin to sitting around tables, as opposed to sitting in rows. I attempted to downplay my lead-person-up-front role and even provided a question-and-answer time.

For many busters, the Christian message itself is divisive. Because community and relationships are their ultimate values, divisiveness is the ultimate evil. They think the Christian message divides people into the haves and the have-nots (which in an ultimate sense, it does).

One of the most powerful pictures for a buster is the global community within the body of Christ. At New Song, we had every ethnic variation imaginable in the service and on the stage. This painted a picture of redemption and reconciliation that cuts across socioeconomic and ethnic lines; it's a compelling picture for a relationship-oriented buster.

Buster discipleship

Busters will have a style of ministry different from that of boomers. To release them into ministry requires different strategies.

Emphasize compassion ministries.   Busters don't want to

talk; they want to respond. This is their great strength. They will avoid discussing the evils of abortion, for example; they'd rather contribute to the alternatives of crisis-pregnancy counseling or adoption work.

Downplay the institution.   Busters react negatively to the notion their church is an institution or organization. At New Song, we never implied, "We need you to keep the institution going." Instead they need to feel ownership of the ministry and that they have a voice in where the ministry is going.

Busters tend to have a lot of disposable income (largely because many are living at home). They're willing to part with it, but they need to believe in what they give to and they need to see results from it. They won't just give to the institution. But they will give to particular projects (through the institution), especially if they feel emotionally drawn to those projects.

Busters demand honesty about what's going on in the church. They want their leaders to be straight with them. If the church communicates *You're supposed to be giving,* most busters will turn a deaf ear. But they will listen if the message comes across as, "It costs $17 every week per chair to advance the kind of ministries you are benefiting from. If you're sitting in that chair and you're not able to contribute, that means someone else is paying for your chance to receive all of this. That's fine if you can't give, but if you can and you're not, then you need to rethink your giving habits."

Adapt what it means to be a leader.   The term *leader* can be frightening to busters. They have a natural suspicion of anyone trying to lead them somewhere. At New Song, we even avoided the word *committees*; instead we used the word *teams*. Busters tend to be the *we* generation: working together is important. We used a team approach even for teaching in worship services. Within a service we might use two or three different *communicators* —one giving a seven-minute presentation, someone else coming up with a twelve-minute presentation, and so on. Everyone would talk about the same thing, but from different perspectives.

Let them fail. Busters tend to be paranoid about failing, but they need to have freedom to fail (and succeed) in ministry. And they will fail you. While busters want relationships, it may take six months or a year for them to trust you. They may test you by staying away from church or activities just to see if you'll follow up on them.

Busters need you to tell stories of your failures; they need to know that God uses imperfect people. At staff meetings, I was honest about my failings. This communicated that I didn't have it all together, just as they didn't have it all together, but God could still use me and them.

Let them lead. I wondered how New Song would do after my departure, given the relational nature of busters. The church mourned our leaving; my family and I mourned the end of our years there.

After we left, the staff and elders formed a pastoral team that now fulfills the role of senior pastor. Under its leadership, New Song has thrived, continuing to maintain its distinctives, continuing to grow, and making plans to plant a spin-off church.

Busters can lead and pastor. They will do so, however, with their values of teamwork, relationship, and community. I am confident that churches such as New Song, led by busters, will teach us how to fashion a ministry approach that will reach their generation.

Busters have paid a high price for their life after God.

"My secret is that I need God," Coupland confesses in *Life after God.* "That I am sick and can no longer make it alone. I need God to help me give because I no longer seem to be capable of giving. To help me be kind, as I no longer seem capable of kindness. To help me love, as I seem beyond being able to love."

We must move beyond seeing busters as a scourge, as slackers and losers. It's my prayer that God would help us understand, accept, and value this generation.

7

What It Takes to Reach Men

One myth of men's ministry is that men won't join. They will join, if it's not forced and if the cause is big enough.

—STU WEBER

Several years ago, I watched a local television talk show about men who had attended a seminar with Robert Bly, author of *Iron John*. I thought, *Now I'll get to see what the men's movement is all about. These local guys will give it to me straight.*

But I was struck by how confused the men appeared. As if in a recovery group, they shared their stories of disappointment and pain.

But they never got beyond them, except to say, "It's been great sharing." *There must be more to being a healthy man*, I thought, *than saying how disappointed you are.*

This yearning has caused the male-identity search to spread to the Christian arena. In 1995, more than 700,000 men participated in Promise Keepers weekends in thirteen cities. This year, twenty-five rallies are planned. This is more than a reaction to prevailing secular winds. This Christian men's movement is an artesian well bursting through all the loose places on the surface of our country. It's a gusher not created by human engineering. It's nothing less than the Spirit of God at work.

I've always wondered why the church had such tremendous ministries to women, students, and children, but nothing to men. When I connect with other guys, I feel fulfilled, vision-oriented, energetic. As I saw what was happening in our culture, a dream began to take shape: Wouldn't it be great to gather a hundred guys who enjoyed being men? And wouldn't it be great to do it in the local church?

Right time, right place

Not knowing where to begin, I decided to preach a series on the family and to start with men. What began as three messages on what it means to be a man turned out to be eight. I can't explain why, but the topic connected powerfully with our congregation. The feeling on those Sunday mornings was electric. I could sense people leaning forward to listen.

The normal number of requests for sermon tapes (from our homespun tape ministry) was thirty or forty per week. The weeks I spoke on the principles of masculinity, the requests shot up to three hundred (which says more about their hunger than about my preaching). But I couldn't continue preaching about men forever.

As an aside, on the last Sunday, I said, "I'll be here at the church next Saturday morning at 9:00. If you're a man and you're interested in discussing more on what it means to be a man, show up then, and we'll talk some more."

You have to understand what I had just asked of our men. Oregon and Washington are the forty-ninth and fiftieth states in church attendance per capita. This is a put-me-on-my-acre-age-and-let-me-be-a-pioneer culture. Saturday mornings are especially sacrosanct in Oregon. I expected maybe ten or twelve guys.

The next Saturday, three hundred men showed up. I was flabbergasted. We stayed till noon, and before everyone left, I said, "We're going to start a men's ministry. You're telling us that much."

Prepare, prepare, prepare

Something worthwhile is worth preparing. In creating a ministry to men, we did not want a false start. The quickest way to a false start was to say, "Let's get on the bandwagon and get some guys together and have a few doughnuts and see how long we can last."

Something substantive would take leadership.

But I knew I couldn't lead the ministry. As a pastor, I was too busy already. I prayed and committed myself to find two or three lay leaders with the vision.

Two guys in their upper thirties, who were best buddies, emerged. One is more of an upfront person; the other more behind-the-scenes. Both are rock-solid believers, and their friendship has been a godsend in rough water, so they understand the power of male friendship.

Those two lay leaders, a staff pastor who would oversee the ministry, and I attended a Promise Keepers weekend in Boulder, Colorado. The rally and worship with 50,000 men were breathtaking; the spiritual fireworks were spectacular. The most helpful part, though, was the three-day leadership conference prior to the weekend rally. The training provided us with the vision for our ministry.

During that week, our group members kept saying, "This is great, but how would this fit in our church?" We didn't want to copy Promise Keepers, though that organization provided some excellent resource material; we wanted to be Good Shepherd Community Church. God changes history when the little people in the little places do what they should. We wanted to be God's men in little Gresham.

So, we looked a little further and dug a little deeper. We also profited greatly from Cross Trainer in Des Moines, Iowa, a ministry that has effectively brought together men from many denominations.

Taking the high ground

The fall before our January kickoff, we invited fifteen men to a series of planning meetings. Some were senior-aged men, some in their middle forties, some CEO-types, some blue-collar men. They helped us form our purpose and our plans for a kickoff event.

Our culture keeps punching at men. We felt the best way to motivate a man is to point to the high ground and say, "That's what the Lord wants of us, and none of us is there yet. Let's lock arms and lean into the wind and climb that mountain together."

We didn't want to heap guilt on men or pressure them into accountability groups. The key for us was affirmation and acceptance: let's learn to be men together. Our purpose statement is "to point men to the High Ground of God's intentions in their relationship with him, with one another, in their homes, their church, and their world by providing biblical teaching, strong encouragement, motivating challenges, and mutual accountability."

For the kickoff, we landed a well-known speaker for a Friday night and Saturday conference. Men lined up to register ahead of time. We even sold gift certificates to the women in our church, saying, "Guys, this is what we're planning (a bunch of us are coming). By the way—daughters, wives, moms—if you want your guy to be here, pay for it and give the registration certificate as a gift."

Men responded, and a surprisingly large number showed up for the kickoff event held in our church.

Platooning

It's okay to go to a battalion meeting, but most combat takes place in the platoons. At the end of our opening weekend, we announced, "We're going to get together every Tuesday morning at 6:15 at the church." In our planning phase, we had decided we needed to funnel the men into smaller groups, but we wanted to offer them freedom to make that decision at their own pace.

We called these Tuesday morning meetings "High Ground" because we live in Oregon where everybody loves to go to the mountains. Here is how we did it last spring:

From 6:15 to 6:30, men arrived and hung out, eating doughnuts (nonfat, of course) and drinking coffee. From 6:30 to 6:55, an instructor, usually another staff member or I, taught. One morning, for example, I told about one of my best friends who died while I knelt beside him in the woods on opening morning of hunting season in Oregon. He left behind a seventeen-year-old son, a thirteen-year-old daughter, and an eight-year-old son. I asked, "Now that his life was over, what had he done that really mattered?" In his case, he'd left a powerful legacy. He was committed wholeheartedly both to his family and to God's family.

After the twenty-five-minute talk, we dismissed the group, giving the men four options:

Leave.   Some men needed to get to work; others were not yet comfortable with the intimacy of a smaller group. We'd say, "It's not even seven a.m.; you can still get to work on time. But if you'd like to stay, here are other options, which will take only thirty minutes."

Attend a newcomers' group.   This is an informal time when men get oriented to the group, meet leaders, and ask questions.

Attend a "Bull Pen."   These are informal groups (ten to fifteen men each) offering the opportunity to discuss the morning's topic. Men can just sit and soak in the conversation or jump into the discussion. Each group has a leader with prepared questions from the morning's talk.

Join a 4-A Team.   These groups, which stress acceptance, affirmation, accountability, and authority, have two to five men meeting once a week (on Tuesday mornings or at another time). This is clearly the next level of commitment, and we want all our men to end up here. We tell them that the highest ground is deep friendship with another man.

The goal is to become accountable with the other members of the 4-A team. The understood rule: confidentiality, which allows men to talk about tough issues.

The next Tuesday, after our kickoff weekend, more than a third of those conference attenders showed up bright and early. We met every Tuesday morning until the first of June. (In Oregon, summers are off limits. You don't fight it; you join it.)

Learning to swim

Our ministry to men is still young; we're just wading into the water. But several principles have helped us:

Model both failure and conviction.   Last spring, I told our men one of my big failures with my firstborn son:

"I had never been a dad before; my son had never been a son before; we were going to school together. One time he made the mistake of violating the two rules of my home of origin: Don't sass your mom; don't sass your dad. When he did, my hand 'involuntarily' hit him in the chest. I say involuntarily because it happened before I knew it was happening. I knocked him backward over the couch.

"As he fell, I realized what I had done, so I fell with him. As we lay on the ground, I began crying and said, 'Could you possibly forgive me?' " That story provided a teaching moment for our men. Father failures, leadership failures, husband failures—every man has failed, so they can identify with failure. Men's speakers must be able to say, "Here's what happened to me. I often blow it."

But transparency isn't enough; you've got to model open conviction, the commitment to grow beyond the failure and in Christ. Both emphases must be there.

Know the men you're trying to reach.   We continually remind our men that they have a choice: we want them to move to the 4-A teams, but they might need to test the waters, and they might not end up staying on the first 4-A team they choose. Some men's ministries, however, demand high commitment up front. For instance, men won't be allowed to attend unless they bring at least one friend and commit to attending each session for the entire year.

The difference in commitment is the result of a difference, I believe, in culture. A more white-collar congregation might rise to an up-front call for high-level commitment; they may not feel threatened by it because, as CEO-types, they've been taking on challenges their entire lives.

But for other congregations, a more open-ended approach, where men are allowed to proceed at their own pace, seems to work better. The point is, each church needs to evaluate its locale in order to create the right program to reach its men.

One myth of men's ministry is that men won't join. They will join, if it's not forced and if the cause is big enough.

Ease men into deeper relationships. We tell the men in our 4-A groups to temper their expectations, that it is not a miracle group. It's a group of guys committed to mutual best interests. It's not a pass-fail test.

At the beginning of each new group, we suggest that the men make a list of four questions, personal and specific, they want to be asked each week. Then, they may hand that list to someone in their group the next time they meet.

This helps to short-circuit the awkwardness that can plague the early stages of intimacy. And it allows for those incredibly bonding "Oh, you too? I thought I was the only one" kind of moments.

Speak to their issues. It sounds obvious, but men need to hear about men. We try to speak to the issue of fathering, for example. Recently, to do that, I told our men about my youngest boy:

> My youngest son is the third of three boys. The first two are high-powered; the third is not any less high-powered, but he's the third out of three. By the time you've had a brother who's all-conference this and another brother who's all-conference that, there's not much left for you to do.

As a father, I worried about our caboose. He is the most sensitive of the three. To encourage him, I spent a lot of time with him in the outdoors camping, hunting, fishing. Anybody who has spent time in the outdoors knows that a pocketknife is essential gear. The man with the best blade gets the job done. So, whenever you're setting up camp, you're always looking for the knife.

My son Ryan had a pocketknife that became his identity. His older brothers always had to ask him to use the knife as we were setting up camp. That became his status in the tribe. He was the man with the blade.

Before my birthday one year, my family was planning a party for me. Earlier in the afternoon, my youngest walked into my office at home where I was studying. At first I didn't hear him; I felt him—I could sense his presence—and I turned around.

He had chosen this moment because he wanted to give me a birthday present, but not at the birthday party. He wanted it to be just him and me. He handed me a present, and I opened it—his knife. As my eyes lifted to his, his eyes looked into mine. This was one of those rare moments when the spirit meets the spirit, with no verbal way to communicate adequately the deep feeling between you.

The story provided the foundation for other men to ask questions about their fathers and how they're fathering.

Train leaders.   C. S. Lewis wrote, "It is painful, being a man, to have to assert the privilege, or the burden, which Christianity lays upon my sex. I am crushingly aware of how inadequate most of us are, on our actual and historical individualities, to fill the place prepared for us."

We believe the leaders of men must be men who are confident of their masculinity. Our leaders must be able to answer, "What does it mean to be a man?" If a leader can't answer, he certainly can't help other men celebrate their masculinity.

For us, the answer to that question lies in the Creation account and other key Scriptures. We believe God holds a man responsible for those near and dear to him. A married man is called to give himself up so his wife can be the woman God intended her to be.

In addition, male leaders must be secure enough in the grace of God to share their failures because that's what opens up the hearts of men.

Modeling masculinity

Garrison Keillor says manhood, once an opportunity for achievement, is now an obstacle to overcome. That's why today, more than ever, men need to know masculinity is to be celebrated. They'll follow anybody who says, "I'm glad you're a man, and I respect you for being one."

A pastor doesn't have to be the athletic, outdoor type to lead men. The real muscle of a man is not on his shoulders or in his biceps. It's in his heart, in his character.

One man who mentored me (I would follow him to the ends of the earth, in fact) has always doubted his masculinity. His father never approved of him, and his mother was a perfectionist. But I'd follow that guy anywhere because he's authentic, a man who is committed in his heart to do right by God.

That kind of modeling gives men permission to be men. They want to know it's not only okay to be a man, it's critical to be a man. That's what it takes to reach men.

8

How to Reach the Premarital Couple

We're presented with an unparalleled opportunity to touch couples seeking marriage with Christ's love.

—Doug Scott

The pattern is familiar: a couple calls the church office to say they are planning to be married and want to arrange a wedding in the church. They are not members of this church (or perhaps they were members years ago but haven't been to a service since confirmation). They may not even be members of the denomination, but they "knew someone who was married at St. Swithin's two years ago."

How should we respond? What are the pastoral possibilities inherent in these situations?

Many clergy dismiss such calls immediately, explaining that they perform services only for members of their own congregation. Others may see some of the couples and make a decision to perform the ceremony on the basis of the couple's rudimentary understanding of the Christian faith. Still others act as ecclesiastical marriage brokers, performing the ceremony for any and all who ask, usually beefing up their discretionary fund in the process.

After struggling with these questions for some time, I have devised an approach, based on a number of theological suppositions, that seems to work well.

The primary assumption

My primary assumption about all the individuals who call is that they have been prompted to call by the Holy Spirit. To be sure, they are probably unaware of this prompting, but in each of these situations, I assume God is giving me an opportunity to do some serious examination with the couple about the nature and quality of Christian marriage.

The couple may have their own reasons for calling the church, and each of them is woefully familiar to every minister:

"Your church is so pretty."

"Your church is close to our reception hall."

"My second cousin was married there by the minister who was there before you."

Their initial reason for calling is unimportant. The Holy Spirit has prompted them to call your church, even if yours is the fourth or fifth on the list of possible places. You have been presented with an unparalleled opportunity to reach out with Christ's love to two people who may have never before experienced it in all its fullness. I don't dismiss such opportunities quickly.

My second assumption when the unchurched call is that this may be the first time they have ever turned to the church for help. If they are a young couple, both sets of parents are probably still living, and there is a good chance, given increasing rates of longevity, that the grandparents are living as well. Consequently, this couple may never have had an opportunity or the need to turn to the church in time of crisis. While they may have attended Sunday school in childhood, their most recent experience of church was probably a Christmas Eve service a number of years ago. For the first time in their lives, they really want something from the church.

Our initial response to their call will determine whether they see the church as cold and unresponsive, or open and responsive to those outside as well as inside its fellowship.

My third assumption is that there are some shreds of spiritual awareness that prompt them to seek marriage in the church. To be sure, a certain percentage of the couples who call want a church wedding only because "it's tradition," or because their parents insist. However, we must also recognize that for others, there are certain events in their lives which they see as "religious moments." While they may want to confine their experience of God to controlled and predictable encounters, there are moments when they feel God should be included.

My fourth assumption (especially if they have no prior connection with the parish I serve) is that there may have been a problem with a previous church affiliation. Perhaps one of them is divorced and is not permitted to remarry in his or her own denomination. Perhaps one was treated harshly by a former pastor. Perhaps they were difficult and alienated themselves from the life of their initial church home and have not since been affiliated with a community of faith. In any event, they may well be spiritually homeless, and they have turned to your church. They may not be looking for a church home, but they are asking to use the house.

On the basis of these assumptions, I have determined to consent at least to meet with each couple who call inquiring about marriage.

The initial telephone call

I attempt to do some initial screening on the telephone, and I include a clear explanation of what can be expected from me. I determine where both parties live, their ages, and previous religious affiliation, if any. I ask if there were previous marriages, and if so, how long the divorce decree has been final, and where it was granted. Is at least one of the parties baptized? Have they sought to be married by another member of the clergy and been refused?

I explain to the caller that I will be glad to see the couple but that my consent does not mean I will guarantee to marry them. I insist that the interview be with both bride and groom, and that no other family members be present or accompany them. I explain that the purpose of the interview will be to determine whether we can speak seriously about being married in the church, and that at the conclusion of the interview I may consent to marry them, but in all probability no decision will be reached for some weeks. I then set a mutually convenient time when the couple can meet with me in the office, explaining that they should expect to be with me for at least an hour.

I do not make the appointment on the basis of a mother's telephone request. When a mother calls, I simply explain that I will be glad to discuss the possibility when her daughter or son calls.

The initial interview

The attitude of most couples with no parish affiliation who come for an initial premarital interview falls usually into one of two categories—apprehensive or arrogant. They are either nervous, not knowing what to expect, or they are openly disdainful of this situation, which they consider a necessary evil. In any event, they are rarely comfortable. While many clergy might not try to dispel this feeling, thus retaining an edge or advantage, I try to make the couple as comfortable as possible, remembering that they will probably judge this "church business" by their impressions of who I am and how I respond to their presence.

After pleasantries have been exchanged, I turn immediately to the form that catalogs all necessary information required by the state and my denomination. I do this simply in question-and-answer form, and include questions of the date they had in mind, the names of their witnesses, and their permanent address after marriage. The last piece of information allows me to contact the church of my denomination closest to them for referral, should they be moving some distance from this parish.

Unless the couple is very young, or there is a great difference in their ages, I do not ask why they want to be married. After interviewing hundreds of couples, I have never found one that gives me an answer other than "because we love each other." Obviously, the age of the couple may make it necessary to determine whether love—not trying to escape from a difficult family or personal situation—is their real intention. However, if they are both of reasonable age, and there are no legal or ecclesiastical impediments, I turn immediately to the meat of the interview.

My initial presentation usually runs as such:

> Let me say at the outset that I am not here to sit in judgment of you. You have decided that you want to marry each other, and because there are no legal impediments to marriage that I can determine, you have every right to do so. You have decided to marry, and I am not going to try to change your mind. Our purpose today is simply to determine whether this marriage should begin in the church. Now the state and the church view marriage very differently. In the eyes of the state, marriage is little more than a contractual agreement—the two of you agree, by contract, to do certain things for each other, and make promises about how you will conduct your life together. The contract is witnessed by two individuals of legal age. At any point in the contract, you may choose to seek to have that contract dissolved through the process we call divorce. That is how the state views marriage, and this can be performed by a judge or a mayor.
>
> The church's view of marriage, however, is very different. So let me begin by asking: What do you really want? Do you simply want to be married, or do you want to commit yourselves to the unique responsibilities of Christian marriage?

This presentation is usually followed by a silence of considerable length as the couple look at me with a blank stare. I have on occasion had a couple respond that they simply want

to be married. At that point I reply, "I'm sorry, I don't perform weddings—I preside at the services of the church. If I
had known that was all you wanted, I could have saved you
the trip. Thank you for coming." On those occasions, the
couple, flustered by the swiftness of the dismissal, invariably
back down and begin to explain what they meant by their
prompt response. The door remains open.

More often than not, however, the couple, after sitting in
silence for some time, ask what I mean. The opportunity for a
teaching dialogue between clergy and couple has been presented. I usually proceed in a question-and-answer format
designed to get at their personal spiritual development and
the impact of that development on their common life. Some
of the questions might take the following form:

How would you define your relationship with God? What
role does God play in your daily life? What does God expect
of a couple who begin their married life in the church? Have
you discussed your mutual responsibilities as a Christian
couple? How would you say Christian marriage differs from
other marriages? Do you worship together? Do you feel comfortable with the idea of praying together? Why or why not?

To be sure, most unchurched couples I've met with take the
attitude, "I try to live a good life and be nice to people," but
this avoidance of the issue must be pointed out. I make a
clear distinction between being a Christian and being "nice"
(or altruistic or philanthropic or compassionate). What I seek
from them is a clear definition of how they see God working
in their lives, and their response to that action. There are
some couples who just don't seem to get the point. Here is a
potential approach for clarifying the issue:

"Your relationship as a couple has a number of different
dimensions. There is a social dimension (you date, share
common activities and friends), an emotional dimension (you
have feelings toward and about each other that satisfy each
other's emotional needs), a financial dimension (you have
made decisions about your common property, how your
money will be handled, who will work, and at what job), a

physical dimension (the sexual expression of your emotions), and a spiritual dimension. How do you see yourselves as spiritual persons, and how do you relate on a spiritual level with each other, and with God?"

Following this exploration, the couple usually come up with one of two answers. Either they realize there is a neglected aspect of their relationship and are anxious to develop that aspect, or they state that their commitment to the Christian faith is marginal at best and that they have no intention of associating with a church following the marriage ceremony. If the former situation arises, I have an opportunity to provide direction about the development of the Christian faith in this embryonic stage. If the latter presents itself, I usually use the following approach:

> I am not a baseball fan. Understand, I believe in baseball— that is, I believe baseball exists and that there are many people whose happiness depends, in part, on the fortunes of a particular team. They go to each of the home games, wear team jackets, and put team decals on their cars. I can believe all of those things, but I am not a fan. I don't enjoy going to baseball games, and whether the Mets win or lose is of no importance to me at all. It would be strange, therefore, if I wanted to have my wedding in Shea Stadium! You see, when you are married in the church, you ask for the blessing, approval, and support of God's family as you begin your married life because God's family is important to you. During a church wedding, you make promises to each other, and to God, about your life together and your life as members of God's family.

At that point, I discuss the specific expectations of Christian marriage and the commitments made by the couple toward the church in that ceremony. Then, "Because you have made it clear that you have no commitment to the church, do you feel comfortable making solemn promises about your future involvement with the church?"

The device is obvious. Rather than making the decision for the couple, you present the couple with the teaching of the church and ask them to make the decision. Most couples have a sense of integrity and say they weren't aware this was what happened in the context of the ceremony. Frequently, they say they would rather be married in a civil ceremony than make promises they don't intend to keep. Occasionally, they say they still want to be married in the church, and at that point, you can justifiably state some expectations.

For instance: "You say you want to go ahead and make these promises to each other and to God. Each of you is willing to make these commitments to each other because you have seen some evidence that those promises are already being fulfilled. If you are serious about making these promises to God, why don't you start fulfilling them now, and see how you feel about making a long-term commitment later. That is, let's say that you are faithful in attending church and working at your Christian relationship and forgo making a decision about marriage in the church until you have had an opportunity to see how it 'feels.' In two months, after you have attended church together for a while, let's get together again and talk about the next step—making a long-term commitment to establishing a Christian relationship."

At that point, some couples say they have no intention of adhering to those expectations. In that event, they have made the decision: they do not wish to be married in the church if it entails attendance and support. I then thank them for their time and wish them well in their life together. They may, on the other hand, agree to those conditions, at which point I have provided the couple with an opportunity for a deep involvement with the community of faith.

Every attempt should be made to integrate the couple into the life of the congregation as soon as possible. Usually, their involvement leads to commitment.

The second interview

The context of the second interview is determined by the response of the couple to the conditions established at the first one. If they have expressed a desire to explore the spiritual aspect of their relationship and have agreed to a trial period of church involvement, we then discuss how they feel about their involvement thus far.

On occasion, couples have determined that church life is not for them, and they decide to forgo a church wedding in favor of a civil ceremony. More often than not, however, they have, through the movement of the Holy Spirit, found the richness inherent in Christian living and want to pursue their faith even further. A small percentage of couples agree to a period of church involvement but fail to fulfill that agreement. If that is the case, I express my confusion, saying,

> You are ready to make lifelong promises to your partner because he or she is already, in a partial way, fulfilling those promises. If you didn't see those promises being fulfilled, you would be skeptical about them being kept after the marriage ceremony. You have not demonstrated to me that you are ready to fulfill the promises you would be asked to make in a church wedding. Let me ask you again, are you ready to commit yourselves to a Christian marriage?

I have rarely had to refuse a couple. Usually they decide on their own either to commit themselves to the church or to seek a civil ceremony. From their response to the situations presented them, I tell the couple, in effect, that they already have made the decision about whether they really want to be married in the church, and that I agree (or disagree) with their decision. We then can plan the wedding itself, including a time for in-depth marital counseling.

The counseling phase

A significant portion of the premarital counseling process involves directing the couple toward full involvement in the life of the congregation. Pastors of other denominations might use a different approach, but I invariably urge the couple to attend adult inquirer classes that lead to confirmation. If they are lapsed members of my denomination, I suggest they request to be transferred from their home parish.

But more important, I emphasize not only technical membership in the church but active involvement as well. Themes centering on stewardship of their time, talent, and treasure fit naturally into the premarital program, and I see that they are directed toward programs or service groups within the congregation that would further heighten their interest and participation. In planning any fellowship or social function, I make sure the couple in question receives an invitation, either a handwritten note or a telephone call, from another member of the congregation, thus making them feel more a part of the parish family.

The congregation I serve is open and responds warmly to the presence of newcomers. The couple quickly feel at home. Should they be moving some distance from my church following their wedding, I contact the nearest church of my denomination and refer them to the pastor.

By using an approach that places the onus of the decision on the couple rather than the minister, I feel I fulfill a number of desirable goals. This approach provides an attitude of openness and caring; offers an opportunity for growth, teaching, and commitment; and most of all, allows the couple to have equity in the nature of all their commitments to each other and to God. They make the decisions and, having made them, are far more likely to fulfill the obligations inherent in Christian marriage.

9

A Game Plan for the Athletically Inclined

Sports create an environment for relationships to be forged and for Christ to be shared.

—GREG ASIMAKOUPOULOS

Jerry Philpott never attended our church. To the best of my knowledge, he never responded to an altar call. But he did to a telephone call inviting him to play eighteen holes.

A retired cop named Jim who loved golf had started attending our church. One Sunday I suggested we tee it up sometime. That afternoon we set a tee time for Tuesday morning.

On the course, Jim introduced me to two of his friends with whom we would be playing, Jerry and Rod. Before we had finished the front nine, Jim told me that Jerry had recently been diagnosed with terminal cancer, though I wouldn't have guessed it by the way he swung a golf club. Jerry didn't say much that day, but I drove back to church that morning determined to stay close to him. Tuesdays became our day for golf.

After our second outing, Jerry broke his silence about his death sentence; he was scared. I sent him a greeting card along with an article on golf written by a Christian friend of mine. I conveyed my concern and expressed my appreciation for our time together.

Each week Jerry and I chased our shots up and down the fairways. Occasionally our chats would dip below the surface.

I continued sending notes. I'd enclose a devotional thought I had come across that week. Jerry relayed his appreciation.

Three months later, Jerry's cancer was strangling his strength. He'd join us for coffee, but not for golf. Rod kept me posted on Jerry's declining condition. Before I left on an extended trip, I asked Jim if he would go with me to Jerry's home to pray with him. That afternoon, we reminisced about golf. We laughed. We prayed. Just before we left, Jerry acknowledged his need for a Savior. When I returned from my trip, Jerry had gone home to be with Christ.

Sports often feel like a rival to church involvement. A recent Gallup poll revealed that 90 percent of the American population is affected by some kind of sports activity each month, and 75 percent are affected by it each week. Americans are motivated by athletic involvement on the field, in the stands, or from the couch.

But sports can also be the church's ally. Sports are a natural way to draw close to nonbelievers. The settings create an environment for relationships to be forged and for Christ to be shared.

I decided to learn the sports-evangelism methods churches are using in order to help fulfill the Great Commission.

Intentional start

Eight years ago, Paul Van Camp, pastor of Ogema Baptist Church in rural Wisconsin, sat in his study scratching his head. What could a church with 150 attenders in a town of less than 150 people do for outreach?

As he walked across the church parking lot to the parsonage, Paul looked across the church lawn and visualized young people playing basketball on the property. The leadership of Ogema Baptist latched on to Paul's dream and voted to blacktop the field. Within months, Hi-Point Christian Basketball Camp was born.

The response was overwhelming. After two years, the old

parking lot was repaved and four portable standards were acquired to accommodate the extra participants.

"After seven summers of camps, the positive impact of our sports ministry can clearly be seen," Paul says. "Even though we've had a number of people join our church (including a coach and his wife), the greatest reward has been all the youth who have made commitments to Christ."

In my former church, the sport of choice was not basketball but golf. We scheduled an annual golf outing that included trophies, food, and novelty-type prizes. We encouraged people to invite unchurched friends and played a scramble format so golfers of all abilities could have a good time. Several men began attending church and committed their lives to Christ.

The key to an effective sports ministry, says Rodger Oswald, director of Church Sports International (a parachurch ministry based in San Jose, California), is that "there is an intentional attempt to involve those who are not yet Christians in your program. The board has to believe that we aren't just wanting to play games. They must buy into the idea that here is a nonthreatening way to reach people."

Ogema Baptist Church even eliminated its Sunday evening service during the summer so the basketball camp could begin on Sunday night. The change was acceptable because the leaders of the congregation were clear about the overall purpose of the sports ministry.

Creative measures

Hope Center Church in Pleasant Hill, California, offers a summer sports camp each July for church kids and their friends. For five days, youth ages ten through fifteen are divided into groups based on their sport of choice. Some practice football, others basketball, others soccer.

During the week, the message of salvation is presented, and devotional materials are distributed. At the end of the week, a

Christian sports celebrity from a Bay Area professional team shares his testimony. Each participant is given an auto-graphed photo and certificate of achievement.

Across town from Hope Center, a Southern Baptist church of 200 attenders has started sports evangelism on a smaller scale. The men's fellowship of Bethel Church sponsors a spring sports banquet.

"It's a chance for our small church to attempt something pretty big," says pastor Larry Baker. "We invite one of the Christians on the San Francisco 49ers to speak at a catered dinner in our church fellowship hall."

The banquet is designed for dads and their kids. The men feel they can invite someone from their work or health club who otherwise wouldn't darken the door of the church.

Here are some other ways churches have used sports means to reach gospel ends:

Opening church space to the public.   For the past ten years, Glen Ellyn Bible Church near Chicago has made its gymnasium available to basketball enthusiasts on Monday and Thursday nights. Members and their colleagues from work meet at the church for pickup games. According to executive pastor Jeff Helton, fifty men and boys show up on any given night.

More than just sweat has come out of those evenings, how-ever. Tom, for example, was brash, his mouth was foul. He had been invited by a friend from work to Glen Ellyn Bible Church's open gym. He was befriended, but his vocabulary was lovingly challenged. During the several years he played on Thursday nights, he experienced the love of caring Chris-tian men who have responded to his loss of a job and finan-cial setbacks. Tom not only started attending worship, he also became a follower of Christ.

A good question to ask is: What space indoors or outdoors would allow you to reach kids and adults through sports?

Renting outside space.   An inner-city church in San Fran-cisco did not own a gymnasium, but its singles wanted to reach the infamous Mission District where the church was located. They contacted a nearby elementary school, which rented their multipurpose room to them to start an adult volleyball league.

Churches limited in their discretionary space can use public parks and school fields. Often corporations also own facilities that can be rented. Even other community churches may be willing to allow use of their gym or field.

A group of men in another church recognized there were neighborhood boys playing catch in the streets, boys uninterested in sitting in a Sunday school class. One man conceived a neighborhood Wiffle ball tournament. He talked the church property committee into painting a ball diamond on the parking lot. Home run lines were painted on the wall of the church that faced the parking lot. The kids stood at home plate and hit toward the building, glass windows and all.

Helping parents parent.   Oswald believes many working parents feel guilt over the lack of time they spend with their children. "We recommend that churches offer Parent-Child Field Days," says Oswald. "It doesn't take much effort or manpower to plan a day for parents and kids to play silly relay games." By printing up a flier and spreading the word throughout the neighborhood, your church may reach non-Christian parents looking for ways to spend a few hours on a Saturday.

A Chicago church bought a block of tickets to a Cubs game last summer. The number of tickets allowed each family to invite a family from outside the church. A tailgate party in the church parking lot preceded the caravan of cars into downtown Chicago. Everybody attending received a box of Cracker Jacks—with a gospel tract written by a Chicago sports celebrity taped to the side.

Piggyback on national championships.   Another creative method is the Super Bowl Party Video Kit ($79.95, Discovery House, 800-269-5727). The kit, produced by a coalition of sports ministries, is designed for Christians hosting a gathering of friends and neighbors to watch the game in their home.

During halftime, an NFL veteran offers insights about what it means to experience a relationship with God.

While Oswald is excited about the video kit, he cautions, "I'd be discerning when showing a video to a nonbelieving neighbor if it's the first time he or she has been in my home. A kit approach assumes a relationship already exists."

Leisurely outreach

In the early seventies, Peninsula Covenant Church in Redwood City, California, purchased a financially troubled swim-and-tennis club adjacent to the church. It quickly gained a reputation as a church where recreation was part of its ministry. Pastor Mike Ryan played for the 1972 national champion USC Trojan football team. "If Christians are going to be relevant in the nineties," he says, "they are going to have to take advantage of our culture's preoccupation with sports and recreation. That's where God desires to speak. Beginning where you are might simply mean taking a long walk around your community to see what kinds of sports kids are into."

Sports is a universal language. Churches finding ways to speak this language may also find people ready to hear the Christian message.

10

A Strategy for Suburbanites

*Whatever programs the church may offer, the community
needs to be led gradually, across the months or years, to see
that the church cares.*

—CALVIN MILLER

Suburbia: the push-button Zion of those who have made it
and therefore have it made. There, amid the water sprinkling
systems and lava rock landscapes, rises the new Eden with
little need for God: *Paradise Found,* where churches ulcerate
themselves trying to sell self-denial to the pampered.

Can the urgency of the Cross ever be made real to those
who cocoon in front of an entertainment center and insist on
defining *hell* as dandelions and *heaven* as the proper side of
town?

Two women from our church once made a church visitation call to a suburbanite. They were fearful but brave and
wanted to extend the gospel to someone in need of Christ.
They were convinced their "prayed up" status would deliver
them from the mouth of the lion. They walked up to a door,
rang the chime doorbell, and waited beneath a plywood-
goose wreath that said WELCOME. It seemed a good omen.
But all too soon they were met by a swaggering young muscle
man—body by Nautilus—clutching a can of beer in one hand
and a remote TV control in the other. Clad only in bikini
briefs, the suburban chieftain spoke brusquely. "Yeah?"

"We're from the church," the tentative women offered.
They had intended to say something more evangelistic, but as

they observed privately to me later, "It's hard to witness to the nearly naked."

The young Adonis, framed in his own middle-class doorway, blurted out a string of profanity, telling them that he wasn't interested in "the church." His profanity and near nudity crushed their spirits. There seemed nothing to do but mumble a "thank you" and say good-bye as the door slammed shut. The plywood-goose wreath lied! They returned to their car, sat down, shuddered, and shed tears over the crushing encounter.

As they told me of the experience, I felt a bit hurt and responsible. After all, as their pastor, I had encouraged them to go into the community and "share the gospel." And for most of us, sharing the gospel is the important part of reaching the unchurched. We want to see the unchurched commit themselves to Christ and become a part of the church. These women hadn't shared much of the gospel they had worked to learn in our evangelistic training class. They had found little joy in an event that I had promised would likely be joyous.

I was reminded that the word *witness* and the word *martyr* were originally one, and while their martyrdom was not as terminal as Saint Stephen's, I could see that it was likely to be terminal in terms of their ever being coaxed into sharing again.

This exhibitionist, loin-cloth secularian has remained for me a symbol: handsome, self-confident, complete in himself—living between the TV control and suburban good times. His needs, as he would likely define them, are more Dow Jones than spiritual. Jesus is not even a remote part of his imagined necessities.

The twins of outreach

Reaching the unreached can be done in many ways, but outreach usually falls into two categories. The first is *confrontational evangelism*. Both the church and the community quail before this kind of evangelism. The reason we so fear this confrontational approach is because the confronted secularian sometimes confronts back. We are thus intimidated by the rude treatment we shall receive, or (more truthfully) the treatment we *imagine* we shall receive. The intimidation is so strong that many pastors have given up altogether on the idea of such direct neighborhood encounters.

Perhaps because of fear, many Christians have created their own ghetto in today's society. They have their own language—with clichés well understood and oft used by those who worship in the new temples that ring our growing cities. Temple language, full of "Praise the Lord" and "Bless you, brother," seems alien to the *Wall Street Journal*-ites, who live in places named Wedgewood, Leawood, Applewood, and Pepperwood. And people who speak a strange language are often feared. Thus the fear extends both directions.

But it's more than the language of Zion that frightens suburbanites. Evangelicals have their own concert artists, radio and television networks, and publishing empires. They have their own subculture heroes, few of whom are well known by the world at large. To those outside the church, all this makes these Christians seem to live in another world.

So what happens when these opposite worlds meet on a Thursday-night evangelism call? Inner terror—on both sides of the door. The worlds have so little in common that bridging becomes a matter of near panic. The suburbanite who lays down his *Forbes* magazine (or his *Playboy*) to answer the door and finds literature-armed churchgoers on his stoop is terrified! These evangelists may be gentle in their confrontation, but the terror of the event is nonetheless great.

The second category of outreach is more relational than confrontive. This *bridge-building* method still emphasizes reaching out, but replaces confrontation with initial friendship. This gentle approach says we must wed the spiritual needs of suburbanites to their sociological needs, giving the first emphasis to sociology. We reach them best by bringing up the eternal issues only after we have talked about softball,

barbecues, and committee slots. In other words, we must so-
cialize before we evangelize.

But perhaps you, as I, have seen what can happen to
churches using this softer approach. As pastor, you find yourself on a treadmill of a thousand "new ghetto" activities. To
the brotherhood, you become the fry cook; to the Cub Scouts,
umpire; to the ladies, bazaar auctioneer. Without a strong
sense of personal spiritual discipline, you can become the
bishop of the busy, and "busianity" may replace Christianity.

The church that leaves off the nasty business of urgency
may wind up "many but not much."

The strokes of different folks

We've wrestled with the challenge of reaching out to suburbia in a way that maintains the urgency without mounting a
campaign that's too terrifying for both the church and the
neighborhood.

We started by realizing that while unchurched suburbanites may seem to be alike and have a single system of values,
they are as different as those already in church, and so they
respond to different methods of being reached.

Some of those who never go to church may be reached by
the church's annual Christmas pageant or Easter musical. The
athletically inclined are more likely to respond to the church's
softball league than its junior choir program. And, yes, we've
discovered that some people still respond well to a knock on
the door.

So we still do visitation (while trying to eliminate as much
of the fear factor as we can). And we offer a variety of ministries (while trying not to fall into a pointless busianity).

We've observed that whatever route a person takes to faith,
he or she tends to stay in that pattern. People who come to
Christ through confrontational means seem to make more
earnest visitors than those who gradually come to faith
through "sociological absorption."

Rick, for instance, became a Christian through Evangelism Explosion, and now that he's a deacon, he remains a firm believer in structured evangelism and is immensely involved in outreach.

Peter came through the subtle and sociological relationships of the church softball team. Now his temptation is more toward busy Christianity.

My challenge as pastor is to help both see the full scope of the Christian life.

The care of community

Community concern sells, even in suburbia. Whatever programs the church may offer, the community needs to be led gradually, across months or years, to see that the church cares. This means public relations, or, to put it biblically, letting your light shine.

I've been interested to see in recent years that major corporations, from AT&T to Exxon to Hallmark Cards, have built empires around advertising slogans that say "We care." Our task is similar: to get the local unchurched to associate our congregation with an image of people who care for one another and the community.

Care has two sides. One is the informal, low-profile, and personal kind of care. A young man, who with his family had just moved into our community and visited our church once or twice, had to have emergency gall bladder surgery. One of the Bible classes in our church heard about it. Class members took casseroles to the family and cared for the children so the wife could visit her husband. As a result, this couple joined our church and quickly became part of the ministry.

The other kind of caring is structured, open, and public. Our youth group went through two neighborhoods of West Omaha a few weeks ago to collect food for the downtown mission and gathered more than a thousand cans. They not only helped the mission, but they also made our community aware that our church cares about the needy.

We also advertise. We have on our signs: "We're there; we care." Sometimes a disgruntled member will say, "Either give me more attention or take that off your sign!" But the message is essential.

We produced a thirty-second television commercial that shows me in front of Methodist Hospital, reminding the community that the staff of our church enters that hospital several times a week in a genuine effort to care about those who are in pain. While I admit TV and radio can lead to caring that's flamboyant and proud, it can be a legitimate way to remind our community of our calling.

Some time ago, I got a call from an elderly woman who had just been told by her doctors that she was dying and possibly would not survive the night. Through the media, she had heard Westside's humble boast that we care. She told me I was the only pastor she knew and asked if I could come to the hospital to see her.

I went. We talked, and I read Scripture and prayed.

She survived the crisis and eventually recovered fully. She is now a faithful member of our church and a close friend.

The focus of family

Whether suburban marriages are harmonious and the children are adjusting, all couples want their families to work better. They are looking for ways to help maintain the family unit.

The gospel offers a lot to people who crave family togetherness. Much of what the church offers is met with warm interest by individuals who believe that families are still a good idea in the world where homes are often falling apart.

This has two implications in our setting.

The first touches the pastor's own family. I realized my

family needed to be an example, to be seen reaching out. So my wife, Barbara, and I work together on visitation night. Every Monday evening, Barbara and her coworkers prepare a meal that will allow other members to come directly from their offices to eat before they receive the classroom instruction and assignment cards. Without this meal, many would not have time to go home and eat and make it back in time.

In addition, we practice hospitality, not just with longtime members of the church, but also with those who are new.

But there's a second implication with the families being reached. I've made it a practice (and I teach this to others) to speak with the man of the family. In a day when sexism is a possible criticism, I do this not because I believe one parent is more significant than the other, but because I believe that in most homes, the man is the key in reaching the entire family. Perhaps it's because he's often the most reluctant; perhaps because he often has more influence on the choice of activities for the *whole* family.

When I do visitation, I ask if I can meet the whole family. I work at including both the husband and the wife in the conversation, but when it comes to asking for commitment (whether praying for salvation or simply indicating their willingness to visit the church), I ask the man for his commitment first. If *he* agrees, it's easier for the rest of the family to make the same commitment.

As a result, on most Sundays as many men as women attend our church (and Bible study hour).

The wait of glory

Waiting on the secular family to be interested in the church's message demands patience. Sometimes it's directly related to need. At seasons of great need, most people are interested in God. If the pastor can lay down the church's availability through advertising or general reputation, when those needs come, the families who thought they were not interested suddenly are.

This posture is not a lazy waiting but an eager waiting to help those who find themselves crying out for help.

We discovered this with one family. I visited them several times over the years, and the husband, an Air Force officer, was quite willing for his family to go to church but never saw a need for it himself.

Then he received a yearlong remote assignment overseas and had to go without his family. When I stopped by, he said, "It'd be nice, Reverend, if the church could stop around and see how my wife and kids are doing every once in awhile. I'd be grateful."

While he was gone, church members helped in a variety of ways. When the automatic washer broke down, we arranged for its repair. Some of the members helped out with home maintenance.

When the year was up and the husband returned, he came to church! One Sunday morning, his face streaked with gratitude, he made his commitment to Christ.

Caring and waiting eventually paved the way to faith. He went on to become a strong member of our congregation.

The fuel of effort

Love is the fuel of our evangelism. Pastors cannot, without loving Christ, find a desire to witness. Without loving people, none of us would stay long at the job.

But pastoral love, whenever it occurs, can prompt the most rigorous sort of action: Love reaches for the hurt and takes bold steps without self-interest. It can accomplish unbelievable things merely because it is so void of self-interest.

Some time ago, a teenager, Arthur Hinkley, lifted a 3,000-pound tractor with bare hands. He wasn't a weight lifter, but his friend, Lloyd Bachelder, 18, was pinned under the tractor on a farm near Rome, Maine. Hearing Lloyd scream, Arthur somehow lifted the tractor for Lloyd to wriggle out.

Love was the real motivation.

We become the most like Christ when our motivation is distilled love. And that *agape* works—even in the suburbs.

11

How to Understand the Rural Mind-set

New life in any amount beats decline and death hands down.
—Stephen McMullin

If you're a rural pastor, as I am, you have probably read books that claim to address the needs of the small, rural congregation, only to discover that to many authors, *small* means a church of less than two hundred and *rural* means a town of less than ten thousand. You've probably heard exciting news about churches adding thousands of members every year, too.

Where does this leave the pastor of a church of forty in a community of five hundred? What does church growth mean in such a congregation?

More than eight years ago, I was called to a two-church pastorate; the smaller church had a membership of twenty-one, the larger a membership of sixty-two. On my first Sunday in the smaller church, I preached to seventeen people: two men, twelve women, and three children. About sixty attended regularly in the larger church during my first year, but sixteen months after my arrival, more than twenty of them left after a lengthy dispute. A lot of people in both churches seemed discouraged.

I cannot tell you that in eight years the churches have been transformed into thousand-member congregations; we are still small, rural churches. The smaller church has 24 members now; the larger church has grown to 99 members. But my experience has convinced me that there are principles that will help the small, rural church grow and have a vital ministry.

Growth hindrances

Only in the past few years have I begun to understand some of the dynamics of the rural church, and I've made some positive discoveries in the process. Let's consider some of the things most important in these churches.

Traditions.   Some traditions are beneficial, and others severely hinder the church's ministry, but in a rural church almost all are considered sacred.

A pastor recently told me that in his first church only the women and girls entered the sanctuary before the service. The men and boys talked outside until the organist began playing "Holy, Holy, Holy," their signal to be seated. Traditions in a rural church will dictate everything from where a family sits to who rings the church bell to where people park their cars.

I've come to realize these traditions aren't frivolous; they're important to the church. I may have the difficult task of helping end some traditions, but it's good to understand that for some in the congregation, it will be like burying a close relative. Wise pastors care for such members with the sensitivity typical of comforting a bereaved family.

History.   Many of these rural churches are afraid to look to the future, but they recall a glorious past. "My great-grandfather made the pulpit" or "Our family members have been deacons here for four generations" are comments that tell us the past is important to the church.

Many of these churches really do have quite a history. In my smaller church, a meeting was held in 1832 that resulted in a decision for a group of churches to band together into what later became our present denomination. In the nineteenth century, the church had more than a hundred mem-

bers, and denominational meetings and Sunday school conventions regularly were held in the church.

The history of your church is no less important to your
people. I've found it wise to take time to find out about my
churches' past in order to better understand how they became
what they are today.

Church officers. Holding an office in many rural
churches has little to do with function. Often there is no
nominating committee; many officers simply serve perpetual
terms.

As a student, I assisted a rural church pastor who was
frustrated with the volunteer organist. After he talked with
her about how the church music might be improved, she
responded by resigning publicly the following Sunday because her position as organist had been "called into question."
She had been church organist for decades, since age seventeen.

Some pastors have talked to me about their frustration with
lifelong officers in rural churches who no longer carry out the
duties of their office. In most cases, other faithful people,
with or without official positions, see that the work is done.
But that's not the way I understand things are supposed to
operate, so it tends to make me uncomfortable.

The Sunday school. The pastor accustomed to Christian
education activities during the Sunday school hour will receive a rude awakening in many rural churches. In a very
small church, the Sunday school often boasts a larger attendance than the worship service. In fact, the Sunday school
opening may well serve as a sort of pastorless worship service
and can last as long as a half hour. Then the church business
has to be handled. I had to get used to the reality that decisions already made by the trustees or deacons had to be discussed again in Sunday school for final approval.

Actually, this no longer happens in my churches. Perhaps
such discussions are only a long-term reaction to strained
communication, so the business gets discussed in Sunday
school because the pastor is often absent. The importance of

Sunday school for transacting church business diminishes when we conscientiously involve the congregation in decisions they fully understand.

Growth principles

Answers to the needs of the small, struggling congregation are not simple. Not all churches share similar circumstances. Not all react the same way. But I've found the following principles effective in enabling my churches to grow and in offering hope for continuing growth.

Forget the short term.   In a congregation of forty, four deaths in one year constitutes a 10 percent decline. Such statistics can be discouraging. I recommend keeping such statistics but comparing them after five years, not after five months. Only after being in my churches six years could I see actual numerical growth in both of them.

Set reasonable goals.   It's easy to arrive at a church of thirty members and say, "I want the church to double in size in five years." We think, *That's only six people a year. Why I can reach that many myself!* The problem is, it's usually not the only problem.

It means changing some of the traditions of the church. We must initiate building improvements. We work at making the offices of the church more functional. And on and on. All this takes time, and meanwhile there are funerals and sermons.

The upshot: the evangelistic calling doesn't get done. So we get discouraged after two years with no results and move on—just before ministry could have had a lasting impact. A better scenario is to set reasonable goals that take into account the unaccountable.

Target areas of outreach.   Small churches don't have the resources to cover all the bases for ministry, so I've learned to concentrate on the areas of greatest need. If men aren't attending church, we can make them the subjects of outreach ministry. If young families aren't being reached, we can lean toward beginning ministries aimed at this group.

The alternative to focusing ministry is to spatter a little ministry everywhere. Then we reach no one effectively and exhaust everyone in the process.

In my smaller church, we decided to try a men's breakfast. Considering that only two men regularly attended the church, it was an uphill battle. But it was the area of greatest need, and it has been successful over the years in bringing men to the church for fellowship, a devotional time, and prayer—men who still feel uneasy attending the Sunday services.

Help members think like visitors.   This strategy is crucial to turning a dying church around. Walk into the church on Sunday morning and ask yourself, *If I were attending for the first time, what would make me want to come back?* Or not want to come back? What catches your eye? What attitudes do you notice? Is the church clean? Do people stare at you as you enter? Is the piano in tune? These types of questions helped me notice things hindering the effectiveness of my church.

We did a survey in the smaller church during my first year. The members all said the church was well kept; the nonmembers said the church was dirty. The nonmembers were right; the members had simply stopped noticing.

Our biggest problem was the church building itself, and I suspect that's true in many other churches. Who wants to begin attending a church where the very physical condition of the building tells you the church members don't expect the church to continue for long?

The community learns much about a church from its building. The members may say that ministry to children is important, but if there are poor nursery facilities and no rest rooms, the community knows that children aren't really a priority. A building that's attractive and meets the needs of community and congregation will encourage visitors to come and remain.

Develop a positive ministry.   I recently read the minutes of a business meeting in a small church. The pastor told the people that they were uncommitted, that he was the only one serving the Lord in the church, and that because of their lack of dedication, the church wasn't growing.

My heart went out to the pastor and the congregation because I know the frustration that can so easily engulf a rural pastor. This pastor was stymied by the church's traditions, and the congregation was discouraged because they couldn't meet the pastor's expectations. Obviously there was little growth in that congregation.

I've learned there is nothing to gain by criticizing the status quo in the church. Instead, I try to get people to focus on how much better things will be once certain changes are made.

For instance, we have accomplished some expensive building improvements in both churches, yet I've been careful not to find fault with the building in its prerenovated condition. I can achieve a much more positive atmosphere by seeking to establish a vision for what we might do, not by criticizing what we haven't yet done.

I won't teach church members to be thankful for one another unless I am genuinely thankful for them. The problem is that sometimes I get frustrated, and I want to push people toward ministry and outreach. At those times, I try to remember that instead I need to lead people to ministry and outreach. And I've learned that I can't lead anyone when I harbor a negative attitude. Once I'm excited about the challenges God has laid before the church, however, I can share that excitement with others.

Increase the church's profile. A growing church has somehow announced to the community that the church is there and people are welcome. Rural churches, I have found, enjoy three areas of special opportunity to attract outsiders.

First, the rural church is potentially the focal point of a small community. The other rural institution—the one-room schoolhouse—is long gone. Today, students from my pastorate attend one of three regional high schools; the school districts were set up with little regard for the boundaries of rural communities.

My rural churches can capitalize on this factor by hosting special events that will attract the attention of the whole community. The community can be included in church anniversary services, building dedications, or Sunday school events. The facilities can be used for other community events such as picnics or musical programs. These events tell our community that we're alive and active.

Second, special days can be used to great advantage. On the Saturday before Mother's Day last year, our deacons went to every home in the communities served by our churches and presented the mothers with a rose and an invitation to the church services.

That's impossible in a community of several thousand, but in a rural community it's feasible and fosters a warm attitude toward the church, which can directly increase church attendance.

Events such as graduation or Christmas offer excellent opportunities as well. Not many people are invited to graduation at the regional high schools, so we have a community graduates' reception after an evening service in June. All the graduates in the area are honored, and the whole community is invited. It's always one of the best-attended services of the year, and the occasion lends itself beautifully to a service that emphasizes the need to trust in God for the future.

Third, our newsletter works to make the community aware of church activities. We send a quarterly newsletter to homes in our communities, and it's amazing to discover how many people who don't attend our churches are quite knowledgeable about our churches' activities because of the newsletter. I also consider the newsletter a great springboard for conversation during pastoral visitation in nonchurch homes.

One often-overlooked factor is the church sign—or the lack of one. Rural church members may think everyone knows about the church, but that's an illusion. Because I can't imagine going to a store that bears no indication of its nature,

I'm constantly amazed at the number of churches that don't have even a sign telling the name and denomination of the church, let alone the times of services or the pastor's name. I doubt if newcomers attend a nameless church. A simple sign in front of the church can make people feel expected—and wanted and welcome.

Growth curve

I've dealt with my share of frustrations as a rural church pastor. When I first arrived, I wanted to see great things happen overnight. What I saw instead was a decline in the smaller church due to the failing health of the elderly members, and a decline in the other church because a key family left after a simmering dispute boiled over. People in the smaller church were talking about closing in five years; in the larger church, people were emotionally drained by the exodus. So was I.

I'm glad I didn't resign. Both churches have survived. The smaller church has not only maintained its membership and improved its ministries, but it also has begun to reach younger families and new residents in the community. And the larger church has grown remarkably, especially in the past three years.

Perhaps in a growing urban setting a net increase of three members in one church and thirty-seven in the other doesn't seem like much, but when I see the people in these communities who have come to know Jesus Christ as Savior and Lord, I realize the frustrations and effort are worth it. New life in any amount beats decline and death hands down.

PART 3

Focus

12

Speaking to the Secular Mind

We can't win non-Christians if we don't know how they think, and we can't know how they think if we never enter their world.

—BILL HYBELS

Driving home from church one day, I pulled behind a guy on his Harley-Davidson. I noticed a bumper sticker on the rear fender of his motorcycle, so I pulled closer. It read: [EXPLETIVE] GUILT.

After the shock wore off, I was struck by how different his world was from the one I'd just left, and even from the world a generation ago. In my day, we felt guilty, I thought. Now, it's not only "I don't feel guilty," but "[Expletive] guilt."

There was a time when your word was a guarantee, when marriage was permanent, when ethics were assumed. Not so very long ago, heaven and hell were unquestioned, and caring for the poor was an obvious part of what it meant to be a decent person. Conspicuous consumption was frowned upon because it was conspicuous. The label *self-centered* was to be avoided at all costs, because it said something horrendous about your character.

Today, all of that has changed. Not only is it different, but people can hardly remember what the former days were like.

Why we need a new approach

Many churches, however, still operate with the understanding that non-Christians are going to come through the doors, feel pretty much at home, understand the sovereignty of God and the redemptive work of Jesus Christ, and in one morning make a complete transition from a secular worldview.

Even twenty years ago that may have been a reasonable hope. The secular worldview wasn't that disconnected from God's agenda. A guy would hear the claims of Christ and say, "Well, that makes sense. I know I'm a sinner" or "I know I shouldn't drink so much" or "I really should be faithful to my wife."

Today, even though we're asking for the same thing—a commitment to Christ—in the perception of the secular person, we're asking for far more. The implications of becoming a Christian today are not just sobering; they're staggering.

Recently I preached on telling the truth, and afterward a man came up and said, "You don't understand what you're saying."

"What don't I understand?" I asked him.

"You're just up there doing what pastors are supposed to do—talk about truth. But my job requires my violating about five of the things you just talked about. It's part of the job description; I can't be 'on the level' and keep the position. You're not asking me to adopt some value system; you're asking me to give up my salary and abandon my career."

We preachers, I was reminded that day, have our work cut out for us. The topics we choose, the way we present Scripture, the illustrations we use, the responses we ask for, all need to contribute to our goal of effectively presenting Christ to non-Christians. Here is what I've learned, sometimes the hard way, about what kind of preaching attracts them, keeps them coming back, and most important, leads them to take the momentous step of following Jesus Christ.

Sensitive training

If we're going to speak with integrity to secular men and women, we need to work through two critical areas before we step into the pulpit.

The first is to understand the way they think. For most of us pastors, though, that's a challenge. The majority of my colleagues went to a Bible school or Christian college and on to seminary, and have worked in the church ever since. As a result, most have never been close friends with a non-Christian. They want to make their preaching connect with unchurched people, but they've never been close enough to them to gain an intimate understanding of how their minds work.

If we're serious about reaching the non-Christian, most of us are going to have to take some giant steps. I have suggested for many years that our pastors at Willow Creek find authentic interest areas in their lives—tennis, golf, jogging, sailing, mechanical work, whatever—and pursue these in a totally secular realm. Instead of joining a church league softball team, why not join a park district team? Instead of working out in the church gym, shoot baskets at the YMCA. On vacation, don't go to a Bible conference but to some state park where the guy in the next campsite is going to bring over his six-pack and sit at your picnic table.

When I bring this up with fellow ministers, I often sense resistance. It cuts against everything we feel comfortable doing. And yet not knowing how non-Christians think undercuts our attempts to reach them. If we're going to stand on Sunday and accurately say, "Some of you may be questioning what I've just said. I can understand that, because just this week I talked with someone about it," then on the Tuesday before we've got to drive to the Y and lift weights and run with non-Christians. We can't win them if we don't know how they think, and we can't know how they think if we don't ever enter their world.

The second prerequisite to effective preaching to non-

Christians is that we *like* them. If we don't, it's going to bleed through our preaching. Listen closely to sermons on the radio or television, and often you'll hear remarks about "those worldly secular people." Unintentionally, these speakers distance themselves from the non-Christian listener; it's us against them. I find myself wondering whether these preachers are convinced that lost people matter to God. It's not a merciful, "Let's tell them we love them," but a ticked off "They're going to get what's coming to them." These preachers forfeit their opportunity to speak to non-Christians because the unchurched person immediately senses, *They don't like me.*

What helps many pastors genuinely like non-Christians is the gift of evangelism. When you have that spiritual gift, it's easier for you to have a heart for non-Christians. Not every pastor claims evangelism as a gift. But I've seen many develop a heartfelt compassion for non-Christians by focusing on their needs. That takes away any intimidation they might feel around non-Christians; it frees them to minister.

When I was in youth ministry in the early seventies, kids wore their emotions on their sleeve. They'd come up crying, or mad, but I could readily recognize their need. When I started ministering to suburban adults, everybody was smooth. Everyone dressed nicely and had a nice-looking spouse, two nice-looking kids, a nice car, a nice home. I thought, *What do these people need church for? Everybody's getting along fine.*

The longer I worked with them, though, the more I realized, *These people have gaping holes in their lives. That pretty wife hasn't slept with her husband in three months. Those kids, if you could ever get close to them, are so mad at their dad they'd fill your ears. That home is mortgaged to the hilt, and that job that looks so sweet isn't all that secure. That guy who looks so confident is scared stiff inside.*

That appearance of sufficiency is a thin veneer, and underneath is a boatload of need that we, as pastors and teachers, are equipped and called to address in the power of the Holy

Spirit. As we learn the way non-Christians think and develop a genuine love for them, we can speak the word of Christ in a way they'll hear.

Creative topics and titles

Unchurched people today are the ultimate consumers. We may not like it, but for every sermon we preach, they're asking, *Am I interested in that subject?* If they aren't, it doesn't matter how effective our delivery is; their minds will check out.

A dozen years ago, the book *Real Men Don't Eat Quiche* came out, and immediately sales took off. Everyone was talking about it. As I was thinking about the amazing success of that book, I decided to preach a series, "What Makes a Man a Man? What Makes a Woman a Woman?" Unchurched people heard the titles, and they came; attendance climbed 20 percent in just four weeks.

When that series ended, I began one titled "A Portrait of Jesus." We lost most of those newcomers. Interestingly, the elders said to me after that series, "Bill, those messages on the person and work of Christ related to unchurched people as well as any messages we've heard." In this case, the problem wasn't the content; the people who needed to hear this series most didn't come because of the *title*.

Since then, I've put everything I can into creating effective titles. I'm not particularly clever, so sometimes I'll work for hours on the title alone. I do it because I know unchurched people won't come, or come back, unless they can say, "Now *that's* something I want to hear about." The title can't be just cute or catchy; it has to touch a genuine need or interest.

Here are some series titles that evoked a good response:

- "God Has Feelings, Too." People said, "What? God has emotions?" And they came to find out what and how he feels.
- "Turning Houses into Homes." When I announced the series (in church the week before it started), I said, "Our area is

setting national records for housing starts. As you drive around and see one of the hundreds of houses going up, ask yourself, What's going to turn this house into a home? That's what we're going to talk about in the next four weeks." I could have used a thousand other titles, but this one seemed to touch a nerve.

- "Telling the Truth to Each Other."
- "Fanning the Flames of Marriage."
- "Endangered Character Qualities."
- "Alternatives to Christianity."

I always begin a new series the Sunday after Christmas and Easter to try to bring back the first-time visitors. One Christmas Eve we announced, "A lot of people are saying, 'Christianity is the right way,' or 'The New Age Movement is the right way,' or 'Something else is the right way.' We're going to talk about the alternatives to Christianity, showcase the competition, and let you decide. We'll make an honest comparison, and if it's not honest, you tell us."

That was an A+ title, as long as we dealt fairly with the opposing points of view. I could have called the series "The Danger of the Cults" or "Why Christianity Is the Only Sensible Religion," but those titles would have attracted only people who were already convinced. From the very first words people hear about our message, we need to communicate, "This is for you. This is something you'll want to hear."

Sometimes people who haven't heard me preach misunderstand this and say, "Yeah, it's easy to attract people if you tiptoe around tough biblical issues and don't get prophetic on areas of discipleship." My experience, though, has been that you can be absolutely prophetic with unchurched people. We all should be like Paul when he said in Acts 20, "I didn't shrink back from giving you the whole counsel of God. I didn't shrink back in terms of the content or the intensity." But to do that with any group, we need to preach in a way they can understand. We need to start where they are and then bring them along.

For example, we have a lot of people attend who can't conceive of a God who would ever punish anybody. That wouldn't be loving. They need to understand God's holiness. So I've used the old illustration, "If I backed into the door of your new car out in the parking lot after the service, and we went to court, and the judge said, 'That's no problem; Bill didn't mean it,' you'd be up in arms. You'd want justice.

"If you went to a Cubs game, and the pitcher threw a strike down the middle of the plate, and the ump said, 'Ball four,' and walked in a run, you'd be out there killing the ump because you want justice."

A person hears that and says, "I guess you're right. I wouldn't want a God who wasn't just." Then I can go on to say, "Now before you say, 'Rah, rah for a just God,' let me tell you some of the implications. That means he metes out justice to you."

You can be utterly biblical in every way, but to reach non-Christians, every topic has to start where they are and then bring them to a fuller Christian understanding.

I've also found it helpful, as many pastors have, to preach messages in a series. With the non-Christian, you want to break the pattern of absenteeism. Over the course of the series, he or she gets in the habit of coming to church and says, "This isn't so bad, it only takes an hour." You're trying to show him or her that this is not a painful experience; it's educational and sometimes even a little inspirational. Sometimes it's convicting, but in a thought-provoking rather than heavy-handed way. Pretty soon, a guy says, "Why don't I come, bring my wife, and stop for brunch afterward?"

I've found I can't stretch a series longer than four or five weeks, though, before people start saying, "Is there anything else you're ever thinking about?" And obviously, if I'm going to talk about money or other highly sensitive issues, the series may run only two weeks.

"Why" explanations

Unchurched people don't give the Bible a fraction of the weight we believers do. They look at it as an occasionally useful collection of helpful suggestions, something like the *Farmer's Almanac*. They tend to think, *The Bible has some neat things to say once in awhile, but it's not the kind of thing I'm going to change my life radically to obey.*

If we simply quote the Bible and say, "That settles it. Now obey that," they're going to say, "What? I'm supposed to re-build my life on some book that's thousands of years old? I don't do that for any other respected literary work of antiquity." It just doesn't make sense to them.

So almost every time I preach, I'm trying to build up the reliability of Scripture and increase their respect for it. I do that by explaining the wisdom of God behind it. When you show them how reasonable God is, that captivates the secular mind.

Most secular folks have written off Christians as people who believe in floods and angels and strange miracles. My goal is to explain, in a reasonably intelligent fashion, some matters that touch their lives. I hope when they leave they'll say, "Maybe there is something to the Bible and to the Christian life."

Consider 2 Corinthians 6:14, the verse that instructs us, "Don't be unequally yoked." Some teachers speaking on that passage will say, "The implications are obvious: Don't marry a nonbeliever. The Bible says it, and we need to obey it." For the already convinced person, who puts great value on the inspiration and infallibility of Scripture, that might be enough. I don't think most church people buy it as much as we hope they will, but let's say they give us the indication that they do.

The secular guy, on the other hand, sits there and thinks, *That is about the most stupid and discriminatory thing I have ever heard. Why should I refuse to marry someone I love simply because her religion is a little different?* So one Sunday morning, I started by saying, "I'm going to read to you the most disliked sentence in all of Scripture for single people who are anxious to get married." Then I read 2 Corinthians 6:14.

"This is that awful verse," I said, "in which, under the inspiration of the Holy Spirit, Paul cuts down the field from hundreds of thousands of marriageable candidates to only a handful. And almost every single person I know, upon first hearing it, hates that verse. What I want to do is spend the next thirty minutes telling you why I think God would write such an outrageous prescription."

During the rest of that message, I tried to show, using logic and their experience, that this command makes terrific sense. We were in a construction program at the time, so I used this illustration: "What if I went out to the construction site, and I found one contractor, with his fifteen workers, busily constructing our building from one set of plans, and then I went to the other side of the building, and here's another contractor building his part of the building from a totally different set of blueprints? There'd be total chaos.

"Friends," I continued, "what happens in a marriage when you've got a husband who says, 'I'm going to build this marriage on this blueprint,' and a wife who says, 'I'm going to build it on this blueprint'? They collide, and usually the strongest person wins—for a time. But then there's destruction.

"God wants his children to build solid, permanent relationships, and he knows it's going to take a single set of plans. In order to build a solid building or a sound marriage, you need one set of blueprints."

Over time, I try to increase gradually their respect for Scripture, so that someday they won't have to ask all the why questions but will be able to say to themselves, *Because it's in the Book, that's why.*

Current illustrations

I've found that the unchurched person thinks most Christians, especially pastors, are woefully out of touch with reality. *They don't have a clue as to what's going on in the world,* he thinks. An unchurched person who does venture into a church assumes whatever is spoken will not be relevant to his life.

That's why I select 60 to 70 percent of my illustrations from current events. I read *Time, Newsweek, U.S. News & World Report, Forbes,* and *Business Week.* Every day I read the *Chicago Tribune* (*USA Today* when I travel), watch at least two TV news programs, and listen to an all-news radio station when I'm in the car.

Why? Because when I can use a contemporary illustration, I build credibility. The unchurched person says, "He's in the same world I'm in. He's aware that Sean Connery and Roger Moore no longer play 007. He's not talking about something years ago; he's talking about something I care about today."

I sometimes joke that one of my goals in ministry is to complete however many years God gives me without ever using a C. H. Spurgeon illustration. Today, non-Christians (and even most Christians) don't know who Spurgeon was. And once unchurched people find out, they wonder why I'm wasting my time with him. They think, *This is 1996, and we've seen war in the Balkans and political turmoil, and he's spending time reading some dead Englishman? If he's got the time to do that, he's not living in the same world I am.*

The second thing an up-to-date illustration does is put the listener and me on an even footing. He heard the same news report I did; he saw the same show. When I quote Saint Augustine, he feels like I'm not playing in the same ballpark. But when I say, "On *Nightline* two nights ago, Ted Koppel was talking with . . ." the guy says to himself, *I saw that! I wonder if he felt the same way about that as I did,* and he stays with me.

I learned this principle from studying the parables of Jesus.

I noticed him saying things such as, "You all heard about those eighteen people killed in Siloam when the tower fell on them . . . " (Luke 13:4). As I charted Jesus' parables, I saw quickly that these illustrations weren't quotes from rabbinic authorities but stories of things average people saw every day. When people feel that somebody's in their world and has been real with them, that's powerful.

Freeing responses

When people walk into church, often they're thinking they'll get the party line again: Pray more, love more, serve more, give more. *They just want something more out of me,* they think. *I wonder what it'll be today that I'm not doing enough of.*

It's easy for us pastors to unintentionally foster that understanding. One pastor asked me for help with his preaching, and we talked about what responses he wanted. I suggested, "List the messages you've preached in the last year, and write either *pray more, love more, serve more* or *give more* next to any message where that was the main thrust of the sermon."

He came back and said, "Bill, one of those was the thrust of every single sermon last year." He recognized the implications. If every time my son comes into the living room, I say, "Do this more; do that more," pretty soon he won't want to come in the living room. But if he comes in knowing there is going to be some warmth, acceptance, a little humor, and encouragement, then on the occasions I need to say, "We've got to straighten out something here," he can receive that.

Often the goal of a message can be "Understand this reality about God" or "Enjoy this thing God has done." One Wednesday night message about spiritual gifts was taken from Romans 12:3–4. I could have pushed people to serve more, I suppose, but that evening I said, "This is the most serving church I have ever seen. You people are using spiritual gifts beautifully. What Paul is telling the church at Rome to get on the stick and do, you people have gotten on the stick and done." Then I gave fifteen or twenty illustrations of ways people in the church are serving selflessly for God's glory.

I closed, "I want to say I respect you as a church. You're an unbelievable group of servants that God is pleased with. Let's stand for closing prayer." Parishioners are people, too, and sometimes people need to be commended for what they are doing already. In the case of non-Christians, we may commend them for honestly considering the claims of Christ, for being willing to listen to what we have to say, and not immediately writing it off.

With the unchurched, though, our primary goal has been determined for us: We want them to accept the lordship of Jesus Christ. Let me suggest two key principles in asking non-Christians for a commitment.

1. Give them freedom to choose. I've been surprised to learn you really can challenge unchurched people as much as you would anybody else—as long as at the moment of truth you give them absolute freedom to choose. At the end of an evangelistic message, I often say something such as: "You've got a choice to make. I'm not going to make it for you. I'm not going to tell you that you have to make it in the next thirty seconds. But eventually you've got to make some decisions about the things we've talked about. As for me and my house, it's been decided, and we're glad we've made the decision. But you need to make that decision as God leads you." I toss the ball in their court.

During one message recently, I made a strong, biblical case for team leadership. At the end I said, "I know many of you own businesses, and you're accountable to nobody. I think from what we've read in the Scriptures today, you would be the primary beneficiaries of following God's plan of team leadership so your blind spots don't cause your downfall.

"But," I said, "it's your life; it's your business; it's your family; it's your future. I trust that over time you'll give this thought and make the right decision. As for me, I've got elders, I've got board members, I've got an accountability group. I feel glad I have a team to accomplish what God has called me to do.

"Let's stand for prayer."

When you give a person complete freedom to choose, he goes away saying, "Doggone it, I wish he would have laid a trip on me because then I could have gotten mad at him and written off the whole thing. But now I have to deal with it." Rather than letting people get away, giving them freedom urges them to make that choice.

2. Give them time to make a decision. Suppose a guy came into my office and said, "I have a Mercedes-Benz in the parking lot. I'll sell it to you for $500 if you write me a check in the next fifteen seconds." I wouldn't do it. By most counts, I'd be a fool not to buy a Mercedes-Benz for $500. But if you make me decide in fifteen seconds, I'd refuse because I haven't had enough time to check it out. I have some natural questions: Is there really one in the lot? Do you have a title to it? Does it have a motor?

But on Sunday we're tempted to tell people who've been living for twenty, thirty, or forty years under a totally secular worldview, "You've got just a couple of minutes at the end of this service to make a decision that's going to determine your eternity. It's going to change your life, and you might lose your job, but come on down." The non-Christian is thinking, *Whoa! This is a big decision, and I've been thinking about this for only twenty minutes.*

When I ask non-Christians for a commitment, I'm trying to persuade them about something that's going to alter radically everything they are. They say things such as, "You mean marriage is permanent? You gotta be kidding—like I have to reconcile with that witch? No way!" or "You mean I have to get serious about child rearing and not just hire somebody to do it?" Everywhere the non-Christian turns, he's finding I'm asking for far more than he first expected. He senses a spiritual need—that's what brought him to church—but he's going to need a lot of time to consider the implications.

Most of the conversions that happen at Willow Creek come

after people have attended the church for six months or more. The secular person has to attend consistently for half a year and have the person who brought him witness to him the whole time. He needs that much time simply to kick the tires, look at the interior, and check the title before he can finally say, "I'll buy it."

I get criticized for this as much as for anything else in my ministry. People protest, "Bill, you had them in the palm of your hand, and you let them get away!"

I've heard this enough times that now I usually respond with some questions. "Do you think people heard the truth while they were here?" I ask.

"Yes, they heard the truth."

"Do you think the Holy Spirit is alive and well?"

"Of course I believe that."

"Do you think Bill Hybels ever saved anybody?"

They quickly say, "Oh, no, no."

I say, "I think we're okay then. If they heard the truth, and the Holy Spirit is alive and active, God will continue to work in their lives, and Bill Hybels isn't the only way he can accomplish his will for them."

Having said that, however, sometimes people need to be challenged. And when I do challenge people, I challenge them hard. Periodically I'll say, "Some of you are on the outside looking in. You've been around here for a long time and have enough information. I'd like to ask you, what is it that's holding you back from repenting of your sins and trusting Christ right now? Sometimes a delay can be catastrophic. It's time to deal with this."

But—and this is critical—when I do that, I always make a qualification: "Now for many of you, this is your first time here or you've been here only a few weeks. You don't have enough answers yet, so I'm not talking to you. You're in an investigation phase, and that's legitimate and needs to go on until you have the kind of information the rest of the people I'm talking to have already attained."

Trying to reach non-Christians isn't easy, and it's not getting easier. But what keeps me preaching are the times when after many months, I do get through.

Once a man said to me, "I came to your church, and nobody knew what really was going on in my life because I had 'em all fooled. But I knew, and when you started saying that in spite of all my sin I still mattered to God, something clicked in me. I committed myself to Christ, and I tell you, I'm different. My son and I haven't been getting along at all, but I decided to take two weeks off and take him to a baseball camp out west. He started opening up to me while we were out there. Thanks, Bill, for telling me about Jesus."

For a preacher, such a joy far surpasses the ongoing challenge.

13

Preaching Evangelistically

I remain committed to evangelistic preaching, not just because of the Great Commission, but also because of its great satisfaction.

—MYRON AUGSBURGER

Since day one, the church has used one method to reach out to people more frequently and more successfully than any other.

It's the way the gospel was brought to Europe by Paul, and the way it spread throughout the West by the Dominican and Franciscan orders, among others. It was central in the life, worship, and outreach of the Reformation. It was the means by which lives were ignited and entire towns transformed in the great awakenings in this country. Today, it remains the one task, more than any other, that most congregations expect of their pastors, because it is the main vehicle for communicating to them and the larger community God's grace and peace.

I'm talking, of course, about preaching.

A church can and should reach out to the community in a variety of ways, many of which are discussed in this book. But we would be remiss if we overlooked preaching, particularly evangelistic preaching. All preaching seeks to communicate God's grace and peace, but evangelistic preaching is unique. In that sense, it deserves particular attention.

The objections

In spite of its noble history, some preachers remain hesitant about evangelistic preaching. Many wonder about the place of the evangelistic sermon in a church setting, where the hearers supposedly are already believers. The four objections I encounter most, and my responses, are these:

Evangelistic sermons don't help believers. Because evangelism is aimed at the unbeliever, and because unbelievers usually constitute only a small minority of a congregation, some preachers reason that the evangelistic sermon is out of place in a worship service. Not quite. In spite of these assumptions, the evangelistic sermon remains necessary also for the believer, for three reasons.

First, it helps believers clarify how they will present the gospel to their friends during the week. When they hear the pastor articulate the evangelistic message, it gives them a model and a message for their own witnessing. Frequently members thank me for a sermon that gave them ways to explain their faith to a friend at work.

Second, the evangelistic sermon gives relatively nonverbal members an opportunity to share the gospel with their friends, without saying a word! Many of our members bring friends to church so they not only can see the gospel at work, but also hear it articulated. Once, members of a Sunday school class invited their unchurched friends to a dinner, and they clarified on the invitation that a pastor would be present to talk about Christ. My presence as a pastor offered a natural way to introduce Christ into the evening.

Third, people who regularly come to church don't necessarily have a personal relationship with Christ and, thus, need to be evangelized—to hear and respond to the good news.

A number of years ago, Archbishop William Temple formed a commission to study evangelism in England. The commission concluded that the church is a field for evangelism when it ought to be a force for evangelism. It has been estimated by

D. Elton Trueblood that two-thirds of the members of American churches know nothing about personal conversion. We may disagree about the numbers, but few pastors will deny the reality.

I once preached at a noonday service in which struggling single parents were being ministered to, both with preaching and with gifts of food and clothing. After the service, as people were filing out, shaking my hand, one woman, well dressed and dignified, said, "Thanks for that message. That was just what they needed."

I held on to her hand and said, "But don't we all need it?"

"Well, maybe sometime I'll be in trouble," she replied, "and then I'll need it."

"Are you married?" I asked. She acknowledged she was. So to make a point, I said, "I guess you needed a man in your life. Is that why you got married?"

She stiffened. "I love my husband. That's why I married!"

"Well, that's the way it is with salvation," I said. "It isn't a crutch we use because we're in trouble. We walk with Christ because we love him."

Those who have never known Christ and those whose relationship has become stale need to hear the good news presented afresh.

Evangelistic sermons are simplistic. Some preachers think their preaching gifts and their congregations demand sermons that challenge the mind. They assume the evangelistic sermon does anything but that, because it aims at people's most elementary need. They are right about the aim of the sermon, but they couldn't be more wrong about its intellectual quality.

An evangelistic sermon will clarify the gospel and highlight its uniqueness in the world today. That means, then, the preacher must understand clearly the alternatives to Christ, many of which are worldviews that listeners hold. In addition, the preacher will have to work at speaking fairly about these other views, for listeners will turn off the one who sounds uninformed or biased.

To put it another way, if you're trying to communicate the gospel in the midst of the modern world, when New Age, existentialist, hedonist, and materialist worldviews compete for people's loyalties, you can be sure evangelistic preaching will challenge preacher and listener intellectually.

Not that we need to sound academic. In fact, we shouldn't. But that makes the task even more challenging. Although we must recognize the complexity of worldviews people hold, and the complexity of reasons for holding them, we need to translate Christian theology into the clearest and simplest language.

I was invited to speak at a weeklong, citywide crusade in Salt Lake City in 1963. Early in the week, a spokesman for the Mormon church went on television and said, "Go to this meeting. We need a revival of religion in America. It'll do you good. But remember, we've got all this and more." I felt my task was to show that they didn't have all this, let alone more.

On the first night I spoke on Hebrews 1, that passage that highlights the uniqueness of Christ so eloquently. In short, the text and the situation demanded that I speak on christology. But I also needed to communicate the uniqueness of the church's christology in ways people could understand.

So, I said plainly that Jesus is not a prophet in a series of prophets. In that setting, they knew exactly what I meant. Then I explained that Christians do not say Jesus is like God, as many do when they speak about their prophet, but that God is like Jesus:

"If my son walked in and said, 'I'm John Myron Augsburger, Myron Augsburger's son,' people might say, 'Well, of course. You're like your father.' But if they hadn't seen me and they met him, they couldn't say that; they wouldn't have any comparison to make. But they could say, 'Ah! So this is what the Myron Augsburger family is like.' "

I concluded by explaining that no other person or prophet is like Jesus, because he is the only one who expresses to us what the Father is like.

Competent evangelistic preaching can be more formidable

than giving a lecture in a seminary classroom. Not all evangelistic preaching will be intellectually demanding. But if we want to challenge people to love God with their minds, much of it will be.

Evangelistic preaching is event oriented. Some evangelistic preachers simply aim to bring listeners to the edge of decision and then go for the jugular at the invitation, using any tactic available. Naturally, some church members hesitate to bring friends to hear such a presentation, fearing the tactics used by the evangelist will alienate their loved ones and put a strain on those relationships.

If that's evangelistic preaching, it's understandable that many pastors want nothing to do with it. Neither do I. Yet I don't abandon evangelism in the pulpit.

Instead, I do it differently. When evangelistic preaching becomes merely event oriented, it becomes unlike the rest of the Christian life, which is a long-term proposition. That's why I take the long view when I preach evangelistically.

When I preach as an evangelist, I recognize that people may have invited friends. Some people present may not know Jesus Christ in a personal way, and some Christians present have ongoing relationships with these unbelievers. My goal is to enhance that relationship by pointing the unbeliever to Jesus, not damage that relationship.

I was scheduled to preach evangelistically in British Columbia last year. The organizers and I agreed to have a session for educators. The idea was to encourage the Christian schoolteacher to invite an unbelieving colleague to a dinner meeting where the Christian message would be presented.

In that setting, then, through preaching and discussion that followed, I aimed to interpret why Christianity makes sense out of life. And when I was through, I wanted the Christian schoolteacher to remain comfortable driving home with the unbelieving colleague he or she invited. So, I tried to present the claims of Christ compellingly but leave people the freedom to think and to reflect about their decision. That means I must trust the Holy Spirit to work in people's lives over time, as he always does.

Evangelistic preaching depends on the preacher. Some preachers quail before the evangelistic sermon. They look at their preaching gifts and the awesomeness of the evangelistic task, and they refuse to do it from the pulpit. There's too much riding on the sermon, they feel, and they don't think they're up to the task.

Well, less rides on the preacher than they think. Naturally, preachers do well to craft their message so that it presents the good news in as compelling a fashion as possible. But we also do well to remember that the effectiveness of evangelistic preaching depends in great part not on us but on the members of the church.

Billy Graham came to Washington, D.C., in 1982 to lead a crusade. Thousands attended, and many became Christians, including a few people connected with our church.

One young woman I baptized as a result told me, "Yes, I came to Christ in the Graham meeting. But that isn't what brought me to Christ." She then talked about two Christian men from our church with whom she worked at the fire department. She said that observing their Christian lives had made her approach them and say, "I need what you've got." So they invited her to their Bible study and then to attend the Graham crusade.

Likewise, people come to our church, hear an evangelistic sermon, and become Christians because first they've been impressed with the witness and friendship of our members.

Evangelism, then, does not depend primarily on the preacher. Certainly, the sermon plays a vital role in the process. But it is a church effort. No one person has to bear the weight of this joyous but formidable task.

The elements of style

The evangelistic sermon has taken many forms over the centuries. Methodist Bishop Quayle said that preaching is not so much preparing a sermon and delivering it as it is preparing a preacher and delivering him. In spite of the many changes in time and culture, that remains especially true of evangelistic preaching.

Fundamental to our preparation, of course, is immersion in prayer and Scripture. But beyond that, I preach more effective evangelistic sermons when I remember the following things.

Practice vicarious dialogue.   Evangelism is not a gimmick. It's not some smooth technique of persuasion. Too many people think of the evangelist as a smooth salesman who comes in to sign people up. Instead, when I evangelize, I'm not trying to manipulate people's minds about their deepest needs and questions and sell them the gospel. Rather, I'm simply trying to describe their deepest concerns and show how Jesus addresses them.

I do that by practicing "vicarious dialogue." As I prepare my sermon, I try to listen to the objections and questions my listeners may have at certain points in my message: "Yes, but what about this?" or "Okay, but so what?" Then I craft my sermon to respond to people's questions at appropriate points. This forces me to think seriously about the people I'm addressing. It also helps them see that I am not just trying to get them interested in something they don't care about; I'm responding to their interests.

Don't put down; lift up Christ.   In 1964, I attended a missions conference in western Pakistan where Anglican Bishop Wolmar spoke. It was during the time when many were suggesting we impose a moratorium on foreign missions. Wolmar said, "We will long want missionaries to come to Pakistan, but not the kind who come reaching down to help poor benighted souls. Instead, we want those who will come and stand alongside them, regarding them as sincerely religious, showing them what Jesus offers that they don't have."

Unfortunately, some preachers misrepresent others' views, seeking to rebut them, or they ridicule their opinions. Instead, I try to understand other religions and worldviews, present them fairly and accurately, and lift Jesus higher.

A friend of mine who has a doctorate in Islamic studies, David Shenk, does this well in a book he cowrote with Islamic scholar Badra Katereqqa, *Islam and Christianity*. David wrote chapters on how the Christian views the Islamic faith; Katereqqa described how the Muslim views the Christian faith. Then they each wrote a response to the other. In the end, they each acknowledged that their disagreement hinged on the Christian idea that God loved us so much that he entered the world in Christ and suffered. For the Muslim that's impossible; for the Christian, it's essential. In sum, David didn't try to condemn Islam; he simply showed the Muslim readers the uniqueness of Jesus Christ.

Use language that connects. I was talking with a man from the inner city of Washington, D.C. When he learned I was a preacher, he demanded in a belligerent tone, "Tell me what difference it makes in my life that Jesus died on a cross two thousand years ago."

Fond of theology as I am, I was tempted to describe to him the theological meaning of the atonement. Instead, I said, "Do you have some close friends?" When he nodded yes, I continued, "Suppose one of them gets in trouble. What are you going to do with him?"

"Help him out," he said.

"How long are you going to hang in?"

"Well, he's your friend. You hang in."

"But he gets in worse trouble still. When can you cop out?"

A little peeved, he said, "Man, if he's your friend, you don't cop out. Even criminals won't cop out."

I looked at him and said, "And God came to us as a friend and identified with us in our problem. When can he cop out?"

"You mean Jesus?" he asked.

"Yes. If he's a friend, when can he say, 'That's it. I've gone far enough with you'?"

All at once, his eyes lit up, and he said, "You mean that's why Jesus had to die?"

"That's one reason. He couldn't cop out short of death, or else he wasn't really hanging in with you."

He stood up and dusted off his pants. Then he grinned at me and walked off down the street, squaring his shoulders as he went. As I watched him walk away, I muttered to him (although he couldn't hear), "You don't know it, but you've been evangelized."

There's more to the atonement than that, of course. But what I did explain of the atonement, I explained in language with which this man could identify. The same sort of thing has to happen for evangelistic preaching to be effective.

The elements of variety

Effective evangelistic preaching also depends on using a variety of elements.

Themes.   All evangelistic preaching aims to bring people to a decision to accept Christ. We make a mistake, however, if we assume that all evangelistic preaching must begin and end on the same note. Christ meets needs in a variety of ways: he's the propitiation for our sins, yes, but he's also the norm for ethics, the Shepherd of sheep, the Bread of Life, the Way, the Truth, and the Life.

I preached a series of evangelistic sermons in Kansas and after the first night's sermon, a woman shook my hand at the door and said, "Thank you for that message. But I didn't hear anything about the blood tonight."

I said, "No, that wasn't my subject."

"In our church," she said, "we hear about the blood in every sermon."

"Well," I said, "you come back tomorrow night."

She did, and she heard about the blood. At the door she

shook my hand and thanked me, saying how she appreciated hearing about the blood of Christ. I kept holding her hand and said, "Madam, you do yourself and your pastor a disservice. The gospel has so many elements. If you insist he preach every Sunday on the blood of Christ, he will never get to other themes that could enrich your faith."

Needs.   Too many times we fail to recognize that people come to hear us for different reasons. Some people come out of fear of death. Others come out of a sense of emptiness— their lives lack meaning, and they're bored. Some want their salvation assured. Others' lives are in shambles, and they need help. And sometimes people are troubled by their addictions, enslaved to chemicals, ambition, or bad relationships. Preaching is better when adjusted to the needs calling to be addressed.

Cultures.   Although largely young, white professionals attend our church, we do have a number of minority groups actively involved. A message that works for one subculture, of course, may not work for another. I need to remember the variety of cultures I address. And it doesn't hurt to get help in doing so.

Sometimes we invite a guest preacher who speaks the language of the black community, or a music group that appeals more to another ethnic subculture. A different part of the neighborhood often turns out for them, one that doesn't come to hear me.

Settings.   I get calls from university campus and community groups to speak or lead in prayer. I often accept these invitations and use them to "preach" evangelistically in a new setting.

I was invited to lead the invocation at a national insurance conference in Washington, D.C. Not all of the conference planners were particularly interested in Christianity, but some were Christians and thought prayer was a good thing to have on the program. So I went to dinner with the group. When they called on me to lead the invocation, I stepped up to the microphone and said, "If I'm going to lead you in prayer, then it's better if you understand where I'm coming from."

Succinctly I indicated that I was a committed Christian. I hadn't come simply as a professional minister who prays for a living, but as one whose walk with Christ is extremely meaningful. I went so far as to invite God to be working in the life of each person at this event. Then I led in prayer.

After the program, a number of people came and thanked me, not for the prayer, but for my introductory comments. I rarely do something along those lines, but in that setting, I felt a touch of evangelism was necessary. Naturally, I don't want to misuse such situations. But if handled with tact, we can use them effectively to present Christ to others.

The ways of measuring

It irks me when, after an evangelistic sermon, someone asks, "How many did you get down front?" Evangelism's effectiveness can't be measured that way. Yet in many churches, the altar call remains the measure of the preacher's success. And that can lead to many sorts of manipulation.

I was in one evangelistic meeting when the evangelist closed his message by asking, "How many of you want to love the Lord more? Raise your hand." Of course, we all raised our hands. Then he said, "If you really mean that, stand up." Naturally, a lot of us stood up. Then he said, "If you really mean that, come down front." And a lot of people walked to the front and were taken to a counseling room and received prayer. Later they were reported as people who responded to the invitation. Yet as a listener, I felt manipulated.

So, giving an invitation can be used inappropriately. Yet I believe at the right time and place it's the right thing to do. It is one way in which people can make a public commitment to Christ.

There are few hard-and-fast guidelines as to the right time

and place. Different churches, different pastors, and different sermons will demand different responses.

Sometimes it's far better to let people pray in silence after a sermon, encouraging them to talk to me after the service or during the week. Other times, in planning a public invitation, I make it clear from the beginning where the sermon is heading. Once in a while, I make a judgment in the midst of the service; I didn't plan it, but by the end of the sermon I sense it is appropriate to invite people to make a public response.

Even though the time and place is flexible, there are two things we try to do to make invitations meaningful for the people coming forward.

First, we prepare the people for the invitation. That means sometimes offering an invitation in nonevangelistic settings. For instance, after a sermon on Christ's power in our lives, we may invite people to come forward to have an elder pray for them about some area in which they need to experience more of Christ's power. That not only gives Christians an opportunity to be ministered to, it also makes an invitation after an evangelistic sermon less threatening. Unbelievers who attend our church become aware that in our congregation, it's natural for people to go forward to pray and to be helped.

Second, in offering an evangelistic invitation, we try to be clear about the level of commitment we are inviting people to make. If we give a narrow invitation just for unbelievers, spotlighting them unduly, we put those people in a tight spot. They may feel awkward about walking to the front of a congregation of committed Christians. That's an unnecessary social hurdle to expect them to overcome. On the other hand, we don't want to play games with people and make the invitation so general it applies to anyone who wants to do better in life.

The subject of the sermon, of course, will determine to a large degree what we invite people to do. But we try to be as specific as possible without throwing up needless social barriers.

The fruit of atheists

In 1980, I spent a year at Princeton Theological Seminary as a scholar-in-residence. Esther and I lived in a seminary apartment during our stay. One of my first mornings there, as I stepped into the hall to get my mail, a young woman approached me and asked, "Are you Dr. Augsburger?" I said I was. "Well, my husband and I live upstairs and I wanted to meet you." Then, just like that, she asked, "Where were you in the summer of 1959?"

I thought a bit and said, "Well, I think I was on an evangelistic mission."

She asked, "Were you in Arthur, Illinois?"

"Yes, I was," I said.

"Do you remember the young Mennonite girl who brought one of her atheist high school friends to talk to you?"

"No," I had to admit, "I don't remember that."

"Well, I was that atheist. We talked for an hour and you gave me all the reasons I should be a Christian. But you didn't push me to make a commitment. When we got up to leave, you turned to me and said, 'Marilyn, I'm sorry for you, because you're going to miss out on so much that Jesus intends for you to enjoy.' "

"Well," she concluded, "I never got away from that."

She had become a Christian. She had earned a doctorate in philosophy and, with her husband, was a guest teacher that year at Princeton. They're both on the faculty at the University of California at Santa Barbara. About two years ago, she was ordained in the Episcopal church.

You can see why, then, I remain committed to evangelistic preaching. It's not just because of the Great Commission. It's also because of its great satisfaction.

14

Making the Invitation Compelling

Evangelistic preaching is challenging because it must remain simple.

—GREG LAURIE

I became a Christian in 1970 during the Jesus Movement. I had been attending Calvary Chapel in Costa Mesa, California, more or less the epicenter of the Jesus Movement, where people from all walks of life came. The church had no formal dress code, so as a teenager sporting long hair, I felt comfortable and welcome. One Sunday I missed the morning service at Calvary, so I decided to attend another local church in the neighborhood.

I arrived late. The preacher was already preaching. As I took my seat, I immediately felt uneasy. I could feel the cold stares of those sitting around me. My jeans and tennis shoes did not match the dress code.

The stares bothered me a little, but I thought, *Well, these people are Christians; I'm a Christian. We're all brothers and sisters.* I sat down near the front and opened my Bible. The preacher was wrapping up what sounded like a great message, so I decided to stay for the second service.

The stares continued into the second service. Even the preacher seemed to be looking at me. Others stole furtive glances at me out of the corner of their eyes.

The sermon was next, and the preacher stood up. He began by saying his message would be different from the one in the earlier service. "I need to preach the gospel in this service," he said. "I think some here don't know Christ."

Does he think I'm not a believer? I thought. "We all have sinned," he said, but what I think he really meant was, "You (yeah you, the one seated in the fourth pew on the left) are a sinner." He riveted his eyes on me while making sweeping gestures. He was sure he had a genuine hippie on the ropes.

I squirmed and brought my Bible to my chest so he could see it, as if to signal to him, "Don't waste your sermon on me; I'm already a Christian." But he preached on and then gave an invitation for people to come to Christ. The choir began singing "Just as I Am." Only one girl walked to the front. The choir kept singing; the verses kept coming like hot days in August.

Finally, the person to the left of me whispered, "Are you a Christian?" When I said yes, she seemed disappointed. Then someone behind me asked, "Are you a Christian?"

"Yes, I am; I'm a Christian." I felt like shouting it.

Then one of the robed choir members with pouffy hair stood up and shuffled down from the platform and edged her way between the pews to where I was seated.

"Are you a Christian?" she asked. I weakly nodded. But I must confess I almost gave in to the peer pressure and became born again, again.

Stories such as mine give evangelistic invitations a bad rap. We've all sat through a hundred poorly sung verses of "Just as I Am," waiting for an alleged someone to gather courage. It's enough to make one wonder whether invitations should have gone out with bell-bottoms and the Carpenters.

Yet I'm a firm believer in evangelistic invitations—especially today, when so many churches attract seekers. I believe invitations can and must be done well. Here is what I have learned in publicly inviting nonbelievers to make a decision for Christ.

Simple and clear

Evangelistic preaching is challenging because it must remain relatively simple. The temptation is to be clever, but it's best to keep an evangelistic message direct and clear. I love exploring the caverns of God's Word, but I try to resist that urge in an evangelistic sermon. An evangelistic invitation depends on clear content, clear language, and clear directions.

Clear content. An evangelistic sermon should include certain elements—most notably the message of the Cross. I recently asked Billy Graham in what ways his preaching today differed from his preaching forty years ago. I barely had the chance to finish my question before he gave his decisive answer: "I preach more on the Cross and the blood. That's where the power is."

Except for preaching a watered-down gospel, the worst sin in giving an evangelistic invitation is making it confusing or overly inclusive. Here are the four elements of the gospel I include in every invitation. (The following outline was adapted from a message given by Graham during his 1957 Madison Square Garden Crusade.)

First, I want my listeners to understand clearly where they stand before God. I say, "Number one, you must admit that you are a sinner. That's hard to admit. But the Bible says we've all sinned and fallen short of the glory of God. You might protest, 'But I live a good life. I'm a moral person.' But the Bible says if you offend in one point of the law, you're guilty of all. Have you ever sinned? Have you ever broken a commandment? Then you're guilty. One sin is enough to keep you out of heaven. You have to admit you're a sinner."

Second, I explain Christ's provision: "Christ died on the cross for you. He died for your sin. He paid the price for you when he shed his blood. The apostle Paul said, 'He loved me and gave himself for me.' Scripture also tells us, 'While we were yet sinners, Christ died for us.' Not only did he die on the cross, he also rose again."

Third, I explain, "You must repent of your sin. The Bible

tells us that we must 'Repent, then, and turn to God, so your sins may be wiped out, that times of refreshing may come from the Lord.' The word *repent* means to do a U-turn, to go the other direction. Now you're going to walk away from sin and walk toward Christ."

Fourth, I lay the choice before them: "Last, you must receive Christ into your life. Becoming a Christian is not just believing a creed. It's receiving Christ into you, into your heart. The Bible says, 'For as many as received him, he gave them the power to become sons of God.' "

Clear language.   Not only must the content of the invitation be clear, so must the language. As a new convert I was bewildered by Christian jargon: "Welcome, brother, you're part of the body of Christ now. Walk in the Spirit and avoid the flesh." I thought, *How can I be a part of "the body" and "avoid the flesh"?* It sounded ghoulish.

Today, many church leaders are sensitive to Christian jargon, but the principle bears repeating: Be clear. Nonbelievers today are always less churched and further removed from Christianity than we think. Christian jargon repels, rather than attracts, nonbelievers. I'm not saying we should avoid biblical terminology such as *repent* and *justification*. We must simply define ourselves as we speak.

For instance, you might say, "To have your sins forgiven you must repent, which means to change your direction—to stop running from God and begin running to him instead."

Clear directions.   I've heard gripping evangelistic sermons bumbled by a confusing invitation. Nonbelievers need clear, simple directions. The prospect of raising a hand or walking the aisle is scary enough without added confusion.

First, people need to know *what* you want them to do. I will often say, "In a few moments, I'm going to ask you to raise your hand if you would like to make a personal commitment to Christ."

I've asked people to stand if they wanted to receive Christ and then directed them to a counseling room: "If you wish to make a commitment to Christ, make your way over to that room. All others, please don't get up or leave early. Let's keep the aisles open for those who are coming to Christ."

I've also had people raise their hands and then said, "Go over to the side room now. We have some materials we want to give to you."

At funerals, I've said, "If you want to know more about following Jesus Christ, don't hesitate to come up and talk with me after the service."

Other pastors have their listeners meet their eyes while heads are bowed in silent prayer.

Second, listeners need to know *why* I'm asking them to stand or make a public commitment. I often say, "Jesus said, 'If you'll confess me before men, I'll confess you before my Father who is in heaven. But if you deny me, I'll deny you.' So you need to make a public stand for Christ."

I might continue, "Jesus said to Matthew, 'Get up and follow me.' And Matthew left his table and publicly followed him. When Jesus saw Zacchaeus up in a tree, he said, 'Come down from there. I'm coming over to your house for a meal.' Philip baptized the Ethiopian eunuch with his entourage watching. These were public stands. Now, I'm going to ask you to make a public stand."

If people reject the invitation, so be it. But I need to make sure what they are rejecting is Christ and not a poorly executed and muddied invitation.

Gentle persuasion

Conversion is a tender, mysterious moment. Who can understand it? I preach intending to persuade people to come to Christ, but only the Spirit gives life and brings conversion. When I give the invitation, I often remember the verse, "As many as were ordained unto eternal life believed" (Acts 13:48). So much of giving effective invitations is just staying out of the Spirit's way.

Yet I want to give indecisive people an opportunity. Persuasion is legitimate. It is the impetus many need to move from the kingdom of darkness into the kingdom of light. Sometimes after giving an invitation, I'll come back with a second appeal and say, "We're going to sing this one more time." (One more time means one more time; I don't play games with them.)

Sometimes I might say, "Realize that this is an eternal decision. Jesus said, 'You are either for me or against me, with me or opposed.' Indecision about Christ is a decision. Make your decision today. In this final moment, if you want to come, come." I want people to understand the implications of what they're doing. They need to know the consequences of rejecting Christ.

Manipulation is a danger; I am not a salesman trying to close the sale. After preaching an outstanding sermon, one pastor asked those who wanted to commit their lives to Christ to come forward. As the choir once again sang "Just as I Am," there was little or no movement in the congregation. The pastor then said, "Perhaps you would like to rededicate your life to Christ. Get up and stand here in the front." One person out of a congregation of 2,500 straggled forward. The pastor finally said, "Perhaps you would like to join the church. Get up and come forward!"

I was waiting for him to say, "Maybe you'd like to examine the veneer of the wood on my pulpit more closely. Don't leave me here alone! Get up here!"

If a person can be manipulated into making a decision for Christ, he can be manipulated out of it. Pressured in, pressured out. Besides, today's communication-savvy attenders will not put up with manipulation. It only makes everyone feel uncomfortable.

The same is true of music. Well-done background music can create the proper mood for people to evaluate where they stand with God. But never should it manipulate. Several more numbers by the backup band is not the answer to an empty altar.

I often think of a Billy Graham crusade in London in 1954.

The first night, the response to the invitation was overwhelming. The next day the British press claimed that Graham was using music to manipulate the people. That night the Graham team used no music during the invitation. All you could hear was the stomping of feet as people came from the bleachers. The response that evening was bigger than the response on the previous night.

The clear presentation of the gospel—not the music or other flashy techniques—must always be the entree of the invitation.

The pastor as evangelist

I don't give invitations every Sunday at Harvest Christian Fellowship. In our church structure, Sunday morning is primarily for feeding the flock (though I'll break that rule if I sense God's leading). Sunday evening is our primary venue for reaching nonbelievers. The service is designed as an evangelistic Bible study. I generally work my way through a biblical text but lace the message with evangelistic statements to confront the listener. At the end, I often ask for a decision.

I've intentionally made the clear presentation of the gospel an integral part of my preaching. I believe deeply in the pastor-evangelist role. Charles Haddon Spurgeon, Martin Lloyd Jones, and Harry Ironside were pastors who did evangelism well. The need for the pastor-evangelist is great today, given our expertise at attracting seekers to our churches. But attracting seekers carries a responsibility to give them opportunities to choose eternal life. For many, all they need is to be asked.

In the final analysis, though, giving an effective invitation depends more on our God-given burden and sense of urgency than any technique we might employ. Spurgeon once wrote, "The Holy Spirit will move them by first moving you. If you can rest without their being saved, they will rest too. But if you are filled with an agony for them, if you cannot bear that they should be lost, you will find that they are uneasy too. I hope you will get into such a state that you will dream about your child or hearer perishing for lack of Christ, and start at once and begin to cry, 'O God, give me converts, or I die.' Then you will have converts."

D.L. Moody once preached the gospel but did not give an invitation; he told the people to go home and think about it. That night the Great Chicago Fire broke out, and many people who had been in attendance at that Moody meeting died. From that day forward, Moody determined never to tell people to go home and think about the gospel. He would ask them to choose each time he preached.

Salvation Army founder William Booth said that he wished he could have his soldiers-in-training exposed to hell for twenty-four hours: If they saw the consequences of rejecting Christ, they would be better motivated.

Moody, Spurgeon, and Booth were leaders who modeled the evangelistic fervor I desire.

I was just a two-week-old Christian when I was dragged into witnessing on a California beach. I was a starry-eyed convert with not much training; I hadn't even memorized the tract I was handing out.

I walked up to a middle-aged woman and asked if she would like eternal life. Then I read the tract to her. When I got to the point where it asked the question, "Is there any good reason why you should not accept Christ?" she said, "No." Suddenly I froze. I finally told her to close her eyes and to pray while I frantically searched for a prayer to read—I hadn't planned on success.

As we were praying, I thought *This isn't going to work. She isn't really becoming a Christian.* After we were through, she opened her eyes and said, "Boy, something happened to me." And I said, "Yeah, something happened to me, too."

A fire had been lit in my soul, and I've been giving invitations ever since.

15

Opening the Bible for Seekers

Discussion Bible studies are powerful agents of change.

—MARILYN KUNZ

It is now clear that large numbers of people have become Christians through peer-group discussions of the Bible. And when unchurched participants become serious about the Christian faith, they normally begin attending church, often the church of their group's initiator.

Whole churches have been built using this method, and the gospel has penetrated neighborhoods and workplaces that likely would not have opened up to other evangelistic strategies.

What are the keys that make these groups succeed, causing the local church to grow? Here are six:

Safe invitation

Instead of being asked to "join" a Bible study, people are invited to a home to hear about an idea: a discussion Bible study group for adults who aren't experts. After dessert and coffee, the host or hostess explains how the group will function, using the method of inductive (investigative) study. A twenty-minute sampler—one incident from the gospel of

Mark—gives a taste of what's ahead. Those interested set a time and place to start studying Mark 1.

The same thing can happen on the job. Any group that meets on neutral territory is less threatening for newcomers than meeting in a church. Lunch-hour groups currently meet every week among Wall Street businesspeople, research scientists at a pharmaceutical corporation, and executives and clerical workers at a chemical firm; there's also an after-work study among garage mechanics with their Christian employer, and breakfast studies (weekday or Saturday) among small-town tradesmen and professionals. Workers who know one another through their jobs but meet in homes range from lobstermen on an island off the Maine coast to astronauts and their spouses in Houston.

Protective structure

An ideal ratio is six to eight people studying the Bible for the first time with only one or two firm Christians. Groups with too many "experts" do not appeal to raw beginners.

A group of six to ten is large enough to stimulate interaction and new ideas but small enough to let everyone speak and respond to the comments of others. If a group is twelve or larger, discussion tends to split into two or three competing conversations. The moderator has to exert strong control and may be tempted to lecture. The quiet people and those who know the least sit back. Sometimes they stop coming.

But when everyone has a fair chance, each participant is greatly influenced by what she discovers and shares in the group. What she hears herself saying about Jesus' claims will be remembered long after she forgets what someone else tells her. We recall only 20 percent of what we hear but 70 percent of what we say. That's why *discussion* Bible studies are powerful agents of change.

Whole book bites

Newcomers to the Bible need to lay a foundation before they can handle studies that skip around. Using selected verses here and there to present the gospel message confuses the person who cannot set them into a meaningful context. They also put the person at risk when approached by a cult using a thematic presentation. If methods are similar, the biblically untaught person has a hard time distinguishing between what is authentic and what is counterfeit.

Those new to Bible study should start with Mark; it's clear, concise, full of action, and does not require familiarity with the Old Testament. No wonder missionary translators usually begin with Mark.

Well-prepared questions

Groups function best with questions that help them observe, interpret, and apply what they find in the Bible text. The questions should be forthright enough to allow each person to take a turn as moderator, moving the group paragraph by paragraph through a chapter. The material must not assume that everyone understands Christian jargon or can easily comprehend a religious mind-set.

Three ground rules

The following ground rules protect a group against misuse of Scripture:

Confine the discussion to the chapter being studied.   This keeps the newcomers at equal advantage. As the weeks go by, of course, everyone's scope of knowledge enlarges, and the group is able to refer back to chapters previously studied.

Expect everyone to be responsible for pulling the group back from digressions.   The moderator's job is greatly eased if others in the group help say, "We've gotten onto a tangent. Let's get back to the chapter."

Agree that the document (Mark, for example) will be the authority for the discussion. People should not be coerced into believing the Bible, but they can be encouraged to be honest about what it says and to refrain from rewriting it. As a group continues to study week after week, most members come to recognize the Bible as authoritative.

These guidelines keep a group on the path of orthodoxy. It is difficult to promote heresy in a group studying a book of the Bible in context.

Nonexpert study

Not every member should attempt an outreach Bible study. A wise pastor will not try to get the whole church into this approach to evangelism. Some Christians tend to tell others too much too soon. The discussion approach requires patience and a willingness to let the non-Christian build a framework of Bible knowledge and discover Christ's claims for himself.

But once this has happened, the person is much more likely to hear and believe a gospel presentation from the pulpit or from a Christian friend.

For those the church wants to encourage in this kind of outreach, a preparation series of four or five Wednesday nights or an all-day Saturday workshop may be used. Such a training program should include:

- An explanation of inductive study.
- Instruction in sensitivity to the non-Christian.
- Practice in introducing the idea of a Bible study to friends and colleagues.
- Participation in an actual Bible study discussion.

Copies of the study questions for Mark should be available as well.

At one such workshop, two men were role-playing the initial invitation. Jim later reported, "When Charlie asked me how I'd like to 'join a group and study the Word of God,' he lost me. I was suddenly aware that a person who had never studied the Bible would not call it 'the Word of God.' It would have been better if he'd simply asked me if I'd like to be in a Bible study for nonexperts. I would have said yes to that."

Outreach can start in a neighborhood with one or two young mothers from the church inviting women on their block. The daytime group becomes so valuable that they want their husbands to share the experience, and an evening Bible study begins for couples. Next, businesspeople start studies at work.

Those who come to Christ through a discussion Bible study are able to reach out to their friends in the same way. Meanwhile, church members mature spiritually and become more effective leaders in the church. Small-group Bible study is a ministry multiplier.

PART 4

Evaluate

16

The Numbers Game

The only value of numbers is in comparison; that's why you find statistics in columns.

—Wayne Jacobsen

Lucy finally met him face to face among the trees in the soft moonlight. She had seen the great lion earlier but had been dissuaded from following him because of the taunts of her friends. Now the lion Aslan, after a gentle rebuke, tells her what she must do: "Go and wake the others and tell them to follow. If they will not, then you at least must follow me alone."

In my office hangs a large sketch of a lion that depicts this scene from C. S. Lewis's *Chronicles of Narnia.* The eyes of the lion, who symbolizes Christ, seem to plead, "Why won't you simply follow me and not worry about what others think?"

I needed that encouragement and correction as I pioneered a new church. I remember the time five people showed up for a Sunday morning service for which I had prepared a keynote sermon on that body's development—and two of those were visitors. Back home I went into my study and wept. Not for ministry lost, not for the needs of people, but in anguish that others would find out about it. I wept wondering if my call had been a mistake.

Though confident about God's work most of the time, I fought feelings of failure whenever I looked at statistics. And believe me, people gave me the opportunity often. Even though we grew from twenty-five to one hundred during this two-year stretch, I came to see how preoccupation with numbers does more to stifle real growth than to nurture it.

Statistic hounds

Our Christian subculture usually focuses on statistics as the measure of pastoral success. I feel it whenever someone asks me how the fellowship is doing. Invariably the next question is "How many people are coming now?" After fighting that question for years, I have found relief now in realizing that it tells more about the questioner than my answer will ever tell about me.

Young pastors, especially, are hounded in their self-image by statistics, their success determined by numbers. Figures can make you feel impressive—or impotent. The pressure is devastating, and though it may lead pastors to do things that will help the church grow, it may not lead them to righteousness. Though they have more people, they may have less of the Lord.

"Do not fret—it leads only to evil" (Ps. 37:8) is as true of ministers and numbers as it is of the psalmist and the wealth of the wicked. Who can resist the temptation to manipulate the responses of people under the guise of developing their spirituality when the monthly denominational report looms ahead? When numbers are our goal, it is easy to prostitute ministry on the altar of results by making pragmatism our lord.

The danger, however, is not peculiar to small congregations. Our focus on statistics can have harmful effects even when the numbers are large. I've heard some incredible things taught by pastors whose only validation rested in the size of their congregation. I've known the spiritual lethargy that subtle pride and self-security can cause when statistics inflate self-importance. And what of the large-church pastor harassed by the pressure "to keep the whole thing going," plagued by tension and stress, wrestling the temptation to be a people-pleaser?

Numerical failures

You would think our preoccupation with numbers would end when we realize the only value is in comparison. That's why you find statistics in columns. How can we indulge ourselves in the same thing for which Jesus rebuked Peter (comparing his calling with John's; see John 21:20–23)? Paul said it leads only to senselessness: "When they measure themselves by themselves and compare themselves with themselves, they are not wise" (2 Cor. 10:12).

Though counting heads can sometimes be helpful in sharing what the Lord is doing, Scripture gives us four other reasons why numerical success can never be a valid measure of successful ministry.

First, the nature of the gospel message tends away from large-scale acclaim. The road is still a narrow one. Jesus warned his disciples that in some cities no one would accept their message (Matt. 10:14–18), even though he had given them the power to work wonders.

Do you know how many of the five thousand who feasted on the loaves and fishes were still following Jesus twenty-four hours later? Twelve. John records the challenging sermon Jesus preached the next day that drove people away in anger. He told them to eat his flesh and drink his blood—that he would have to become the very fiber of their existence. His popularity waned when the bread stopped and truth began. Jesus didn't design the gospel to be attractive.

We're often told there is a large harvest waiting in every city if we'll just meet the needs of people. God doesn't call us to meet needs; he calls us to confront our world with the reality of his kingdom. Though his compassion meets needs, it doesn't always do it in the way people desire. Much of the gospel presented today befits less the God of the ages than a fairy godmother offering people by God's hand what they've been unable to achieve for themselves: wealth, fame, comfort, and security.

Second, shaping our ministry to suit the masses neglects the nature of this evil age. Paul clearly warns that multitudes love to have their ears tickled by teachers who say what they want to hear (2 Tim. 4:3).

It is a simple fact: good teachers know how to drive away a crowd when they hang around for the wrong reasons. Where I previously pastored, one of the staff members who most reflected the character of the Lord rarely had large classes. Crowds look for clever language, humor, high interest, but not always for life-changing truth, especially when it confronts uncomfortable areas.

Third, reaching large numbers of people may not always be God's priority and is certainly not synonymous with successful pastoral ministry. One source of encouragement I've had over the past two years was from an offhand comment I heard at a pastor's conference. A speaker used an illustration of an encounter he had with a parishioner seven years before while painting the rail on the front steps of his small Indiana church. I couldn't imagine this pastor ever painting rails, much less only seven years ago. He was now pastoring a church numbering close to 5,000.

You may think he was wasting time, but God was forging a vessel. Paul spent at least seventeen years of life-preparing growth before God launched him to Asia.

Fourth, though we can say with confidence that righteousness leads to fruitfulness, can we say with equal certainty that fruit will always be immediate or external? A success-oriented society defines success only by desired results. In church work it has come down to numbers and budgets.

Paul had to reemphasize to the Corinthians that you cannot rate the quality of anyone's ministry on a tally sheet because we are called to different tasks. Some plant, some reap. The day of judgment will reveal the quality of work each has invested in God's kingdom. But Paul does make clear that the planters are rarely reapers.

Dietrich Bonhoeffer's obedience led him back to Germany to serve his compatriots as World War II was beginning. "I shall have no right to participate in the reconstruction of Christian life in Germany after the war if I do not share the trials of this time with my people," he wrote to a friend. He didn't go back to a large church pulpit, but eventually to a prison camp and execution only days before it was liberated by the Allies. Any regrets? "You must never doubt that I am thankful and glad to go the way which I am being led," he wrote from his prison cell.

True success

If not by statistics, how can we measure success? After all, we must know who to invite to our conventions, whose formula to follow, and whose book to read. Bonhoeffer demonstrates clearly the true measure of success. It is simple obedience to the will of the Master, not for results, but regardless of them. If he was playing the numbers game, would Martin Luther have posted his ninety-five theses? Would Saint Francis have abandoned his family's wealth? (After all, he could have used it for Jesus.) Would Corrie ten Boom have hidden Jews from Adolf Hitler?

I know that doesn't help us judge people. If only that ministry could be evaluated by quotas, sales contests, promotions, raises, or finished products. But it can't. That's why ministry can be a frustrating profession for those who seek accomplishments. Obedience is our only motivation, and nothing as trivial as size (or lack of it) can ever measure it.

How freeing this should be to ministry people when their calling is challenged. You sit alone in your study trying to pray and read the Word, but instead you're churning inside, wondering if you're successful. You feel left out by those who think your labor insignificant. You don't feel like a celebrity, and maybe you don't need to, but the pressure to produce flashy statistics eats at you daily. Another family leaves the church, and you doubt your calling or the quality of your service. Pats on the back come few and far between, or they don't come at all.

Be encouraged to trust obedience above numbers and the corresponding human affirmation. Seek only the Lord's approval. Without it, no one else's will really matter. With it, you'll need no other.

This is Paul's example in 2 Timothy. At the end of his ministry, Paul writes confidently, "I have finished the race." Success! What's incredible about this statement is that it was written in a prison cell after "everyone in the province of Asia" had deserted him. These were his banner churches in Ephesus, Troas, and Colossae. And in Rome at his trial, "no one came to my support, but everyone deserted me."

Though his ministry had been extensive, now he could count his supporters on two hands. Yet still he writes, "Now there is in store for me a crown of righteousness which the Lord, the righteous Judge, will award me on that day." Paul lived every moment in this life for his first moment in the next. The accolades of people would never be its substitute.

Often in my present pastorate, what we perceived to be pleasing to God and what would have quickly increased our numbers have been two different things. Deciding not to invest large sums into our facility, or not to manipulate people to do busy "church work," or not to make our services less controversial have cost us more people than we've gained. The choices have not been easy. The pressure to grow is ever present. The desire to have colleagues believe in what I'm doing is strong. But faithfulness to Jesus must be stronger.

Pastors must be free to follow their calling, whether it leads them to serve among repenting multitudes as Jonah did, or to preach as Isaiah until all who hear reject the God you preach. We can't predetermine our lot. What matters is that our calling is deeply rooted in our relationship with the Father and our actions in obedience to his Word. Sure, Jonah had a larger following, but do you think he was the better preacher? His obedience was characterized by malice and mistrust, Isaiah's by loving submission.

"The full flood of life is . . . not in seeing God's work succeed, but in the perfect understanding of God, and the communion with him that Jesus himself had," Oswald Chambers said in *My Utmost for His Highest*. This is where success is measured—not in externals, but in a quiet heart before the Lord. Though others can't know that, we can be free to live for the first moment he embraces us and says, "Well done, good and faithful servant."

17

Our Sufficiency for Outreach

My calling as pastor is to lift God's people before the Lord, to bring his Word to his people, and to equip them for their calling. Unbelievers, in a sense, are incidental to that primary purpose.

—JOHN MACARTHUR JR.

I receive many letters from pastors who feel intimidated by today's church trends. They see the exploding seeker church, but the bottom line is, they're not in the same league as its pastor. They can't pull off the techniques. And they can't afford to do it. The creativity isn't there, the money isn't there, and the crowd isn't there.

One pastor who read my book *Our Sufficiency in Christ* called me in tears. He said, "I was beginning to wonder if what I have always believed about ministry was wrong. This helped me realize that what I've always been committed to is what I need to stay committed to. I just needed to hear that what I'm doing is okay."

Pastors hear the therapists on the radio and they read the books of renowned Christian counselors who say, "Pastors often do more harm than non-Christian counselors," and they get intimidated. So these pastors think, *I can't counsel anybody. Somebody's going to kill himself; I'll get sued and be in court for ten years. I better not say anything.* They hear about the mystical experiences of the charismatics, and they've never seen a sign or wonder in their life. They wonder why they're in ministry if they can't make the lame walk or see a mystical vision.

All across our nation pastors who are godly and well-trained are wondering if they are competent for the task of ministry. What is our sufficiency for ministry? How can we carry on successful outreach in our contemporary culture? I believe the answer lies in a few key principles.

A church for saints

Many people come to church for less than ideal reasons: to be part of something exciting, big, and thriving; to be entertained or inspired; to get a spiritual lift to help them through the week; to give the kids some religious training; to see the preacher they've heard on the radio.

So thinking up a strategy to get an unbeliever to church isn't difficult. All you do is find their hot buttons and press them. If they like dancing elephants, you get dancing elephants. If they want to be successful in their business, you hold a business-success seminar. If they're worried about their kids, you hold parenting workshops.

I'm not guided by that. My calling as pastor is to lift God's people before the Lord, to bring his Word to his people, and to equip them for their calling. Unbelievers, in a sense, are incidental to that primary purpose.

I would never think, *How can I structure this service to accommodate unbelievers?* or *How can I make unbelievers want to attend?* because that's not our purpose—unless we are gearing a special meeting for evangelism. We do have an evangelism outreach on some Saturday and Sunday nights. But we would primarily ask our people to bring those they know.

The biblical pattern is that the church *gathers* to worship and be edified. It *scatters* to evangelize.

Although my preaching in a regular church service is focused on those who are already believers, the effect is often evangelism. One recent Sunday night in our baptism service, the last guy to come into the water announced during his testimony that he had been a homosexual for twenty years. He was HIV positive, and he knew he was going to die.

"I came to this church," he said, "because somebody told me that this was the church that preached the truth for a desperate man. When I walked in, the first thing out of your mouth was Psalm 107, which you stood up and read during worship. God directed that at my heart; that whole psalm described me. Before that hour was over, I had heard enough of the gospel to commit my life to Jesus Christ."

What primarily attracts newcomers to Grace Community Church is personal relationships. The strength of the church has always been people bringing people. In our first six years, the church doubled every two years, without our doing any advertising.

So I basically instruct people: "Honor Christ with your life, take every opportunity to present the gospel, be aggressive in scattering your seed. It isn't the skill of the sower; it's the state of the soil."

It isn't a marketing strategy; it's letting others see the obvious benediction that Christ has become to your life, your marriage, your family, that makes the gospel attractive. Christians have something non-Christians want. I trust that by giving our church people a clear understanding of the gospel, they will be able, when doors open, to start where people are and lead them to the good news of forgiveness and salvation.

A transformation for believers

From the outset we have concentrated on life-changing truth. People had their lives changed and began bringing others, and that continues today. Our church continues to have a tremendous response from unbelievers. I give an invitation every service, and there's not a service after which we don't have people coming into the prayer room to respond to Christ. We baptize anywhere from five to twenty people on a

Sunday night, every week, 90 percent of them led to Christ by somebody else in the church.

Even when we hold a special concert, we don't advertise; we just let our people know that this is a special time for them to bring unbelieving friends.

It's easy to get sidetracked from our purpose, which is spiritual transformation. One diversion is an excessive focus on felt needs.

A man came up to me one night after a recent sermon and said, "I'm not a Christian. My marriage is falling apart. My business is going bad. Can you help me?"

I could have offered some thoughts on marriage enrichment or business principles, but that wasn't the real issue. Instead I replied, "It sounds like you need an invisible means of support."

"Yeah, that's it!" he said. "That's exactly what I need." So I started from there, explaining how Christ could come personally into his life and circumstances.

Unbelievers come in different shapes and sizes, with all different kinds of felt needs. The most compelling—even more than "How do I fix my marriage?"—is sin. By sticking on a Band-Aid, we may fail to address the need for a transformation of life.

We do need some point of contact with a non-Christian, however. I'm not saying we never address felt needs. We just don't want that to become a diversion.

A second diversion is entertaining people in church. Of course to bring about spiritual transformation we need to be adept at keeping people's interest. When we explain the Bible, we need to focus on the things that people find significant. We need to illustrate well. But the difference between maintaining interest and merely entertaining is the purpose: Is it for the sake of being interesting? Or for the sake of truth and spiritual transformation?

It gets back to the preacher's motivation. I'm not concerned with whether listeners think I'm novel, witty, or entertaining. I'm concerned that they get the truth.

I'm not really a student of communication technique, but I have learned how to keep people's attention. What rivets people is anticipation, the expectation that I'm about to say something they want to know. As long as they think I'm about to say something funny or helpful or informative, I will have their attention, and as soon as they decide I don't have anything worthwhile, they're gone. So I don't try to hold listeners by entertaining them in some superficial way, but by giving them the sense that I'm going to say something worthwhile.

A worship for God

The galloping pragmatism I see in the church mitigates the confrontive character of the gospel. When the church becomes enamored with influence and image as the key to evangelization, it is no longer depending on Christ. The philosophy in some churches is, *If they really like us, they'll like Jesus.* I'm not sure there's any correlation whatsoever.

Therefore, I have trouble with the idea of a "user-friendly church." We don't want to be personally or institutionally offensive, but we cannot buffer the offense of the Cross.

At Grace Community Church we do everything possible to let visitors know we're thrilled they're there. We put high priority on treating visitors with real love and care. We have a host ministry that moves throughout the campus identifying people that look new and integrating them into the flow. In the service I take special care to welcome first-time guests. We give them a booklet that explains things in which our church is involved. In the worship service I think most are impressed with the music, which is exceptional. If they are offended, it is always the message that does it. They don't get offended until I get up to preach!

I've often encouraged pastors, "Don't let your church look like anything but the most well-cared-for property in town. If the bank looks better than your church, you're in trouble.

The bank is saying, 'We care more about you than the church.' "

We have a beautiful, well-manicured facility. In fact, I remember one couple visited, came to Christ, and later said, "We thought if you took care of flowers, you probably cared about people."

I read a study that ranked the things that determined where people would go to church: Looks of the facility was number one. Parking, two. Nursery, three. Friendliness, four. Pastor, five. So yes, I think our parking, our shuttle service, and our nursery care are crucial.

So there's nothing wrong with being creative, doing things that make outsiders take a look at your church, things that attract needy unbelievers, as long as it doesn't mitigate the message that God is central. God has given us a beautiful world, and we ought to do everything we can, as Adam did, to dress the garden. In addition we want to keep as nice as possible the things that represent him.

All of this is based on our understanding of human nature: people gravitate toward things that are nice, things that are lovely. I have no problem with anything that doesn't compromise the message or depreciate worship. What happens when churches are so concerned about unbelievers' reactions, though, is they depreciate worship. They put God-centeredness somewhere down the line.

There's a big difference between appealing to human nature's attraction to beauty versus human nature's attraction to entertainment. We are here to demonstrate the beauty and the graciousness of God. We're not here to entertain people. When you move to entertainment, you've taken a major jump.

I object to the user-friendly church idea because even though its proponents may assume the spiritual foundation of ministry, the presentation tends to make people think that the methods are essential. I would rather see a book or seminar say, "Preach the gospel, and by the way, don't forget to provide ample parking." Much of the time it's a matter of emphasis.

The bottom line: Our sufficiency isn't in our techniques, skills, or experiences. Our sufficiency is in Christ.

18

Coming to Terms with Technique

If we really desire the deepest healing for others, we must eventually help move them beyond felt needs and prod them with the goad of the Word into a life of obedient love.

—Donald McCullough

By what power do we minister? Pastors have always needed to answer this question, but never more than now. At one time the pastoral office carried a heavier weight of authority; the pastor was often the best-educated, most respected leader in the community. Not so today.

We have degrees in theology, a subject no longer considered "the queen of sciences" but evoking the same bemusement as Sanskrit. We are generalists in an age of specialization. We work with words in a video culture. We lead institutions in an anti-institutional era. We can't help wondering what good we do as we refer parishioners to doctors and psychologists and lawyers for concrete help.

What is the basis of our authority? Where do we find the necessary power? I have three assumptions.

First, the theological answer is that we minister through the power of the Holy Spirit. But we are not limp puppets; we must do something, and our choices of what we do places the issue of power on a very practical level.

Second, I assume for most of us the difficulty is not a simple choice between success or faithfulness. We all struggle with mixed motives, to be sure. But most of us, down deep, want to be faithful stewards of the gospel.

Finally, I assume we want to build congregations where Christ is glorified through caring fellowship and evangelistic outreach; we want to draw men and women into the family of faith.

The question remains: Where do we find power for this work? As a pastor in modern America, I'm as tempted as anyone to seek it at the altar of technique.

The temptation of technique

Americans have always loved technique. Our most famous homegrown philosophy is pragmatism, the belief that the value of all ideas is determined by their practical consequences. In other words, truth works. William James (1842–1910) and John Dewey (1859–1952) gave erudite expression to this notion, and their writings found receptive soil in a nation built by "Yankee ingenuity" and a "can-do" spirit.

Our national dedication to practicality has had beneficial consequences. We have split the atom, walked on the moon, and developed more efficient shaving creams. Every day we enjoy the comforts of technique's benedictions. By now we don't doubt its power; where there's a will there must be a way. Faced with a problem? Get the experts working on it and before long they will find the solution. If something such as AIDS persists, it can only be because we haven't spent enough money on it. If the national debt keeps growing, it must be because of incompetent, corrupt politicians; we simply need someone with enough courage to descend on the problem with something akin to the Nike swish and "Just Do It."

It's never easy to transcend the gravity of culture. The church, made up of nothing but ordinary people, always reflects the values of Canaan about as much as the law of Israel.

In the church world, technique means an idolatrous faith in practical means to achieve efficient ends. Technique's bible is the how-to manual of successful methods. Technique's creed is the conviction that research will lead to improved means, which will lead to successful ends.

This false god, with extravagant promises of efficiency, too often seduces us into sacrificing the integrity of our ordination to the ministry of the Word.

We have had special difficulty staying away from the Baals of pragmatism. We're not much interested in theology unless it works. "Leave the abstractions to professors; just tell us how to get on with the business of being Christian. The simpler the better."

So lining shelves of Christian bookstores are improvement manuals (on everything from spirituality to sexuality) and books that show how to get out of any problem in no more than twelve steps.

Given the inclinations of culture and congregation, pastors are easily lured into the shrine of technique. The church, wheat and weeds growing together, saint and sinner in every individual, is a messy affair that seems impossible to lead much of anywhere, let alone toward growth. So I would like to think there must be some method, some new means of operation, that will help me manage the three-ring circus into the greatest show on earth.

Now that my theological degrees hang in their frames, volumes by John Calvin and Karl Barth tend to gather dust while I study the latest books on church sociology and cultural change. And the conferences I attend are less likely to be about "Approaches to Biblical Interpretation" than about "How to Grow Your Congregation Beyond the 2,000–Member Barrier." I'm tempted to be more interested in the medium than the message, more interested in strategies for marketing than the Savior I've met.

The tyranny of technique

Technique does bestow its blessings. It works, at least within a particular field. No doubt one reason our congregation grew from five hundred to two thousand in a dozen years is that we tried to think strategically about such things as meeting felt needs and advertising in more creative ways.

The use of good techniques, however, differs from reliance upon technique. Herein is the problem. Technique seems to have a life of its own, drawing us more and more under its influence. Unwilling to remain a servant, it becomes a tyrant.

Jacques Ellul pointed out that means will always overtake ends. A church building, for example, can facilitate corporate worship, but so much congregational time and money may get committed to its maintenance that it becomes an end in itself. In the same way, improved methods, though legitimate as means, tend to become ends. Invite technique into the sanctuary and before long it takes its place on the altar.

A world of difference exists between saying that truth works and saying that what works is true, if by truth we include what ought to be. This distinction gets lost as technique grows in influence. What works, we think, must be right. Our goal, for example, should properly be evangelization and discipleship. But too often growth itself becomes the end, and whatever creates growth becomes authoritative.

Thus, preaching that never confronts the listeners' self-centered lifestyle might enhance growth. But just because it works doesn't make it right. Yet if we rely on technique to supply power for our ministry, we will naturally follow where it leads.

Getting more people into our sanctuaries may be of some value, but numerical growth itself cannot be the goal. Growth simply for growth's sake is cancerous. The only growth that finally matters is growth in Christian faith and the fruits of obedience.

Are the people to whom we minister deepening their trust in the grace of Christ? And are they demonstrating this by loving God with all their heart and soul and mind, and by loving their neighbors as themselves?

I praise God for full pews in the congregation I serve, making necessary three services. But in itself, this doesn't mean much. The growth that counts shows itself when Matilda says, "God really loves me, and I want to be his woman, his holy woman."

Or when Bill, eager to share the gospel with others, commits himself to raising enough money to start ten new churches in San Diego in the next ten years.

Or when Marilyn finally forgives someone who has wounded her deeply.

Or when Aubrey convinces farmers in the San Joaquin Valley to donate surplus crops to the poor and has about 80,000 pounds of food transported each week into the inner cities of Los Angeles and San Diego.

For growth such as this to occur, we need something far more powerful than technique; for this we need nothing less than the Word of God.

Whenever I'm tempted to find power for ministry in technique, I try to remember three basic theological convictions.

The power of the Word

First, the Word of God has all the power necessary to accomplish the will of God. In fact, it is the only power able to do this.

God creates and re-creates through the Word. In the beginning, God spoke to nothing, and it became something ("God said, 'Let there be light' " in Genesis 1:3). In response to human rebellion, God speaks forth the re-creation of all things through the enfleshed Word ("the Word became flesh and lived among us" in John 1:14). And the Word's work of creation and re-creation continues through the apostolic witness of Scripture and its proclamation.

Technique may create more empirically verifiable results in the short run, but the Word alone has power enough to cause growth that will endure for eternity. Power for ministry, therefore, comes from preaching and teaching the Word, from building congregations that are Word-saturated and Word-shaped.

Why then are we ever tempted by technique?

Because the Word takes the way of humility, often the form of weakness. Who would have guessed all things came into being through the baby lying in a manger? Who would have guessed the world was saved through the broken figure on a cross? Who would guess that lives are transformed into holiness through words written in Scripture? "God chose what is foolish in the world to shame the wise; God chose what is weak in the world to shame the strong" (1 Corinthians 1:27). We have no choice, therefore, but to find our confidence and authority and power in the Word.

My most recent inner conflict between the temptation of technique and the integrity of my calling as an ordained minister of the Word came during a recent political campaign. Technique told me to keep quiet, at least in the pulpit, about the election. Conventional church-growth wisdom cautions against controversy in sermons. No matter what I said, someone would be unhappy. Liberals would dislike the biblical pessimism about human rulers; conservatives would dislike the biblical call to care for the poor.

On the other hand, our nation was focused on the election, and silence would imply a docetic gospel that has nothing to do with daily life. So with some fear I chose Psalm 146 as my text: "Do not put your trust in princes, in mortals in whom there is no help. . . . God executes justice for the oppressed, gives food to the hungry . . . lifts up those who are bowed down . . . watches over strangers."

The following week I received a letter from a member telling me that she and her husband had brought their neighbor to church that Sunday.

"We appreciate your ministry," she wrote, "but you should know that he left in anger and will not be back."

I felt horrible. I immediately castigated myself for insensitive stupidity. But when my emotions settled down, I reminded myself that I was not ordained to be popular or to grow a large church; I was ordained to witness to the Word in all its fullness, and I must trust it still has power for creation and redemption.

The number of people drawn inside church walls doesn't mean much. What really matters is how many are exposed to the Word. One congregation may draw a Sunday crowd of 5,000 to inspirational talks as a way to get 500 into a mid-week Bible study (an honorable strategy). Another church may draw five hundred to Sunday services with high-protein doses of the Word.

Both churches, I submit, are effectively the same size. If concern for numerical growth has a place in ministry, it is here, in the passion to reach as many as possible with the life-changing power of the Word.

The incarnation of the Word

My ministry is also shaped by the conviction that the Word not only became flesh but becomes flesh. The Word did not remain a disembodied idea, but took the form of a human being, Jesus of Nazareth, who lived in a specific time and place. The Word dressed itself in the clothing of culture.

It still does. Not only were the apostolic witnesses to this Word children of their time, with concrete ways of thinking and speaking and writing, so are contemporary proclaimers and hearers.

Ordination to the ministry of the Word, therefore, calls for the work of translation. Faithful communication of God's Word cannot remain abstract but must always be incarnational, always connect with actual people and their hopes and fears, their ecstasies and anxieties.

Here the insights of church growth and cultural analysis and church sociology can be helpful. After placing confidence in the power of the Word, after exegeting the biblical text to hear the Word—then comes the creative task of speaking the Word in a manner that will most likely be heard by our contemporaries. If the first two conditions are met, then it's time to be seeker sensitive and aware of felt needs.

I make no apologies for striving to be winsome and even entertaining in my proclamation of the gospel. I prepare sermons, for example, constantly reminding myself that we live in a video age; the people who hear me will respond more readily to the visual than the audio. So I sweat and fret, and I often think the most difficult part of preaching is finding images that picture the truth and thus clothe the Word in a contemporary fashion.

But we are called to translate, not transform, the Word. We may not modify its message or adjust it to the culture for the sake of technique. The Word alone, and not our clever presentation of it, has power for ministry.

A recent cover story in *The Atlantic* was titled, "Dan Quayle Was Right," and presented results of research studying the consequences of the breakdown of the American family. The statistics revealed that many children suffer painful, long-term consequences when parents divorce.

Shortly after reading this article, I came across 1 Kings 16:34: "Hiel of Bethel built Jericho; he laid its foundation at the cost of Abiram his firstborn, and set up its gates at the cost of his youngest son Segub."

The flint of culture and the steel of the Word came together, and the sparks ignited a sermon. Child sacrifice suddenly seemed a not-so-ancient practice. We have modern ways of laying the foundation of success and happiness at the expense of our children. And how this contrasts with the New Testament image of Jesus drawing little children to himself to bless them!

The message of God's Word was clear to me, and I knew I had to remain faithful to it. But how could I craft this into a sermon that would be heard by a congregation filled with busy people, not to mention many who had at one time taken their children through the pain of divorce?

I needed to speak the truth in a way that forthrightly challenged parents who were neglecting children because of careers, or who were contemplating a marital split, naively assuming "the kids will adjust."

Yet how could I do this without alienating those already feeling guilty, those coming to church seeking help? I feared adding to the burdens of single parents by making them feel condemned by the church.

I began by asking Susie's advice. A single parent, she works with our ministry, "Single Parents and Co."

"Tell me," I asked, "how this might be heard by a single mom struggling against tough odds? How can I say this in a way that will actually be encouraging?"

Her candid comments provided a fresh angle of vision. I knew I couldn't transform the biblical truth; I knew the congregation needed a prophetic word of challenge about the importance of children. But I also knew I had to translate the Word in a way that would be heard, in a way that would allow the Word to penetrate defenses in order to do its business.

So as I wrote my sermon, I imagined not only parents sacrificing children, but also single parents struggling against the odds, sacrificing for the children. I ended the sermon by stressing that the primary family unit, from a biblical perspective, is the church, and that we want to surround both children and parents with the love of Christ.

The call of the Word

The Word of God meets people where they live, but it never leaves them there.

First it says, "Follow me," and then eventually it says, "If any want to become my followers, let them deny themselves and take up their cross and follow me. For those who want to save their life will lose it, and those who lose their life for my sake will find it" (Mark 8:34–35).

The Word travels the road toward Golgotha on its way to the empty tomb; it experiences the horrors of Good Friday before the joys of Easter. And those who follow the Word must take the same journey. We gain ourselves by losing ourselves; we enter life through the death of self.

Though our witness to the incarnational Word may begin with felt needs, showing compassion for hurts and speaking to longings, it must never end there. The Word aims for salvation, deliverance from sin, and thus works for the destruction of self-centeredness. A person may attend a church, finding help and inspiration for problems, but remain every bit as self-centered as ever, albeit religiously self-centered. Faithful communication of the gospel, for this reason, cannot neglect the call of the cross.

This will often create discomfort. A few years ago, in a sermon on Romans 5:15–21, I spoke of how Christ has fundamentally altered the human situation. While all had been marked by Adam's disobedience, now all have been re-marked by the grace of Christ's obedience. This means, I went on to say, that along with Paul, "we can regard no one from a human point of view." Christ has been crucified and raised even for those we don't much like. To be concrete (to enflesh the word in the particulars of our culture), I gave a representative list of some people for whom Christ died: illegal migrants, the homeless, homosexuals. Nothing profound, certainly nothing prophetic in my view.

But the next day, I was chatting with someone at the church. He said, "Don, about yesterday's sermon . . . I hated it." Coming from a man for whom I have deep affection, this hurt.

"I hated it," he repeated, in case I missed it the first time. "The part about homosexuals. I can't stand them." His voice was getting loud, very loud.

There was nothing but silence for a few seconds, and then he said in a soft voice, "But don't stop preaching the Word, because I need it."

A few weeks after that, following a worship service, I noticed him speaking with two members of the congregation, a father and his homosexual son who is fighting a battle with

AIDS. Then I saw three heads bowed in prayer as the man put his arms around his brothers in Christ. The Word was doing its business, and the man was being changed.

Meeting felt needs is not enough because people do not always feel their deepest needs. Faithful ministry will both comfort the afflicted and afflict the comfortable. A painful dislocation must take place before one can be relocated in the center of God's gracious but demanding will.

My colleagues have been sensitive to human hurts and creative in ministering to them. They generated programs faster than rabbits make bunnies. We helped the sick, divorced, grieving, hungry, homeless, and addicted. We counseled confused adolescents, frustrated parents, and lonely seniors. We offered seminars in financial planning, disaster preparedness, and effective parenting. It's all good, and it's one reason we ran out of space.

But a few months ago, I asked them to ponder something: In being so focused on meeting the needs of people, are we inadvertently baptizing their self-centeredness in pseudo-spirituality? Have we created a congregation of religious consumers who come to us for help with problems, even as they visit doctors and psychologists and exercise therapists, but all the while maintain control of their lives on their quest toward personal fulfillment?

We discussed whether a therapeutic model of ministry might not encourage people to remain focused on themselves and therefore leave them with the worst of their problems. Jesus not only healed the sick, he called them to follow him in discipleship; he delivered them from one form of death to summon them to another.

If we really desire the deepest healing for others, we must eventually help move them beyond felt needs, beyond their self-preoccupation, beyond their comfort zone. We must prod them with the goad of the Word into a life of obedient love.

Where all this will lead, I don't know. We're still in process, still struggling. I know of no technique to help us. But I am confident we can minister with authority and effectiveness, for we have the Word—a Word with power, a Word that descends to every human need, and a Word that calls us to the only Life worth the dying.

19

Confession of an Evangelistically Impaired Pastor

Conversion experiences have never excited me—at least as I felt they should have.

—JIM ABRAHAMSON

I am a pastor with a terrible confession to make: I do not get excited about "soul-winning."

I can't help it. I feel guilty about it. I have tried to repent of it. I will go to therapy over it. But in the end I must honestly confess that altar calls and "Just as I Am" leave me cool if not cold.

Don't get me wrong: I have a passion for Christ, the gospel, and people. I believe that faith in Christ is essential to eternal life. But bringing people to pray to receive Christ is not what lights my ministry fire.

I can recall my student days at a leading Midwestern university where, as part of a campus parachurch group, I "led fellow students to pray to receive Jesus as their Savior." What could be more exciting, right?

Why did I not share the joy my staff worker did over one more lost sheep coming into the family of God? What was wrong with me? I loved God. I was serious about following Christ. I made sacrifices and took risks living out my faith. I even went to seminary and entered the pastoral ministry.

But to this day I am not an impassioned soul-winner. To be sure, people have come to faith as a result of my ministry, but conversion experiences have never excited me—at least as I felt they should have.

It has taken nearly twenty years for me to come to terms with my condition. Here are my reflections for those who may share my lot and for others who may not be sympathetic but need to understand that I am not a lost sheep.

Killing the sacred cow

The early days of my spiritual life were lived under the motto, "You are either an evangelist or you need one." I had to conform to this motto.

My discomfort with this sacred cow, I'm sure, has something to do with my spiritual history: My conversion was not dramatic. My awakening to growth and maturation was far more exciting. Even today, I love to see others grow. I get excited about seeing the church in my community become the church envisioned by the apostle Paul—a mature bride. I am motivated by seeing people come to maturity in Christ.

Intellectually, I know that not every believer will have the gift for soul-winning, that one person plants, another waters, and God brings the increase. So I try not to be intimidated by my mild evangelistic passion. The New Testament affirms that new birth is an important step but only the beginning of a bigger process. Jesus commissioned his followers to make disciples but did not restrict their work to baptizing; it also included "teaching them all things."

The evangelist and I are not serving in different armies; we are simply occupying different battle stations.

Although evangelism is not my passion, cross-cultural missions and evangelistic outreach have become an important part of our church life. Why? We have cultivated factors that draw nonbelievers to Christ in a congregation that is not focused on evangelism.

Open inquiry into truth. Nonbelievers are drawn to Christ when the church provides an atmosphere where it is safe for people to have questions answered and answers questioned. For nonbelievers to stick around long enough to see Jesus in us and hear the good news, they must feel welcome. Our worship services are prepared for believers, but we try not to offend unnecessarily the non-Christians who are present. For example, we approach sensitive subjects such as social justice, homosexuality, gender roles, and sexual ethics with respect for how non-Christians feel and why they feel the way they do.

We then introduce the light of God's kingdom in the context of a whole new way of thinking. As a result of this 'safe setting,' we attract and keep a number of those who wouldn't ordinarily come or stay.

Our board of elders is made up of a number of people who started attending our services as cynical skeptics. The openness and safety they felt in our meetings was an important factor in their changed lives.

"I don't feel preached at here," said one skeptical husband. "I have been preached at enough in my early contact with the church, and now I want to learn what the faith is about." This guy, who refused Communion just two years ago, has professed faith in Christ.

Open recognition of struggle. Nonbelievers are drawn to Christ when believers speak humbly and honestly about their spiritual process. Whenever I hear someone suggest that loneliness, depression, abuse, and anger will be cured by simply praying to receive Christ, I want to stand up and shout, "Baloney! It's not that simple for many of us."

It is important that the leadership of the congregation be painfully honest if they hope to gain a hearing with people in modern culture. We must acknowledge we have many unanswered questions in our search for truth and light in Christ. We tell people we want a chance to answer their questions and give them a chance to question our answers without feeling ignorant or rejected.

As I was writing this, a member of our congregation walked into my office seeking help for her elderly mother who had a stroke while in a church meeting. It seems this mother expected believers to be immune from injustices such as strokes. Her expectations are all too common and seldom challenged.

I'm careful never to give the false message that Christians don't have problems; I explain that along with the trials of life they have forgiveness, a powerful Comforter, a living hope, and a family that loves them.

Open confession of faith. Nonbelievers are drawn to Christ when they are forced to reflect on the state of their relationship with God. In our meetings, we draw clear lines between those who are in Christ and those who are not. This indirectly challenges seekers and believers alike to examine themselves to see if indeed they are of the faith.

When we take up the offering, we make it clear that this is for worshipers of Christ. "If you are present and not committed to Christ, we are not asking you to give but rather to consider the gift of life offered in Jesus."

When we celebrate the Lord's Table, we make it clear that this is reserved for believers only. "We don't want to embarrass you, but we ask that you receive Christ by faith before you receive the bread and cup that he offers his followers."

Water baptism is another place where the distinction between believer and nonbeliever can be emphasized.

New members go through an orientation class and then meet with two elders for an interview. One purpose of the interview is to hear about the prospective member's relationship with Christ. In some cases it provides an opportunity to present the gospel and even lead the person to a faith commitment.

Frequently in the message of the morning I will talk about the unique blessings of forgiveness, the Holy Spirit, and the Christian family that belong to believers. I explain, "These words are for those who have a living faith in Christ. If you are outside the faith, this is a chance for you to get an idea of what life is like on the inside. We expect that you will be drawn to Christ as we have been."

Open joy in worship.   Several people have told us that they first came to our church because a friend brought them but that they came back again because they were impressed with the sincerity of our people in worship. Worship plays an important role in communicating both the objective and subjective aspects of the faith. When done in spirit and in truth, it is an evangelistic tool. People united in praising God from different ethnic, economic, educational, and class backgrounds is a powerful apologetic for the faith. When natural barriers are broken down by the Spirit of God, people in the world want to know why.

Open expression of compassion.   Nonbelievers are drawn to Christ when God's grace is sensed.

A professor at the University of North Carolina started coming to our worship services because two students from our church visited his aging mother every Sunday afternoon. This elderly woman was losing her sight, so they read her mail to her and wrote the letters she dictated in response. For a period of more than two years, they read the Bible to her and befriended her. Her greatest disappointment in being transferred to a nursing home in a different city was that she would never be able to attend the church where her two young friends were members. She never was able to attend, but her son was so impressed with the compassion of these two young girls that he visited the church, was renewed to the faith that he had thrown away, and became an outspoken witness for Christ in the university community.

One of the greatest compliments I have received in my twenty-three years of ministry was by a young convert who spoke of his pastor as a person who "was at peace with himself and God's people." That is a victory of God's grace.

Evangelism can be alive and well even when the passion for soul-winning is not. The best evangelistic tool is a healthy church.

Section 2:
Growing Your Church Through Outreach

Every generation is strategic. We are not responsible for the past generation, and we cannot bear full responsibility for the next one; but we do have our generation. God will hold us responsible as to how well we fulfill our responsibilities to this age and take advantage of our opportunities.

—Billy Graham

PART 5

Enlist

20

Ordaining Every Member

The pastor as coach is not satisfied with good ritual and good buildings; he is satisfied only when people are being recruited into the ministry of daily life.

—D. ELTON TRUEBLOOD

I meet hundreds of strangers while traveling, and I nearly always ask, "Are you in any church?"

The usual answer is "Sometimes I go to such and such a church." It sounds like going to the theater or the ballpark. Once in a while someone will say, "Yes, I'm deeply involved in . . ." but it's rare. I'm afraid the majority still think the church is something you go to.

When we look at the state of Christians and the church, at our values, beliefs, and lifestyles, there is certainly room for holy dissatisfaction. We are too easily satisfied with conventional success. We fall into an Old Testament mind-set in which we look mostly at how many people come to the temple for the ritual. Meanwhile we forget Jesus' words in Matthew 12:6, "I tell you, something greater than the temple is here."

Cheap Christianity can usually pull a pretty good attendance on Sunday morning. It is cheap whenever the people think of themselves as spectators at a performance. I'm always shocked when I hear Christians talk about being "in the audience." Audiences are fine at the opera or the symphony concert, but worship is another matter.

In Christ's clearest call to commitment, he didn't say,

"Come join the audience." He said, "Take my yoke upon you, and learn of me." The yoke refers to the operation of a team. Early Christians called each other yokefellow (Phil. 4:3) in order to signify a practicing Christian engaged in a team effort.

So when leaders ask how the general operation is going, they must not be too easily satisfied with numbers. You can always get a crowd if you demand little and put on a show. Rather, we need to be asking ourselves, "Are we increasing Christ's kingdom? Are we doing what he intended when he invented the church?" I use the word *invented* deliberately because there was no church before Christ. An amazing invention it was, something far more revolutionary than we normally suppose.

The church can only accomplish its revolutionary purpose, however, when it has certain characteristics.

Rank-and-file ministers

I heard a true story about a preacher who came to Laymen's Sunday and preached on the lay ministry. (That was his first mistake; he should have had one of the members do it.) He was persuasive, however, because at the end when he said, "Will any men who are willing to dedicate themselves to the lay ministry please come forward?" a hundred men responded. Someone who was close to the pastor heard him mutter softly, "O God, how can I use a hundred ushers?"

He entirely missed the point of his own sermon.

I call pastors to engage not in Operation Addition but in Operation Multiplication. This is the point of Ephesians 4. For the pastor to think he is the only minister is to minimize the task. Whenever we make *minister* synonymous with *clergy*, we are pre-Christian. A clergyperson is a professional—one who takes on a responsibility and gets a certain prestige for doing so. One pastor actually said to me, "I know lay Christians need to be developed, but I'm not going to

have a book table because I don't want them to know where I
get my stuff!" He thinks of himself as part of an upper class,
which is precisely what the priests did.

All cultures before Christ had priests. They enjoyed great
prestige. They were always closely allied with the monarchy,
whether in Mesopotamia or Egypt or Israel. Julius Caesar was
made *pontifex maximus* in Rome, even though everyone knew
he was an immoral man. It didn't matter; he had the title.

Christ turned all this around, and we tend to forget how
drastically he did so. "You know that the rulers of the Gen-
tiles lord it over them," he said in Matthew 20:25, "and their
great men exercise authority among them. It shall not be so
among you." Then he made his revolutionary statement about
coming not to be served but to serve. He turned the world
upside down that day.

Unfortunately, we tend to forget, slipping back into the
pre-Christian model of priests and temples. Jesus sent out
teams of workers not to perform a ceremony but to liberate
and to heal. Instead of employing the priests, who were numerous, he entrusted the future to ordinary persons. Have
you ever thought what a good joke it was when he gave
Simon the nickname "Rocky"? That's like our calling a tall
man "Shorty" or a fat man "Slim." Certainly others laughed
when Jesus said it, because Simon was anything but solid. He
was more like rubble than rock.

When I talk with rank-and-file church people, I don't call
them laypeople. A layperson is a second-class citizen. I am a
layman in regard to law because I have not passed the bar;
thus, I am not allowed to practice law. There is no place in
the church of Jesus Christ for those who cannot practice. I
said to people, "You are not a layperson. You are a minister of
common life."

I would be willing to ordain people to the ministry of jour-
nalism, banking, or photography. Why not? What an opportunity they have. They meet people I never will. Think of the
chances a loan officer has to minister: he can keep young
people from ruining their lives by overborrowing.

I was pleased when I saw one signboard outside a church in South Carolina. It read:

> MINISTERS: ALL THE MEMBERS
> EQUIPPER: THE REV. JOHN SMITH
> The true ministers were the folk in the pews.

Penetrating people

A healthy fellowship is a redemptive fellowship. It is penetrating the world not for its own aggrandizement but to change the world. Almost all of Christ's metaphors for the church are *penetrators:* salt to penetrate the food and keep it from decay, light to penetrate the darkness, leaven to penetrate the lump. The emphasis is never on the instrument but on the function. So a successful church is one that is changing the world, chiefly through the action of its members.

The true church is not the structure on Jackson Avenue; it is where one person is teaching philosophy and another is cobbling shoes and another is teaching kindergarten. If you had gone to ancient Corinth and asked where the Christian church was, nobody would have sent you to the corner of Eighth and Main. They would have sent you to where Paul and his friends were making mobile homes—tents, that is. He himself explained this on Mars Hill: "The God who made the world . . . does not live in shrines made by man" (Acts 17:24).

This is why the Quakers call it "meetinghouse" instead of church. We've lost on that one as far as the general speech is concerned, but the term does preserve the distinction between the redemptive fellowship on one hand and the building on the other.

The most exciting thing I know here in Richmond is a soup-and-salad luncheon every Thursday for men, all of whom are ministers in common life. Physicians, lawyers, factory workers, businessmen of all kinds, and even a few pastors meet at the library of the First Friends Meetinghouse exactly at noon. We begin with prayer, led by someone in the group, not an imported professional. We eat our simple lunch, prepared by people of the church, and leave our $2 on the table. At 12:20 we introduce new people, and then one of the group speaks for sixteen minutes, sharing something that has strengthened his life in the ministry. Last come questions and answers and a closing prayer. We average more than the Rotary Club in town—sixty-five men on a normal Thursday.

All of these men are not from the Friends church. That would destroy the idea. The mayor, who is Roman Catholic, is nearly always there. The only thing we have in common is we are all ministers in daily life. We have no officers, no structure, no budget, no minutes, no reporting—that's what wears people out. We simply want to help each other penetrate the world.

I suppose I'm acting as sort of a pastor to the local group, in that I take more responsibility. But I am simply a coach. The pastor as coach is miles away from the idea of pastor as priest. The pastor as coach is not satisfied with good ritual and good buildings; he is satisfied only when people are being recruited into the ministry of daily life.

Certainly this recruitment can happen in public meetings. Lives are changed there, but not as often as we might think. I led a retreat in northern Ohio for twenty-two people, and I went around the circle asking each one to tell what had brought him or her into a full Christian commitment. I assumed some would mention a public meeting or a sermon. Not one did. They told about little people—the shoe repairman whose life was such a testimony that it made a deep impression—inconspicuous people.

Nobody said Billy Graham or Elton Trueblood. I didn't expect them to say Elton Trueblood, but I thought someone would mention Billy Graham. Lives have certainly been changed by his public preaching, but my experience is the great majority are changed in a much less obvious fashion. If the church could make members realize this, that *they* are the team, what a difference it would make. How it would raise their sights!

Someone might question whether my friends on Thursday are actually penetrating the world or just showing up for lunch. Well, here's one measure of penetration: How many of them are visiting in the jail? We got a fellow out of jail who apparently had been arrested unjustly. I went to the prosecuting attorney in Richmond and persuaded him to drop charges. The point is, I could go to bat for the man because of my life in the city. I was heard, while he never would have been.

At lunch the next Thursday I told what had happened and gave the man's name and address. One of the group said, "I'll go and see him." He found the man, his wife, and child in a poor little shack with almost no food. So my friend got the members of his church to stock their pantry.

This is no big thing, but it's concrete. At other times, those in our group who sell cars have arranged decent transportation for people who otherwise couldn't afford it.

This kind of penetration is not easily put into an annual report. Attendance and money are easy to write up for the annual business meeting, but you can never have a full report of the ministry of penetration. What people need to realize is that this is expected, this is what the church requires.

Church is more than an hour a week. That is what I was trying to say when I wrote *Your Other Vocation*—that the Christian always has a two-pronged life. He or she must be a competent journalist or lawyer or industrialist, and must also be a minister of Christ in the world.

Trained minds

I once wrote, "An untrained ministry is potentially harmful." There's more to being a healthy church than just mobilization.

Faith has three essential aspects: the inner life of devotion, the outer life of service, and the intellectual life of rationality. The third area needs lifting, too; all three legs of the stool are essential. We must teach people to *pray,* to *serve,* and to *think.*

Jesus said not only, "Take my yoke upon you" but also "Learn of me." The church must become a seminary if it is going to have a universal ministry. The pastor is the ideal person to be the dean of the seminary, drawing out the ministry of others, equipping, enabling. Those potent words of Christ, "Learn of me," will change our whole focus on ministry.

I spend a lot of time with laypeople, often when their pastors are not in the room. I hear them saying they are dissatisfied because they are not getting the kind of education that would develop them. They assume these great courses are going on in the theological seminaries, and they think their minds are equally as good as the students there, so they want to know why they're being cheated. They are tired of the tough questions being avoided.

Often a pastor will feel as though he is the dean of a seminary, but he has no faculty. Still, he must not fail to make a start. He has to develop his faculty by training some of the members to train others.

In the curriculum of this seminary, the first task is to deepen the spiritual lives of the people. So many live superficially. They can be awakened and enriched through the classics of Christian devotion, a rich body of material that is mostly unknown. If I were a pastor, I'd spend most of my time teaching, and I would start right off with a class on these books: *Confessions* by Saint Augustine; *The Little Flowers of Saint Francis; The Imitation of Christ* by Thomas à Kempis; *Pensées* by Blaise Pascal; *The Journal of John Woolman; A Serious Call to a Devout and Holy Life* by William Law; *Doctor Johnson's Prayers; The Christian's Secret of a Happy Life* by Hannah Whitall Smith; and *Testament of Devotion* by Thomas Kelly.

All of these are in paperback in modern-English editions.

Any ordinary person can grow tremendously through this type of material.

Most people don't know how to pray, for example. What better way to teach them than through Samuel Johnson's prayers? At the end of his life, in desperate sickness, he asked his physician how many more days he would live. The doctor estimated two, barring a miracle. "Very well," he replied. "Stop all medication, though the pain be terrible, for I would meet my Maker with a clear mind." He then wrote this prayer, the last thing he penned:

> Almighty and most merciful Father, I am now, as to human eyes it seems, about to commemorate, for the last time, the death of thy Son Jesus Christ our Savior and our Redeemer. Grant, O Lord, that my whole hope and confidence may be in his merits, and his mercy; enforce and accept my imperfect repentance; make this commemoration available to the confirmation of my faith, the establishment of my hope, and the enlargement of my charity; and make the death of thy Son Jesus Christ effectual to my redemption. Have mercy upon me, and pardon the multitude of my offenses. Bless my friends; have mercy upon all men. Support me, by the grace of thy Holy Spirit, in the days of weakness, and at the hour of death; and receive me, at my death, to everlasting happiness, for the sake of Jesus Christ. Amen.

That teaches not only the devotional life; it teaches theology. No wonder Malcolm Muggeridge called him the greatest Englishman who ever lived. Johnson even wrote a prayer when he commenced work on the dictionary. Reading prayers such as this gives people ideas for their own lives. They learn that prayer befits all occasions of life, not just the church. If we don't raise the sights of people with this kind of training, they will pray in strings of clichés. We must soak them with great models.

There are other parts of the curriculum for a healthy church, of course: the Old and New Testaments, theology, the history of Christian thought, Socratic logic, Christian ethics. I have dwelt upon the devotional classics only because they are so often ignored.

We teach people to think chiefly by dialogue. That's what Plato said. One person's thinking stirs another person's thinking. My great teacher at Johns Hopkins, professor Arthur Lovejoy, said, "All the history of philosophy is one continuous dialogue."

Tonight I have a group of young pastors and their wives coming here to talk. We're going to deal with hard intellectual problems so they could return to their churches and do the same. We're going to talk about how to be fair to other religions without compromising Christ's claim to be the only Way. This is the hardest intellectual problem many of them face. So I must help them.

Why? Because the Christian must outthink the world. We must not leave good thinking to the pagans. We've got to get in there and fight if the common opinion is ever to be changed and the Christian cause to prevail. Christians must be better thinkers if they are going to penetrate the world.

It is more important than ever for the church to be healthy. It is often poor and dull, but it's the best thing available. However sick the church is, this land would be much sicker without it.

If Christians could see the church as a society of ministers in the world, they would approach the radical change Christ sought to initiate. If that were generally accepted, the change would not be small. It would be enormous.

21

Incorporating People on the Move

*In a transient setting especially, a pastor's own commitment
plays a vital role in a church's long-term ministry.*

—STEPHEN W. SORENSON

A few years ago, the national media touted Colorado Springs
as a place of growth and opportunity. Plentiful high-tech jobs
and mountain beauty attracted thousands of people. Military
assignments brought thousands to Peterson Field, Fort Car-
son, and the Air Force Academy. Housing starts reached all-
time highs.

Then the recession hit. One-third of the city's population
has moved out of state during the past five years, making it
one of the nation's most transient cities. Area pastors were
caught in the middle of turbulent change.

Ministering to a transient culture, however, is not just a
Colorado Springs phenomenon. It is becoming the norm, it
seems, for our mobile culture. In many suburban areas, for
example, one-fifth of the population may turn over yearly.
Pastors throughout the country know the difficulty of trying
to build a church on shifting sands, trying to minister to
nomads without going mad.

After interviewing pastors from the Colorado Springs area,
I found that churches are adapting to the transience. The
pastors have learned a great deal and in the long run are
actually benefiting from the process. Here are some of the
lessons they've learned.

Challenges intensified

Transience is not a new phenomenon, of course. America has been a mobile culture from its beginnings, so most pastors have learned to live with it, even appreciate it. But when transience intensifies, so do many of the typical church problems.

Loss of leadership.   Tony and Susan were very involved in First Presbyterian Church. They had two sons, each active in Sunday school and youth ministry. Tony was a church leader. But when the economy fell apart, his real estate and development business evaporated.

"He tried for months to find another avenue of income," says John Stevens, senior minister, "and then he was offered a fine position in the Chicago area. So they left. I could name a hundred couples like this."

Jim Pearring, pastor of Living Word Church, lost fifty people to out-of-state moves late last spring—elders, Sunday school teachers, worship leaders—out of a congregation of 275.

"Last May we were making plans for two services in the fall. The exodus changed our whole course," he said. "One of our elders moved last summer, and it wasn't until after he moved that I realized what a tremendous asset he had been. Within two months, we had to radically change the concept of what our elders were doing and raise up another elder board."

Harvey Martz, senior minister of the 950-member Calvary United Methodist Church, also knows the pain transiency can bring. "About twenty-five active families left between April and August of 1990," he says. "We lost talented leaders. I miss them."

Lack of loyalty.   "The whole fabric of the church is affected," says Roc Bottomly, pastor of Pulpit Rock Church. "Transient people often have a consumer attitude toward church. They attend one church as long as it meets their needs better than another. You don't know who you can count on. People are fickle and tend to be critical. Rather than saying, 'We're part of this and we're going to make it go,' they act as if the church is on probation.

"When a church is constantly gaining and losing people," Bottomly laments, "you feel you have to be more careful about the way you do things. The church's ability to weather struggles—a change of pastor, a building program, any type of turbulence—is greatly lessened. A pastor's margin of error is thinner."

Bottomly speaks from experience. When the previous pastor of Pulpit Rock Church left, the congregation dropped from 1,300 to 600 people.

Stevens adds, "In a transient community people think, *I won't be here all that long,* so they hesitate to get involved, to put roots down too deeply."

Discouragement. High turnover can discourage those who remain.

"When people move out of state, those who remain think something is wrong with the church," explains Pearring. "They look around, don't see as many people, and think the church is falling apart. And when it's their friends who move, it weakens their roots in the church. That can snowball: we've had people leave as a direct result of others' moving.

"One young lady said to me, 'We want to be involved in a church where people stay twenty-five years.' Obviously that's nearly impossible to find nowadays, but she kept searching anyway."

Budget uncertainties. Pastors in transient communities quickly discover that it's difficult, if not impossible, to develop accurate budgets.

"Last year, because of the increased transience, we set a three-month budget," says Pearring. "We have no idea what will happen after three months. We've had so many changes that trying to plan a year's budget is suicide."

Bottomly has a different problem. Now that the church has a full-time pastor, people who left during the transition are returning, but their financial loyalty is unclear.

"We've grown 50 percent in six months—four hundred new people," he says. "But giving is up only 10 percent. In our transient church, it takes people a while to trust us enough to give. There are more people, with less institutional commitment. As a result, our income is below average for a church this size, so we have to run our operation with fewer staff."

First Presbyterian Church has also had to cut staff.

"The finances of our church today are much more difficult than they were five or ten years ago," says Stevens. "For the last five years, we've been cutting back on staff, streamlining procedures, increasing productivity, and using resources more efficiently. Last year we underspent our budget by nearly $40,000 simply by watching expenditures carefully. If we can find a cheaper way to do something and still get it done in an effective, acceptable way, we do it."

Attractive word

The flip side of ministry in a transient area is that churches must aggressively cultivate first-time visitors and potential members.

"I have to constantly stay on my toes. As a church, we must welcome newcomers," says Pearring. "If we don't, there won't be a church anymore. Two or three weeks ago, a man was upset with me and said, 'The church is focused on newcomers.' I agreed. It has to be."

So churches have extra incentive to do all the things necessary to attract newcomers.

"We spend lots of money on Yellow-Page ads to let people know we're here," says Martz. "Also, at Christmas and Easter we print 2,000 invitations to advertise our services. That's a time when people are open, when they have a spiritual awareness and longing. The best method, of course, remains personal invitation."

A home visit to newcomers also becomes more important than ever.

"Everyone who visits our church is personally contacted the very next week," says Stevens. "We work hard at that."

Martz adds, "A layperson is at the visitor's doorstep on Monday evening with information about our church and a loaf of homemade bread. We thank them for coming, ask how they learned about us, answer questions, and invite them to return. Then we track their attendance. After they attend a few Sundays, we follow up with a phone call inviting them to a new-member orientation session. We've found that the earlier we contact visitors, the greater the chance they'll return."

Leadership moves

Transience forces pastors to put people new to the church in leadership positions.

"In my last church in Oklahoma," Bottomly confesses, "most of the elders, deacons, Bible study leaders, and Sunday school teachers were people who had been and would be around for years. Someone almost had to die before a new person could have a ministry opportunity.

"Here in Colorado Springs, we are constantly losing Sunday school teachers, elders, deacons, Bible study leaders. So we're forced to put new people into those positions. I've noticed, though, that these new people do a better job than we thought they would. In fact, this approach has improved the quality of our programs."

That's not as easy as it sounds, however. In many churches, it's hard for transient people to work into significant levels of responsibility. Ironically, even as pastors lament the ongoing loss of gifted people, some overlook people in the congregation who have previously taught Sunday school, been elders, even attended seminary or pastored churches.

"When these people move to a new church," says Bottomly, "it's not easy for them to communicate gracefully that they'd like to labor at a significant level of responsibility. So the leadership must find these people quickly and communicate,

'You don't have to earn your stars or spurs here. We respect what you've done in the past.' "

So pastors in a transient community look for ways to spot potential leaders and aggressively recruit them. The old way of letting people simply rise to the surface and prove themselves doesn't have time to work.

Sometimes simple approaches work well. "We give people a talent survey when they join the church, and then again once each year," says Martz. "They can sign up for anything they're interested in, and another member follows up their response. Using a computer readout of the surveys, our nominating committee contacts people when needs or positions arise. If you count typical roles like Sunday school teachers and choir members, more than 200 people in our church are involved."

Still, transience hurts. When a church loses veteran leaders, pastors spend lots of time training. The burden also grows heavier on church leaders, who must carry a bigger load until new leaders are recruited, trained, and in place.

In addition, constant turnover hurts one-on-one contact ministries, such as lay visitation.

"Our lay ministry deals with inactive people who start to drift away from the church," says Keith Hedstrom, pastor of Ascension Lutheran Church. "That ministry depends on volunteers who will make ongoing contact, to follow up those who've undergone a death in the family, a divorce, or whatever. When those lay visitors move, we lose that continuity."

In the end, though, these churches are seeing good come out of their situation.

"God provides," Stevens says confidently. "As I've watched this passing parade over twenty years, I've seen people leave and wondered how we'd ever find people to replace them. Even though we never get people exactly like them, God brings others who have great commitment and ability. If I'm patient enough and don't panic, God sends people who are right. Sometimes he doesn't send them as fast or as well prepared as I'd like, but he provides."

Pastoral anchor

In a transient setting especially, a pastor's own commitment plays a vital role in a church's long-term ministry.

"I've always seen myself as a pastor of a local congregation," Stevens says. "I travel seldom, take few outside speaking engagements, and have not written a book. I make hospital calls, attend meetings, preach, teach classes. I have never viewed this church, regardless of its size, as a way to propel me into greater ministry. My job is to serve this church during good times and bad times.

"These are hard times," he admits. "The church needs my leadership more now than it ever has in the past. I'm determined to give it the best leadership. If we're gaining members, that's wonderful. If we're not, that's the way it is.

"Pastors move too often," Stevens warns. "The average minister stays less than ten years, and the smaller the church, the more often pastoral leadership changes. Many pastors do not develop a real sense of commitment to their church and the community. They sit loose in the saddle because they don't expect to stay too long."

When pastors come and go frequently, congregations respond more slowly to a new leader's vision.

"They tire of bouncing back and forth between pastors and visions of what the church should be," says Stevens. "It's difficult for a church like that to develop a consistent approach to ministry, a long-range plan. Our church, in fifty years, has had two pastors. That's one reason it has 5,000 members and why it is what it is today."

Success redefined

Confronted by the challenges of ministry in a transient city, pastors I spoke with have had to reexamine their views of success.

"A pastor's self-image can be tied too closely to the size of the church," says Pearring. "Mine is, and God has ripped that.

But I'm still having a tough time with that. Go to any pastors' conference, and who are the guys speaking? They never ask a pastor of a 100-member church to speak. That custom just reinforces that mentality. So if your church goes from 200 to 250 you feel great, but when it goes from 200 to 150, you feel like trash.

"If I realize, however, that success from a biblical point of view is obedience, faithfulness, servanthood, love, purity, and teamwork, I again ask, 'What are we trying to accomplish?' It's to make disciples, and we're doing that.

"Not all of them stay in Colorado Springs, but we're having an impact. I have to get back to the basics: What has God called me to do? Am I doing it as best I can? Am I giving my all to it?"

Pearring is not alone in the struggle.

"I have had to look at my needs," says Hedstrom. "If I need to be successful and develop ideal programs that appeal to everybody and fill the church, I will be frustrated because it won't happen here. It's hard to 'do church' in a traditional sense in Colorado Springs. On the other hand, if what I am about is helping people grow and become more Christlike than they were yesterday, then I can find fulfillment."

He recalls a young man who, as head of the youth program, was too shy to ask the congregation about holding an activity. "After eight years of involvement, he became a lay preacher! That is the goal of our church—to train and equip people, not to maintain a program."

Vision plays a key role. "A church has to have a vision of what God wants it to be about," says Stevens, "and it has to hold to that vision. It cannot be dependent on where a community is in its cycle. As pastors, we must ask, 'Where do we need to be in order to position ourselves to do what God is calling us to do?' understanding that ministry is long-term, not short-term."

Uttermost parts

After investing so much in training and equipping people for ministry, do pastors in Colorado Springs feel discouraged to see so many people move out of state? Sometimes, frankly, yes.

"There has always been an enormous turnover here," says Stevens. "In the past, though, while we were losing some people, we were gaining others. Now, new people aren't coming into town the way they used to. It's more difficult to watch people leave because I don't necessarily see others replacing them. And now when I see those talents, gifts, commitments, and ministries departing, I feel a sense of loss. I may even panic if I'm not careful. The last couple of years have been very difficult for me."

Still, in spite of battles with discouragement with the local situation, pastors have learned to see the big picture.

"It's easy to become discouraged and say, 'Let me go someplace else,'" Pearring admits. "Now I view departures from a broader perspective. Our church is able to have an impact on people across the country and world. Three of our members are in Saudi Arabia right now, leading small groups.

"Whatever we give people that is good, right, and helpful— introduce them to a new ministry tool, give them a solid, biblical philosophy of ministry—they will take away from here and multiply it elsewhere. So it's not a total loss. In one sense we're privileged. We've become a sending church."

In that way, churches in transient settings know firsthand what it's like to be a mission church, one that gives its life for others. It often hurts and often complicates church life, but the potential impact knows few bounds.

22

Keeping Lay Workers Fresh

Perhaps there would be less burnout if more churches could adopt some of the training and support techniques that volunteer organizations use.

—VIRGINIA VAGT

"I don't want to go to church tomorrow," I moaned to myself Saturday after Saturday during my final months at Resurrection Church.

It wasn't the pastor, his sermons, or a lack of warmth in the congregation that caused me to dread driving up the church's gravel driveway every Sunday. I was twenty-six years old and trying to find my place in church life. My problem was that I was in over my head in a program called Women's Outreach.

The founder of this program, Margaret Schiller, did lay mission work in Honduras every summer with her dentist husband. Her lifelong commitment to outreach was exciting. When she asked me to be one of her workers, to make weekly visits to a poverty-stricken young widow, I eagerly said yes. The extrovert in me and my need to find a meaningful ministry seemed to have found a good match.

Margaret put me in touch with Karen, who lived with her three-year-old son in a nearby low-income apartment building. What exactly was I supposed to do in my visits with Karen? Other than befriend her, I didn't know, but I felt reassured; Margaret told me the Lord would lead me.

At first, the dreary apartment building with its dark halls didn't deter me. Karen would open the thin, scuffed door each Saturday and offer me her warm smile. For several weeks we just sat and talked the way new friends do. Karen seemed grateful to see me, and I felt I was doing God's work.

As I drove back and forth, however, I questioned myself: What is my purpose? Is Karen's life supposed to turn around and improve because I visit her? Is Karen supposed to become a Christian through my friendship? Should I convince her to come to church? With no answers, I just waited to see what would happen.

As the weeks went by, Karen came up with all sorts of things she wanted me to do. One was baby-sitting for Tommy, her son, while she and her cousin went off for an hour—or most of the day! It was unsettling not knowing how long I'd be alone with Tommy in that apartment. On other occasions, Karen asked me to drive her places so she could shop and visit. I never knew how long we'd be gone or where exactly we'd be going.

On some Saturdays, five or six of Karen's friends and cousins would come over. Men would sit together on the plastic-upholstered couch while the women talked and laughed and looked at me as I played with Tommy. On those days I felt conspicuous, outnumbered, and filled with self-doubt.

In frustration I wanted to say, "I didn't come here to baby-sit for you, drive you places, or be a specimen for your friends to look at." Before the words could come out, however, I answered them myself: *Then why did you come here?* Since I didn't know, how was Karen supposed to know?

On Sundays, in the church basement next to the coffee pot and Styrofoam cups, Margaret would ask me how my visits with Karen were going. I wanted to have a good report, to be able to say I was being helpful to Karen or "We're making progress."

I felt too guilty to say to Margaret, "I don't know what I'm doing. I'm afraid of being in Karen's apartment building. And I wish I never had to go back." Instead I said, "Well, I don't really know what to say or do specifically, and I feel a little lost."

Margaret responded with suggestions. One was for me to teach Karen how to shop for values and not waste money on junk food. Theoretically, that was a good suggestion. Karen did need to learn things like that. But I never felt comfortable suggesting to Karen that I knew how to shop and she didn't.

Margaret also suggested that I do a Bible study with Karen. A Bible study sounded good; that was the kind of thing I had imagined we'd do together. And yet, which one? How would I start? If I found a good one, would Karen think I was turning the tables on her, setting my own agenda? The Bible study never happened.

At the two-month point, I felt panicky about visiting Karen. Without any goals or guidelines, the program was always in her hands. I felt caught between the possibility of Karen's rejecting me and Margaret's feeling I could do more. I was also unhappy that my Saturdays were being eaten up by a rocky friendship in which I had no real sense that the Lord was leading me.

Looking back on it, there are many things I should have done differently. But it was early in my adulthood and early in my experience in church work. Back then, I thought that if someone was in need, God wanted me to "give till it hurt." While I still believe there's some truth to that, my problem wasn't giving too much or too little but not knowing what I was doing and not having any hope that the situation would improve.

So, one Saturday, after sixteen weeks of visits, I said good-bye to Karen, and powered by the twin engines of guilt and fear, I never went back to Resurrection Church—and never said good-bye to Margaret, the pastor, or anyone else in the congregation. My guilt came from feeling I had failed. The fear was that Margaret would talk me into giving it another try.

The one thing I knew was that I wasn't going to visit Karen anymore.

Immature of me? Yes. Cowardly? Yes. And I doubt the pastor at Resurrection Church ever knew or even guessed why I left.

Learning how to do church work

After my flight from Resurrection and several years of church hopping, my new husband, Peter, and I landed at a little stone church called Saint Mark's. We attended for ten straight weeks and received a warm pastoral visit followed by a phone call. Would we like to team teach the high school Sunday school class?

Peter was a high school teacher, so that was a good fit, but I had never taught any kind of class. In spite of my lack of experience, however, panic didn't result. Teaching together sounded like a good idea.

The "good idea" stretched into a four-year success experience. In addition to teaching, we took the kids on retreats and spent time with them after church. Peter and I grew spiritually. By having to prepare material for them, we learned more Bible ourselves than we ever would have on our own. The high school kids even christened us "the sunshine family." It felt good to get that kind of affirmation from kids. We kept asking ourselves, "Why is this week-after-week, time-consuming commitment working so well?"

As I look back, these are some of the factors that made our teaching at Saint Mark's work well, and that by their absence had made my involvement in Women's Outreach a failure.

Someone as mentor. At Saint Mark's, I wasn't thrown into cold water without a life preserver. Peter already knew how to teach. He knew what he was doing and was there to help me week after week. I could observe him in action before I had to do the same thing myself.

Going slowly. That first Sunday morning when large and small teenagers began to walk into our classroom, I felt scared. But in those early days, Peter let me solo for just five minutes at a time. As the weeks went by, I took ten-minute segments, then fifteen, and so on until I was able to take half the class time.

Regular debriefing.   Each week we'd go home and talk over how our teaching went. Skits didn't work, but drawing posters on the spot to generate discussion did. With our weekly postmortems, failures became something to learn from and laugh about together. Successes made us glow.

The buddy system.   For Peter, an experienced teacher, working with a novice had additional rewards. He wasn't just given another group of kids to teach. Instead, he also gained the satisfaction of sharing what he knew about teaching. He saw someone else—me—start to succeed as a teacher as a result of his modeling.

A supervisor to help.   When we both ran into problems, the Sunday school superintendent was available for consultation. Teaching Christian sexual ethics to teenagers on Sunday morning, for example, wasn't something we felt confident about. Our superintendent spent several evenings on the phone helping us plan our approach. She kept in touch when she knew we were struggling or trying something different.

Avoiding a rut and passing the baton.   Forgive the mixed metaphor, but after four years, it seemed time for a break. We could tell we had lost our freshness with high schoolers. Both of us were being asked to take on other church responsibilities, too. So we asked if we could train other adults to take our place.

The idea was accepted.   Before packing up our Magic Markers and discussion-starter games, we met with other adults who wanted to begin working with high schoolers. At the close of our teaching years, we both had the satisfaction of training others the way Peter had trained me.

Preventing burnout

Eight years after leaving Women's Outreach, I began ministry visits to another woman. But this time, our visits worked.

As with the above Sunday school teaching, the secret was in training and ongoing support. Without that, I might have thrown up my hands with Sarah, a tired eighty-two-year-old caught in the crucible of old age.

The primary source of help to me in this instance was our local senior citizen center's "friendly visitor" program. The program gave me guidelines and people to call when I wasn't sure what to do, such as how to be helpful to Sarah during the week she moved from her duplex to a nursing home.

As a result of monthly volunteer meetings and the program guidelines, I've been able to maintain my commitment, listen to and smile with a lonely person, and be a fresh face in the world of the elderly. This time, we do talk about God and Christ, and we pray for each other's needs. It just took time.

Perhaps there would be less burnout if more churches could adopt some of the training and support techniques that volunteer organizations often use and that Peter and I unconsciously discovered at Saint Mark's. Here are some of the important principles I saw in action at the friendly visitor program:

Screening.   Before becoming a friendly visitor, I was interviewed. The director wanted to know why I wanted to minister in this way. Apparently most volunteers do want to help people, but they also need to feel the work is satisfying to them. If they don't, they'll quit.

My motives were wanting to improve my listening and empathic skills. Also, being without extended family in this state, I wanted a relationship with an older person. I saw it, too, as part of my Christian responsibility to visit those in need. The director thought my reasons were a good match to the purpose of the program, and I was accepted.

After that interview, I thought, *No one at church has ever asked me why I want to teach or be on the Stewardship Commission.* Perhaps if screening questions were asked at church, more people would end up in the right jobs and would last longer in those positions. At the very least, it would help clarify what we want and what we'll need to do the task.

Purpose.   It sounds so simple, but how often in church do we nail down our purpose? The friendly visitor director told us our purpose was not to do grocery shopping or to clean the kitchen for our seniors. Our purpose, rather, was to listen and be a bright spot in their week. There were other community services such as Meals on Wheels and Dial-a-Ride to provide daily necessities. If we spent our time cleaning kitchens, how could we be good listeners and empathizers?

In the high school ministry at church, we realized our purpose was not to become "overgrown high schoolers" ourselves, but to be adult role models for them, to help guide them in their spiritual and social growth.

Signing on the dotted line.   All friendly visitors have to sign an ethical statement and promise to meet their commitment by not being a no-show and by arriving on time for their visits. Putting it on paper and signing your name brings home the importance of what may seem like a little volunteer job. It also forces those coordinating a program to distill the purpose and requirements into a paragraph.

Since then, I've discovered that many churches also ask ushers, Sunday school teachers, and coffee hour coordinators to sign an agreement to serve, usually for one-year renewable terms. It helps solidify the commitment.

Training.   For six weeks, the senior center provided new volunteers with role-playing exercises, question-and-answer sessions, and insights into the typical problems of the elderly. It felt great to be prepared.

Again, many churches utilize the same approach. In training sessions, Sunday school teachers role-play how to handle the disruptive child. Ushers discuss how to handle late arrivers. Committee chairs role-play how to deal with the committee member who won't stop talking.

Follow-up.   It helps to discuss the challenges and questions that come up as we minister to others. Quarterly follow-up meetings came in handy, such as the time I told the group about my difficulties with leaving Sarah.

Just when it was time to say good-bye to Sarah each week,

she would suddenly open up and talk about her problems, often with tears in her eyes. But until then, conversation would be very difficult. So, not wanting to leave during a meaningful moment, I'd end up feeling manipulated into staying longer than we had arranged.

In the follow-up sessions, the other volunteers told me I was being manipulated. From then on, when Sarah opened up as I was preparing to leave, I felt comfortable saying, "Sarah, I'd like to stay and talk, but I have to leave for another appointment." And I left. After that, Sarah opened up before the end of my visit.

By implementing some of the principles I learned the hard way, we can do much to avoid burnout.

23

Maintaining Momentum

Discouragement becomes a problem when it blurs vision for ministry.

—MYRON AUGSBURGER

D. L. Moody, the great evangelist, was said to have prayed often that the Lord would "keep me from ever losing the wonder."

Anyone who ministers for Christ knows that wonder, as did Moody. We are filled with it when people we serve respond with joy to Christ's love. But the same ministry that fills us with wonder sometimes makes us wonder. Enlivening the souls of others often tries our own. We can become disheartened, and ministry gets mired.

There are a number of things that can stall outreach ministry—fatigue, boredom, a change of priorities, church squabbles, to name a few. But perhaps the most significant is discouragement that accompanies the loss of purpose.

Throughout my ministry, I've tried to sustain not only my own momentum, but also that of people I've walked with, led, or pastored. Here are a few things I have learned.

What brakes momentum

Because Christians are in the business of spirituality, so to speak, we are apt to blame a slowdown of momentum on lack of devotion, some moral lapse, or, perhaps, the devil. Such things can and often do discourage us from reaching out. Naturally, in such cases, prayer and spiritual renewal go a long way toward building momentum again.

On the other hand, we've learned that physical factors also play a role. If I've been up until midnight three nights in a row and then have to get up for a six o'clock appointment, it affects my mood. I become more clipped with others, work seems an effort, and the slightest problem can demoralize me. To put it another way, ministry bogs down when I don't lie down enough.

Aside from spiritual and physical factors, however, I've found people are usually discouraged from reaching out by one of four factors:

Unrealistic goals. In their yearning to be faithful to Christ, churches often set goals that are unrealistic. We think we are being faithful to the upward call, when all we are doing is making the call impossible. If we vow to eradicate poverty in our area of the city, discouragement is inevitable. Better to say, "We will help families in poverty with the means we have available." That is hard enough, but it is something we can do.

Goals also become unrealistic when we insist on perfection: we will help every family in our area, at every opportunity, using adequately all our resources. We cannot do that. We're going to overlook some needs. We're going to waste some of our resources. We will have to turn away some needy people. We might as well admit it up front and save ourselves some discouragement.

Also, some goals prove inaccurate measures of the success of ministry. To aim to give a bag of groceries to every family that asks will dishearten us if we see the same people coming to us month after month for more food. We may have succeeded at giving out groceries, but we will not have succeeded at helping people feed themselves without our aid.

In short, unrealistic goals will discourage us, and that will stall our outreach.

Unmeasurable ministries. Only a few things can be measured in Christian ministry—attendance at meetings, dollars raised, dollars spent. Often the most important things cannot be measured.

Washington, D.C., has one of the highest murder rates in the United States. Naturally, we would like to lower the number of murders in our area of the city, but how do we measure success? Even if the murder rate goes up, we may, nonetheless, have been instrumental in stopping another dozen murders, which would have made the rate even higher.

The same is true of other goals we might set. How do we know how many people we've kept from suicide? How many teenage pregnancies have we prevented? How many people have been kept off drugs because of our ministry? The list goes on. There are many aspects of ministry that cannot be measured, for which number goals cannot be set. But sometimes when people cannot measure the effect of their work, they get discouraged.

Ministry, of course, is sometimes noticeably successful. Attendance at services is one of the easily measured achievements. But frequently the success is subtle, like salt that seasons food: You can't see it. You cannot measure with the naked eye. But it makes a difference.

Most of the friends of one teenage girl in our church either are or have been pregnant. But not her. She says her lifestyle is different; she is not going to live that way. Where did she get those convictions? Not from her neighborhood, which inadvertently conspires to undermine them. Her convictions have been molded and reinforced by her mother and the Christian community. That is success, but it can't be put on a graph.

Inflexible temperaments. Some people claim that overwork brings discouragement in ministry. That is true to some degree, and we try to deal with that problem when it arises. But it is also true that hard work, in itself, never discouraged anybody; it's the sense of worry, futility, isolation, or lack of appreciation accompanying hard work that will bring discouragement. The deeper issue, then, is not that people are busy, but how they handle their busyness.

I've found some of the most discouraged people tend to be inflexible. The people who accomplish the most and find the greatest satisfaction in it, tend to be flexible people.

Why are we told that if we want to get something done, we should ask a busy person to do it? Because they are flexible; they know how to adjust their schedules to meet new demands.

The unoccupied person, on the other hand, often is inflexible. Such people live by routine: they rise, shower, eat breakfast, read the paper, go to work, have lunch, come home, eat dinner, watch TV, and go to bed, all at appointed hours. If their routine is interrupted, they become flustered. If given an extra task, they can't figure out how to change their schedules to accommodate it.

This, of course, is a caricature. But if we can model flexibility and encourage that trait in others, we will help defeat discouragement.

Inappropriate jobs.   If you put a multitalented person in a job for which he has no talents, you're looking for discouragement. Conversely, if you put a person with only one skill in the one job that will use his talents, you'll see motivation for years to come.

One young man connected with the college where I was president taught chemistry, but he was not succeeding. He was a good chemist, but he didn't do the one thing teachers need to do: get his students excited about learning. Naturally, his teaching meandered.

However, he was a gifted researcher, and his ability to analyze and sift through information to find the most relevant data was outstanding. So, the dean and I negotiated with him and moved him from teacher to director of institutional research. He not only worked with enthusiasm, but his work became recognized widely among small liberal arts colleges.

Community burnout spotters

Actually, discouragement is not, in itself, a problem. Anyone who engages in challenging work will become discouraged from time to time. Discouragement becomes a problem, however, when it blurs vision for ministry. That's when it can lead to burnout. When people are so discouraged they're ready to quit, outreach ministry will limp along.

Signs of burnout are many: Physically, people often experience more headaches and are lethargic about work. Mentally, they lack creativity, become easily impatient with coworkers, forget to do jobs or meet appointments, and find it difficult to follow through on projects.

However, although it's easy to list signs of burnout on the printed page, it's often difficult—in the scurrying about of weekly activities—to notice the signs in others. That's why in our church, spotting burnout is a community affair. We use our small groups to determine when someone is on the edge.

Our elders have long met every other Wednesday morning for an hour of prayer only for the congregation. The other Wednesday we meet in the evening, mostly for business. But we begin with a devotional and then share concerns for the church.

Each week, then, elders have an opportunity to share what they have sensed and seen, and others will either confirm it or mention extenuating circumstances (perhaps the person under discussion simply has been up for two nights with sick children—not a long-term problem). If we agree that someone is under undue stress, after we've shared and prayed about it, we designate a couple of people to spend time with that individual. They will, in turn, offer any help that will improve the situation, such as arranging a break in the person's church duties.

Three ways to maximize motivation

Naturally, we want to do more than respond to discouragement and burnout. We want to avoid it, or at least minimize it. Our goal is to make the most of people's motivation, to build healthy momentum for outreach.

We have three strategies to do that: spread the load, help people help themselves, and model dependence.

1. Spread the load. If overwork or mismanaged work is causing discouragement, then spreading the work load becomes a logical way to overcome discouragement. Specifically, that means:

Diversify. As with most churches, we have a number of commissions that do the work of the church. For us, it's five: worship, Christian nurture, fellowship, stewardship, and mission. Our very structure then, assumes that about one-fifth of our time and energy is spent on outreach.

It's easy to understand one of the reasons most churches organized this way: Not everybody can sustain momentum in outreach year after year. Some are not yet ready to do it at all. To give members a variety of avenues of service ensures that outreach doesn't overwhelm any individual.

Give them a break. We not only spread the work load, but also the time load. We'll give people permission to take a break from a ministry, perhaps a year or two, to spend more time with family or to recharge spiritual batteries. The attitude we set is not "This person just couldn't handle the job," but "People have the right and freedom to take a sabbath rest in ministry." That way people can exit a job without feeling they have to exit the church.

That is easier said than done, of course. About three years ago a young woman bowed out of work because of a health problem. A number of people from the congregation had to encourage her regularly afterward, reminding her that she didn't have to feel guilty about it. If they hadn't done that, she might have quit sharing altogether.

Then again, sometimes the process works cleanly. Recently, a young man released from a responsibility eight months earlier told me how good he felt about it. Once rested, he was anxious to get back to work.

Know when to say when. Another key to spreading the load is limiting the number of tasks members attempt. We don't like to see an average member take on more than two significant jobs at a time. For most people, one is enough.

We have some people, for instance, who participate in our praise band. That involves a weekly practice and playing during our Sunday service. Most of these people are also members of a commission, and one or two sit on a board. If they should announce that they want to start an outreach ministry, we'd likely discourage them—unless, of course, they give up another responsibility.

2. Help people help themselves. Because a minister can't be with people in every ministry situation, it only makes sense to help people help themselves in ministry. In this respect, we do the following:

Let members do the talking. Members need encouragement not just from their pastor, but also from their peers. We let that happen during a time called "Windows of Service." Once a month in worship, we have individuals talk about how they are sharing Christ's love in their workplace or neighborhood.

About a year ago, the learning center lacked sufficient volunteers. But after a member of the congregation mentioned this during Windows of Service, things turned around. Since then, the learning center has been owned increasingly by the congregation.

Enable laity to minister. One of my former associates has been impressed continually at how people stay motivated in our church. I once asked him, "What would you say has been the key to maintaining momentum?"

"More than anything else," he said, "the leadership has been committed to enabling others rather than controlling them." Enabling has, of course, become a buzzword in church circles in the past two decades. Let me clarify what I mean.

First, it means encouraging others to reach out and evangelize instead of doing it all myself. Not only does this get more ministry done, it also lets members enjoy the wonder of ministry.

Second, enabling means teaming people in the congregation. Experienced people work with those less experienced, but no one is sent out as a lone ranger. Our pastoral team of three is committed to modeling this pattern.

Third, enabling means training people. For example, we run seminars for people who want to help lead worship services. We teach them our theology of worship and how to use language and mannerisms appropriately. We also hold seminars on discipleship in daily life. The point is we try to offer training in areas where people want and need training to do effective ministry both in and outside the church.

Support small support groups. Every person needs a sense of achievement, worth, and fulfillment. When people in ministry become independent and cut themselves off from close relationships, they become susceptible to discouragement. They don't have people who can regularly give them encouragement and guidance.

Esther and I belong to a covenant group of thirteen that meets every Thursday evening. Over a six-month period, we take turns sharing with the group our schedules and priorities for the coming months. For instance, when it's my turn, the group discusses how I'm using my time and energy, and how that accords with my gifts. In some areas they encourage me to move ahead; in others they prompt me to slow down. This group counsel has helped me sort my priorities and it has given me a tremendous sense of freedom to say no to people: "My friends tell me that I'm doing too much and should cut back."

Furthermore, we encourage people to get support from others who participate in similar ministries. For a number of years I have attended three prayer meetings: one with people who minister in the inner city, one with my denominational brothers and sisters, and one that consists mostly of suburban pastors. Naturally, there is an altogether different feel and perspective in each group. It's not surprising that the inner-city prayer meeting nourishes me most.

3. Model dependence on God and others. We can prevent discouragement from becoming burnout, but, as I mentioned, we cannot eliminate discouragement. It comes with the territory of a challenging ministry. But we can help people maintain momentum in ministry in the midst of discouragement if we, ourselves, model for them how it is handled. I do that in two settings.

In small groups. There are some things that pastors need to talk about freely without feeling it's going to be misread or misused in the church. These I don't mention in settings where members are present. Yet I still can talk about a number of things in small-group settings that show people I'm struggling and need their encouragement and prayers.

Esther and I felt torn inside when one of our children went through a divorce. During that time, as I sat on the front pew in worship, tears often would run down my cheeks as I asked God for strength to stand up and preach. Of course, our congregation knew what we were going through.

One evening, three people from our congregation came to us and said, "We want to pray with you." We went into my study at the church and prayed. Then they said, "You are carrying all this burden by yourself. We would like you to disengage emotionally for a while. We don't want you even to talk, think, or pray about it for several weeks. We promise you we will do the praying in your place. While we pray daily about this, you unhook."

Their love helped us through our crisis. It also helped the congregation to know I was willing to accept their help. If we can practice that type of openness and trust with each other, ministry momentum will be maintained.

From the pulpit. I think it's wrong for a pastor to say, "Pardon a personal illustration." That's the only kind he really knows. (Actually, it would be more proper to say, "Pardon my borrowing this illustration.")

Although we should remain cautious about using ourselves

as illustrations of success, I have fewer qualms about showing people my struggles and God's faithfulness. It is another way of showing that it's normal for people active in ministry to get discouraged, and that we need to depend on God's strength for our momentum.

Staying motivated

Before ordination, I volunteered to go to China as soon as I finished college in order to do relief work. That was in the late 1940s, and I didn't know the Communists were about to take over and close the doors to missionaries. I received a letter from the secretary of missions for my denomination, who knew the situation, telling me I couldn't go, and that surely the Lord would have something for me later in life.

He enclosed in his letter an article by Dick Hillis, "I Was Never Called to China." But Dick had, in fact, been in China for eighteen years. Curious, I read it. He believed he was called to a certain kind of ministry; the location of that ministry, however, was open. If the door closed in one place, he would practice his ministry elsewhere. His ministry wouldn't change, only the locale.

From that day, I've practiced that philosophy. By remembering the purpose of my ministry is to glorify Christ and enhance his kingdom, I stay motivated whatever the place, program, or position. Through disappointments and discouragements, I have yet to lose the wonder.

PART 6

Target

24

Ministry to Newcomers

The most gratifying welcome a visitor can receive is from someone she wouldn't expect to welcome her, in a place she didn't expect it to happen.

—CALVIN RATZ

Newcomers don't come with the glue already applied. It's up to the congregation to make them stick.

But that's easier said than done. Experience shows that not everyone who attends church once wants to return.

Visitors arrive at a church's doorstep for a variety of reasons. There are disgruntled church hoppers, unsaved people genuinely seeking either spiritual or material help, newcomers to town, recent converts, and spiritual prodigals returning to God. Each comes with a different set of fears and expectations. All must be handled carefully if they are going to come back a second time.

At times, church insiders fail to realize how intimidated newcomers feel when attending church. Insiders, familiar with the traditions, the rubrics of worship, the machinery of church programs, and even the layout of their facility, tend to forget that outsiders see these smoothly flowing activities as intimidating barriers to becoming part of an unfamiliar church.

It's a big job

A study by the White House Office of Consumer Affairs indicates that 96 percent of dissatisfied business customers never take their complaints to the offending company. In other words, for every complaint a company hears, twenty-four complaints are never received. The study's most frustrating finding, however, is that each of those dissatisfied customers will tell an average of ten friends about the problem. People who attend church aren't much different.

I know the reasons some people stick with our church. Those who've stayed tell me about the friendliness, the opportunities for ministry, and the sense of God's presence in the services. But how do we find out why others never return? Moreover, those who don't return are the worst advertisements for our church in the community.

Track records in getting first-timers back for a second visit aren't good. One pastor of a church that works meticulously to follow up visitors and who even has a secretary assigned to help integrate newcomers, says perhaps 2 to 3 percent of first-timers ever return. Most of us think we're doing better than that, but we probably aren't.

Furthermore, the need to work at assimilation is greater than ever. In particular, denominational loyalty is eroding. One researcher discovered that of Christians moving from one city to another, 50 percent switched denominations. Even within a community, there's a shopping mall mentality toward church attendance. People go where the action is, regardless of denominational affiliation. That means transfers aren't assured.

And assimilating newcomers involves much more than placing warm, friendly greeters at the door. It's spiritual conflict. The devil doesn't want people in the church, and with a variety of subtle innuendoes and imagined thoughts, he works to make people feel they don't belong. He's constantly pulling people away, not only from God, but from the church. Assimilation needs to be a matter of prayer.

It's hard to define a successful rate of assimilation. The apostle Paul didn't keep everyone. Some who heard him came back only to throw stones. We need to accept without rancor the fact that not all will consider our church worth joining. That's only realistic. But I don't want to be the cause of someone's not returning. Although we'll never meet everyone's needs, we can work to make newcomers feel welcome and to arouse social and spiritual appetites that make them want to return.

Our family has attended many kinds of churches while on vacation. In the car after a service, I've frequently asked, "If we lived nearby, would you want to go back to that church?" I've heard mixed responses. When I've asked why, I've received a string of answers:

"Everyone seemed so happy."

"Unfriendly."

"No sense of God's presence."

"The place was alive. Everyone was involved."

"I didn't know the words to the music."

"No one showed us where to go."

"The preacher was cold."

"The preacher told some great stories."

"I felt like everyone was looking at us all the time."

Looking back at scores of churches I've visited, I've classified three broad factors that determine a newcomer's willingness to return. In management terms, they are "the critical success factors": obstacles, atmosphere, and structure.

Obstacles

A church's composition, history, or philosophy of ministry can erect a wall newcomers have a difficult time scaling. Here are some of the situations a congregation may face that can place barriers before newcomers.

Large family networks.   In our church, three family circles with a chain of relationships connect more than 175 people.

These networks have their own social gatherings in which outsiders aren't included. The Thanksgiving dinner table has little space for strangers. These families enjoy built-in care. News about needs spreads internally, apart from the church. Relatives often are so busy taking care of family needs, little time remains to consider the needs of outsiders. Such networks can be deadly to assimilating newcomers.

We've done two things to deal with this issue. First, we tactfully alerted some in these families to the potential problems, challenging them to take care to include outsiders in some of their social gatherings. Second, we've outgrown the family circles with new growth, so they no longer dominate our fellowship.

Existing friendships.   The fellowship of churches known for friendliness and care can sometimes be difficult to crack. If the energy of the congregation is given to caring for existing members rather than identifying the needs of newcomers, love becomes ingrown.

Even pulpit statements about friendliness can irritate newcomers. I remember visiting one church and hearing the pastor talk about their friendliness. The church was friendly. I watched people in animated conversations with their friends, but the whole time, I sat alone on the pew feeling like an ice cube. No one talked with me. The pastor's comments and the excited conversations around me only accentuated the fact I was an outsider. A time for greeting newcomers would have structured a way for that church to share the warmth outside already-established circles.

Facilities.   The design of church buildings, especially poor layout of the foyer and other entrances, can be an obstacle to a newcomer's welcome. In some churches even finding the sanctuary is a challenge. No signs direct you to entrances, the nursery, or rest rooms. Such inconsideration makes newcomers uncomfortable. Indirectly, but forcefully, the church is saying to visitors, "We weren't expecting you."

However, facilities can communicate warmth and friendliness. In order to create a feeling of intimacy in a large, old building, one small congregation removed the pews, placed padded chairs in a cozy arrangement, and brought the platform closer to the congregation. These people knew a small congregation in a large room makes newcomers feel uncomfortable, so they contrived an intimate atmosphere, even in a cavernous space.

People respond to crowded facilities in a variety of ways. Some outsiders interpret a full sanctuary as a good sign. They think, *Something's happening here, and I want to be a part of it.* Others see it as an indication there's no room for them and they aren't needed. Researchers believe a congregation generally won't grow above 85 percent of the sanctuary seating capacity. Unless the church is a going concern in a generally lackluster spiritual community, a packed sanctuary communicates, "We don't care to make room for you."

A church's history.   Some congregations seem more interested in the past than in the future. Sermon illustrations and announcements constantly refer to past events and cherished traditions. Continual references to names of former members and leaders are meaningless to outsiders and say the church is more interested in its past heroes than in newcomers.

Even excessive denominationalism can hinder assimilation. People seeking help today don't go to a church because it belongs to a historic denomination. They go because they believe they will receive help.

What people seek is a refreshing alternative to the world outside. No one returns for a second visit because a denominational flag has been waved; they come back because they experienced God's presence and the acceptance of God's people.

Special events.   Some folk fail to stick because the event that first attracted them to the church is not the regular diet of the church. For example, a guest musician may pull in a crowd, but the crowd he attracts comes with taste buds for a certain type of music. If the church doesn't deliver that type of ministry on a regular basis, the person feels hungry.

Generally, people expect as a norm the kind of ministry

that first attracted them to a church. This, of course, is one of
the major problems in integrating new converts who've come
through TV and radio ministries. Normal church life doesn't
match expectations caused by the media ministry. People attracted to a church by special events likely will stick only if
the kind of ministry that first attracted them is sustained—a
difficult undertaking.

Philosophy of ministry.   If the pastor or congregation believes church life is generated from the platform on Sunday
morning, integration means getting as many people into the
sanctuary for Sunday mornings as possible. In such situations, allegiance is to the pastor and not to the congregation.
Both strong preachers and flamboyant personalities can build
a following, but they may be only attracting a crowd, not
assimilating members into a church body.

If, however, a church's ministry emphasizes interaction
among members and shared ministry, integration means providing facilities and programs for people to build friendships
and to become involved in service. Church life is what happens among members, as well as in the public worship service.

A woman was converted and started attending our services
regularly. Her husband drove her to church each week and
picked her up afterward. The first time he attended a service
at our church, he said, "You people are so different. You never
want to leave the church. Church is something you do together. In my church, I go to Mass as a stranger. I can be a
good Catholic and not know anyone else in the church, let
alone talk to anyone. You can't do that in your church!"

Ministry of the body is as important as ministry on the
platform, not only for nurturing the saints, but also for assimilating new members.

A reputation of tension.   Strife among members is picked
up quickly by newcomers. And animosity is a poor advertise-
ment. Newcomers want no part of a church torn by dissen-
sion.

Awhile back I was called to mediate a church fight in a

small but divided congregation. A visitor from that community who had attended just one service told me about his icy reception and how both sides viewed him suspiciously. The following week, he was visited by members of both sides in the dispute, each trying to recruit him to their side. Naturally, he never went back.

The answer, of course, is an emphasis on forgiveness and reconciliation. A torn church cannot weave in new members. Until strife becomes the exception rather than the way of life, the church cannot expect to attract and hold new members.

Confusing service styles.   Visitors often feel uneasy when they first attend church. They're on strange turf. Much of what we do in our services, though familiar to members, is intimidating to visitors. An expressive worship style frightens someone who doesn't understand; a highly liturgical service loses the uninitiated. Choruses sung without a hymnal exclude newcomers unless the words are printed in the bulletin or projected on a screen.

Our Sunday morning service includes the reading of Scripture. While most of our people bring their Bibles, visitors often don't. Therefore, we print the Scripture passage in the bulletin so outsiders aren't excluded. (It also solves the "which translation" issue.)

Offerings may make visitors suspect that the church only wants money. So, during the offering at special events, where we have a significant number of outsiders, I usually say, "If you are a visitor, you're our guest, and there's no obligation for you to participate in the offering. However, this is one way the people of our own congregation express their worship to God."

Even during our recent building program, I said little about money from the pulpit. Our special appeals were made primarily through literature we mailed. Many people new to our church have commented on how they were initially impressed by our financial discretion.

Class and cultural distinctions.   There are rich and poor people. There are retirement communities, university communities, and working-class communities. There are farm towns, inner-city ghettos, and suburbs. People aren't all the same. Even if they speak English, they don't all talk the same language. And while those differences shouldn't affect how people interact, they do make a difference in how comfortable outsiders feel when they come into a church.

Some churches try to be all things to all people. But most churches have difficulty providing an environment in which everyone feels comfortable. Usually one social culture dominates.

Poor attitudes.   Perhaps the greatest obstacle to newcomers' integration is the attitude of insiders. Not everyone is as blunt as one person who told me, "Pastor, our church is big enough. We really don't need anymore folk in our church!"

Negative attitudes toward outsiders come from many quarters. Church power brokers, fearing a threat to their base, may resist newcomers. Members can resent the financial cost of providing space and staff to care for the needs of newcomers. Church pioneers can withdraw emotional support from the church. No matter how strong the appeal from the leadership, such attitudes, even if expressed by few, freeze newcomers out of the church.

Atmosphere

Another critical factor in holding newcomers is atmosphere. Some churches exude an atmosphere that says, "Visitors are welcome here." It isn't derived from handouts or slogans. It's not particularly what happens up front, though that helps. It's an air that permeates the whole congregation, an intangible that says to first-timers, "We've been expecting you, and we're glad you've come."

Growing churches are service oriented rather than product oriented. In the words of Ken Blanchard, author of *The One Minute Manager*, "Large and small companies alike are learning that in today's competitive marketplace, it is often good

service—not product superiority or low pricing—that deter-
mines success." In other words, it's not the companies with
the best products that succeed, it's those who take the best
care of their customers that become profitable.

The same can be said of the church. Growing churches
make a commitment to meet the needs of newcomers. They
create an environment where everything is designed with the
newcomer's experience in mind. They remember the human-
ness of their visitors.

For example, I can become so caught up in sermon preparation and delivery that I forget the needs of the very people
the sermon addresses. That's like a quarterback trying to
complete a pass while eyeing the scoreboard. The sermon and
other aspects of the church's ministry need to focus on the
quality of the newcomer's social and spiritual experiences,
providing the subtle yet overriding message: "Newcomers are
wanted and needed here."

How is that done? For one, by pastors when they tune
vocabulary to outsiders; when ordinances are explained in
the language of nonchurched people; when the leadership
style is warm, personable, and conversational. There's what a
friend of mine calls "pastoring from the pulpit."

He says he accomplishes in those moments some of the
pastoral care he is unable to achieve throughout the week. He
also says it's the time in the service when visitors come alive.
His vulnerability and openness as he chats pastorally with the
congregation partially breaks down the barrier between the
pew and pulpit that newcomers often feel.

The atmosphere of warmth and acceptance, however, is
expressed most effectively by people who hold no official position. That's because the most gratifying welcome a visitor
can receive is from someone he wouldn't expect to welcome
him, in a place he didn't expect it to happen. It may be a
warm comment by the person in the next pew. It might be
several smiles and a lot of eye contact in the foyer before the
service. Certainly there's touch. We might not kiss as they did
in New Testament days, but at least as J. B. Phillips put it in

his translation, there should be "a handshake all around!" Welcoming isn't just something done at the door; it's something everyone does all over the building.

Such an atmosphere can't be structured, but it can be fostered. Here are some things we encourage to create an atmosphere of warmth:

We have men directing traffic on our parking lot as people arrive for services. This not only heads off a lot of confusion, it also tells newcomers we want to make it easy for them to find their way. There's a warm smile even before people get out of their cars.

Several people are assigned to minister in the church foyer. Our greeters shake as many hands as possible. Others, our hosts and hostesses, watch especially for visitors. They're prepared to answer visitors' questions and to give directions. They also attempt to get first-timers to sign the guest book or a visitor's card. We also have a staffed information counter. In addition, we train our ushers how to be friendly and sensitive to outsiders.

Assigning at least one or two staff members to serve in the foyer—before, during, and after every service—has been our most productive means of identifying and welcoming visitors. The presence of a pastor in the foyer models the atmosphere we want. In fact, the staff person primarily responsible for the integration of newcomers has been dubbed "pastor of the foyer."

Two other methods help foster the atmosphere we seek. First, I talk about visitors often. I use them in sermon illustrations. I remind the congregation how uncomfortable visitors may feel. I liken our congregation to the staff of a large department store. We're there to serve newcomers.

Second, during a time for greeting in our services, we suggest people welcome at least six to eight people. I encourage people to start their greeting with the words, "Hi! I'm . . . " There's something personable about a first name. It also saves embarrassment by helping people learn the names of others in the congregation.

Structure

What happens if people like the atmosphere of a congregation but then find no group of people with whom they can relate? Churches of all sizes share this woe. Small churches sometimes become cliquish or ingrown. Larger churches may seem impersonal, making the newcomer feel insignificant.

But this need not be a problem if a structure is in place to identify and place newcomers into smaller groupings in which they can minister and find a place of belonging.

Several years ago, we adopted C. Peter Wagner's concept of "celebration, congregation, and cell." Basically, the idea is that the Sunday morning celebration can continue to grow indefinitely if two other groupings exist within the church. In addition to the Sunday celebration (everybody gathered for worship), there needs to be a number of both congregations (a subgrouping of forty to one hundred people) and small, intimate cells (informal networks of friends; intimate, task-oriented groups; or structured small-group gatherings).

We've paid particular attention to building the congregations; they've been invaluable for integrating newcomers. These groupings are large enough not to intimidate newcomers, yet small enough for them to get to know others. We're convinced that if we can get newcomers into one of these congregations, there's a high probability they'll remain in our web of love.

We have about thirty of these congregations, some based on fellowship, some on special interests, and some on ministry. For instance, each of the choirs is a congregation. The workers of many of our programs also become little congregations in which there is a network of friendships and accountability.

Our most important congregations for integrating newcomers are our age-divided adult fellowship groups. We've divided our church by ten-year age spans and placed each person in one of these congregations. Each has its own lay leader and committee as well as its own pastor. These groups meet weekly as Sunday school classes, hold regular social activities, and provide a caring ministry for the needy within the group.

But how do we channel people into these congregations?

Assimilating churches build structures that ensure newcomers are identified, cared for, and integrated into the fabric of the church. Here's how we go about it:

Identifying newcomers. We identify newcomers in a variety of ways. Counselors fill in response cards for those who respond to an altar call. Greeters and hosts get names, and addresses if possible. They're trained to write down the names so they're not forgotten. During services we ask each visitor to fill in an information card. Pastors working in the foyer carry visitor cards that they fill in on the spot.

Some newcomers don't want to be spotlighted; it's the anonymity of a larger church that attracts them in the first place. So we try not to overpower them. But we know that if we don't get a name and phone number or address, our chances of holding and helping visitors is greatly diminished.

One yardstick of success for a Sunday is the number of new names and addresses of first-timers we garner. New names and addresses are our prime contacts for ministry through the week. Without those names and addresses, midweek ministry to newcomers suffers.

One interesting source of information about newcomers is our offering envelopes. It's amazing that with all our efforts to contact visitors, some are missed. Yet some not only keep attending, they also start using offering envelopes! Our bookkeeper alerts us to these people.

Making midweek contact. Follow-up ministry starts Monday morning. My secretary helps me send a letter of welcome to every visitor. For a while, we didn't send the letter to out-of-town visitors, but now we do. We discovered some out-of-towners were in the process of moving to our city, and it was important to give these visitors a feeling that they were noticed and appreciated.

A staff member processes these names on Monday and

Tuesday. He makes an initial phone call, welcoming the people to our church and asking if it would be possible for someone from the church to visit the home. He attempts to gain further information, such as the approximate age of the adults and children. He completes a family information form as the call is made.

Following the call, this pastor may visit the family or assign it to one of the other pastors. He matches the family with the most suitable staff member, taking into account age, spiritual need, and special interests.

Copies of the family information sheet are shared during our staff meeting on Wednesday mornings. From that point, one pastor is assigned and responsible for each newcomer. In addition, we see that the appropriate lay leaders in the youth department, ministry programs, and Sunday school are notified of the new family.

Each of our adult fellowship groups has lay members who assist in the ministry of integration. Each pastor works with his lay leaders to watch for recent newcomers on Sunday, make midweek contact, invite them to informal coffee gatherings, and introduce them to other members of the class.

Maintaining a newcomers' directory. We keep all newcomers in a separate directory for six months. This list is reviewed at staff meetings, and pastors report on progress. After six months on the list, a decision is made to (1) place the name in the church directory as an assimilated family, (2) delete the name as someone unlikely to come back, or (3) leave the name on the list for another six months since their status is still undetermined.

Providing a "Welcome to the Family Class." This class is an invaluable tool for making newcomers feel a part of the church. It's promoted as a class for all newcomers, not just new converts.

I lead this class during the Sunday school hour. We believe newcomers are attracted to a class led by someone with a high profile in the worship service. Two lay couples also work with me, befriending and encouraging newcomers.

The class is a relaxed and informal opportunity to get acquainted. Over coffee, we try to make newcomers feel at ease in the church. The content of the class varies depending on who is present. We spend a great deal of time prompting and then answering questions about what we believe and how our church functions. During a six- to eight-week period, we cover the basic teachings and practices of the church.

I spend considerable time outlining how the church functions and how to build church friendships. Mostly, I watch for specific needs, spiritual problems, and questions newcomers may have. Through our lay leaders, we reach out to meet these needs. We strongly encourage people to become involved in the church's activities, stressing that friendships are built as a by-product of doing things together.

After someone has attended the class for about two months, our lay leaders introduce the person to the lay leaders of the appropriate adult fellowship group and the pastor assigned to that group. Responsibility for integration is passed from the Welcome to the Family Class to the adult fellowship group. Newcomers are encouraged to attend Sunday school.

Each convert is encouraged also to attend one of the midweek home fellowship groups designed for new Christians. Each newcomer who is not a new Christian is introduced to the leader or host of one of our regular Neighborhood Bible Study groups.

Integrating into ministry.   We believe it's critical for newcomers to become involved in the church's ministry as quickly as possible. In fact, we feel that until newcomers assume some ministry responsibility, they won't feel emotionally one with us. They will think of the church as *them* rather than *us.*

Newcomers must not only feel wanted, they also must feel needed. Some people think that as a church grows larger, there's less opportunity to be involved in ministry. That's just not the case. Awhile back, we surveyed our congregational involvement in ministry and discovered there were 995 ministry jobs being done by 602 people. That's a vast army. Yet we easily could use another 150 workers today. The key is to let the newcomer become involved in meaningful ministry. I want newcomers to expect to make a significant contribution to our ministries. So we talk regularly about ministry opportunities. We highlight what's being done. We share our vision. We explain the diversity of ways people can become involved. Though critical recruiting is done individually, from time to time we encourage the congregation to fill in a ministry opportunity sheet. These sheets are of little value for longstanding members, but they give newcomers an opportunity to express their interests.

Those who stick

Some people don't want to be integrated into any church. They may lack a basic commitment to God, and no amount of friendliness will make them stay. Others bear the imprint of our culture that recoils from commitment to anything.

Such people drift through every congregation. Seeing them fall away can be disappointing, especially when we work so hard to show them the challenge and benefits of commitment to a local church.

The thrill of pastoring, however, is to look over a congregation on Sunday morning and see the people who have come and been helped and assimilated:

—Glen decided to become a Christian at a drama presentation. Today, he's an usher.

—Sarah was delivered from a difficult spiritual environment. Today she works in one of our children's ministries.

—Paul accepted Christ in my office. He's active in the church with his wife and two children.

—Russ and Cathy prayed for forgiveness and salvation with me in a restaurant over lunch. They became involved in our sound ministry.

—Ed and Karen felt they were part of the church when they were asked to serve on one of our adult fellowship committees.

These special souls—and a host of others—are all part of each Sunday's celebration. They're there, not because of a specific program but as a result of an entire congregation's spinning a web of love—a web that helps newcomers stick.

25

Ministry to Missing Members

We call not to get people to come back to church; we call because people are in pain.

—JOHN SAVAGE

I was sorting slides I had used in an every-member canvass in my church. When I held some to the window, I was shocked. Pictured in the first three slides were three couples who had held key offices in the church my first year there. Now, four years later, those couples were totally inactive.

These people no longer attended worship, except maybe on Christmas or Easter, made no financial contribution, didn't participate in the life of the church, and had a negative attitude about the congregation.

How could people move in just four years from active involvement to total inactivity? I wondered.

I thought of times I had visited inactive members and seen absolutely nothing happen. In fact, often they were more convinced to stay away after I made the call. I knew I needed to figure out how to keep current members active and enable inactive ones to return.

Anxiety-provoking events

I went to work on these questions as I pursued a doctorate and have continued to search for answers during the past decade.

I tried to find studies about the phenomenon, but I dug up nothing. So, with a psychologist and a theologian, I designed a research project. Thirteen trained pastors and I interviewed inactive members from four United Methodist congregations to find out what caused them to disappear from church life.

We found 95 percent of the people had experienced what we now call an "anxiety-provoking event"—an APE. Subsequent research showed these events usually come in clusters, several APEs compounding within six months to a year.

Anxiety is the emotional alarm system triggered when we're in disequilibrium, when we've been hurt or feel that unless a change is made we're going to get hurt. The inactive members we visited revealed high levels of anxiety, which when unresolved drove them from church membership. Gradually we saw their anxiety fell into four categories.

Reality anxiety.   This anxiety is based on some real, historical event; you could have videotaped what caused it. Normally the event is a snub or an utter lack of church care when a member most needed it.

Suppose a pastor preaches his first sermon at a new church and someone says, "Pastor, we've had some lousy preachers here, but I think you're going to be the worst." That's an anxiety-provoking event for a pastor, and it's reality anxiety.

Awhile back I preached in a church in Vancouver. Two days prior, a family from the church had their home burn to the ground, and their two- and four-year-old children died in the fire. The father, in an attempt to save his youngest, dashed into the bedroom. The walls and curtains were on fire, as were the bedding and the child's clothing. Leaning over to snatch the child out of the fire, severely burning himself in the process, the father tried to pick up his child. The child's body fell apart in his hands.

How many people went to visit him and his wife? Maybe the pastor, but probably not many parishioners. Most would confess, "I wouldn't know what to say," as if they had to say something. A family experiencing the horror of this kind of tragedy would have a hard time returning to a church they felt let them down when they needed them. That is a reality anxiety-provoking event.

Moral anxiety.   This next type is more difficult because it isn't always as obvious. Moral anxiety arises when people experience in themselves or others behaviors they believe aren't right.

A layperson called me once and said, "I understand you work with churches where people are leaving."

"That's true."

"Well," he continued, "our senior pastor has admitted having an affair with a woman in the congregation, our associate pastor confessed a homosexual affair with our organist, and we have choir members involved in affairs."

That large church has lost more members over moral anxiety than most churches will ever have.

Moral anxiety can also be private, yet still drive people from the church. In *Meetings At the Edge*, Stephen Levine tells the story of a devout Christian nurse who cared for Evie, a woman who was given permission by her family to end her life because of the extreme pain caused by cancer. Helen, the nurse, refused to participate in such an act. Yet Evie persisted. She planned to take barbiturate-laced applesauce at nine P.M. Helen reluctantly agreed to arrive at ten and do whatever she could if Evie were not yet dead.

As Helen entered the house, Evie was crying. She was frightened and could not take the applesauce alone. She asked Helen to feed it to her. Helen said, "I cannot," and walked out to sit in her car.

Ten minutes later, Evie hobbled to the door using a chair like a walker. She was vomiting. "Please come help me!" she begged. "I don't want to be trapped in a coma and only partially die. Please come!" Helen walked into the house, fed her the rest of the applesauce, and held Evie until she died.

There's a good chance Helen was not in church the following Sunday, and no one would know why. Her moral anxiety-provoking event was private.

Neurotic anxiety.   The types get more difficult to handle as we go down the list. Neurotic anxiety is pain caused by the imagination. Someone may claim, "I don't go to church because the pastor doesn't like me." If you check it out, the feeling might be based on reality, but the chances are it's only in the person's head.

A man goes into the hospital, expects you to visit, but doesn't let you know he's there. Then he gets angry when you don't call. Months later when you do call, you may trace his problem to that hospital stay. The man is convinced you don't care about him. That's neurotic anxiety.

Even more frustrating than the fact that the person's grievance is imaginary is that we can inadvertently foster it. For example, a pastor regularly calls on a couple who are potential members. He spends time with them and makes them feel important. All the time they're thinking, *Look at all the personal attention you get from the pastor around here!* Then they join the church, and the attention they receive drops almost to zero. They wonder what happened. The pastor has accidentally encouraged unrealistic expectations, which give rise to neurotic anxiety.

Existential anxiety.   Existential anxiety is that feeling brought about by the thought that someday you may not exist, or that even if you do, your life may be meaningless. We hear the refrains, "The church has lost its meaning for me." "The sermons don't mean anything anymore, pastor." "My kids are bored stiff in church school."

I visited a family that had been active church members but had dropped out. As I talked with them, I learned that when they were preparing for marriage, someone from a church said to the bride, "I believe you're a born-again Christian, but I'm not convinced your fiancé is. If you marry him, your first child will die." I was talking with them months after their toddler died.

They experienced existential anxiety at its height. Twenty minutes into that conversation, the couple cried as hard as two adults could cry. Tears running down the cheek begin to say something of the nature of the pain encountered when visiting an inactive member.

Clustering events

Most often people who drop out have run into at least one of these four types of anxiety in clusters. For example, a man in one congregation lost his job, and the family income plummeted. His wife, under stress, ended up depressed. Soon after, this couple—active leaders in their church—were told they were doing an inadequate job as Sunday school teachers and then were abruptly dismissed. They became angry and quit coming to church.

When a layperson and pastor visited them some weeks later, the woman was reading a newspaper. She put it down, said hello, and picked it right back up. That's called resistance. The visitors talked with her husband, and in about five minutes she slammed the paper into her lap. They had before them a red-faced, angry woman.

The first thing inactive people mention is usually the last event in the anxiety-provoking cluster. "We're just as good Sunday school teachers as anybody else up at that church!" she informed her visitors. "If we aren't good enough for that, we aren't good enough for anything."

It's easy to assume that's the sole or primary issue, but it's not. The unresolved anxiety of the cluster of events has made this final event intolerable. Until we uncover and deal with the original pain of the cluster, even if it happened twenty years ago, people will likely remain outside the church.

The pastor and lay visitor talked for some time with these

people. I heard they did come back to church and eventually accepted new leadership responsibilities.

Identifying conflict

Anxiety—of whatever variety—arises from some problem. The most common is intrafamily conflict. Husband and wife square off on some issue; parents and kids squabble. This kind of conflict is the most consistent characteristic of people who have left the church.

Conflict with pastors is the second most common problem, and the main cause is avoidance. When pastors avoid dealing with people's anxiety, the people simply avoid the pastors and their churches.

Family against family, interfamily conflict, is the third arena. It's the Hatfields against the McCoys; people don't get along with one another.

Overwork, or at least the feeling of it, presents a fourth problem area. Volunteer church service, too much, too soon, or too long with no reward, will drive people from the church.

Suppose you discover a family whose members are having troubles at home, seem to be avoiding you, are feeling disappointed about the way other church members have treated them, and think they're overworked and unrewarded. You will usually find they are experiencing reality, moral, neurotic, or existential anxiety—often simultaneously. Then you can predict the next stage: they cry for help.

Answering cries

If we learn to hear and respond to people's cries for help, we can usually prevent their dropping out because most of those still crying for help will respond to our efforts to reach them. But cries don't last forever. Some cry longer than others, depending on their bond to the congregation, but when the cry goes unanswered, eventually members leave. Then the damage is much greater and more difficult to repair.

So how does a cry for help sound? It comes in all forms, sizes, and intensities. A verbal cry for help may sound like this: "I don't know if I want to continue coming to this church. If there is one thing I can't stand, it's hypocrites!" Or it could be more subtle, such as the one I heard years back: "You know, all the men but me in our Sunday school class have had promotions at work."

The cries for help are more numerous than we realize. At one large church, I asked people to listen at church for cries for help. Thirty-three people listened one Sunday morning. The fewest cries anyone heard was two. I heard twelve. The group was shocked by the scores of cries we tallied.

Pastors can respond to cries in one of three ways.

First, they can listen and respond to the pain the cry represents, and that can be amazingly beneficial.

Second, they can ignore the cry, not realizing how serious it is, until the cry moves into anger. The person gets more agitated and says, in effect, "Hey, what do I have to do around here to get you to hear me? Somebody help me! Can't you see I'm about to leave the church?"

Third, they can shoot the person with the gospel gun: "Hey, Buddy, what's the matter with you? You losing your faith or something?" That's a mistake of confusing the symptom with the disease, the behavior with the cause. But surprisingly, even if we react to the immediate anger rather than the anxiety behind it, we'll still recover about 80 percent of the people. Even hesitating steps in the right direction can help.

If we miss the verbal cries for help, we at least have a whole string of nonverbal cries to alert us to the problem. The cries for help become behavioral. The person either leaves or begins the process of leaving.

The first behavior change is leaving worship. Second, people leave major committees and boards. They either don't show up or they begin to show up sporadically. Both of these indicators can be seen on an attendance graph. The one who was always there four Sundays a month drops to three to two to only rare appearances. Or the board member makes one or two meetings a year after nearly perfect attendance in past years.

Third, people begin to leave Sunday school. This may vary from denomination to denomination, but most adults have their closest friends in their Sunday school class. Backing away from friends is a major change.

Fourth, the kids are pulled out of Sunday school. The parents decide they don't even want to bring them, let alone come themselves.

Fifth comes the letter of resignation, and finally, interestingly enough, the pledge is dropped. That's the final gasp for help, the last commitment to be given up in most denominations.

The sad thing is, these dropouts are hurting. They've experienced not only a private cluster of anxiety-provoking events, but now they're also grieving the loss of the church from their lives.

Understanding skunks and turtles

In our original research, a full third of the inactive people we called on had tears running down their cheeks once we dug out the original cluster of pain. Uncovering that hurt caused them to cry before perfect strangers.

These people need desperately to be heard, and when they aren't, helplessness overwhelms them. They begin to blame something external—the church or the pastor. We've nicknamed them skunks. When you call on these people, you get sprayed. It's what happened to me when the woman slammed the paper into her lap and lashed out at me.

When these people drop out, they wait six to eight weeks and then psychologically seal off the pain and anxiety produced by the original cluster. They back away and by all appearances become apathetic. But the pain of that cluster remains in the unconscious and acts as the block to returning to church. In order to get the person to come back, we must deal with that pain. Otherwise we'll hear every excuse under the sun for not returning.

After they seal off the pain, people reinvest their time, energy, and money in other pursuits. Half reinvest themselves in the family; they buy tents, trailers, and snowmobiles and go away on the weekend. You visit them and you hear, "Now our family is just as close to God up fishing on the lake as we were back at church with that bunch of snobs." This family still consider themselves Christians. Guess who they consider unchristian? If we go to them in an attempt to save them, we're in for the scrap of our lives, because they consider themselves more Christian than us.

The other 50 percent reinvest themselves in other institutions: hospitals, PTA, Girl Scouts, Boy Scouts, Rotary. So if we call on them, they'll point their fingers at us and say, "I've gotten involved with that volunteer ambulance crew. I'm a dispatcher on Sunday mornings. You know, we really help people now." That's a skunk speaking.

Another set of dropouts experiences a different emotion: hopelessness. It's the antithesis of helplessness. It's the sense of being incapable of generating any inner motivation. As a result, these people withdraw and become inactive. We call them turtles.

Turtles have incredible power to hook other people's guilt. A turtle's cry for help might sound like this: "I'm sure you could get Mrs. Green to teach the class. She would do a much better job than I could." The turtle drops out, waits six to eight weeks, and seals off the pain, much like the skunk. But turtles point the blame internally, toward themselves.

Whether it's skunk spray or turtle timidity, various cries for help can be addressed.

Reconciling the pain

So what do we do for these people? We need to teach ourselves and our laypeople to hear the pain of inactive people. It helps, too, if we learn how to intervene in the stages leading up to inactivity, before the people disappear from sight in a whirl of emotion.

One way we did this in a church I served was to take fifteen minutes at the end of every board meeting for the board members to report who, in their estimation, was crying for help. We collected those names and gave them to a team of twenty-four trained callers. Pastors can never do all the calling, so as a pastor I aimed for a corps of up to 10 percent of the congregation that I delegated to visit the inactives.

I also extended my secretary's hours so she could stand near me at the door on Sunday mornings to listen for cries for help. She was good at picking them up, and I could inconspicuously indicate others for her to note while I managed the flurry of smiles and handshakes and small talk. By the afternoon, she would alert the calling teams, who would reach out to these people before their cries turned to the silence of absence. Prior to that, I'd often hear several cries on a Sunday morning but fail to remember or follow up on them.

When we call on an inactive family, or one heading that direction, the chances are strong we're going to have to deal with anger. Turtle anger will make us feel guilty, and skunk anger will make us mad. Because calling on an inactive member is often painful, it's easy to enter a cycle: People leave because they're angry; I'm angry because they left; I punish them by letting them sit in their pain; they punish me by not coming back.

That's where reconciliation must enter. Active members of the church go to an inactive member on behalf of the community. If we are willing to bear some pain with the inactive person, reconciliation will often occur.

Look at what God did. We wouldn't listen to him, so he made a pastoral call to his inactive members. He sent his own

Son, who called on us and suffered on the cross for us. That kind of self-giving love got our attention and enabled us to be reconciled to him.

We will not get inactive members back by avoiding pain. We have to take the initiative, go to them, uncover the anxiety-provoking cluster, hear and often bear their pain, and thus pave the road for them to return.

Ultimately, we have to remember we call not to get people to come back to church. We call because people are in pain. If they come back as a result of our ministering to their pain, that is good. But if they don't, we have still reached out to them in the name of Jesus Christ.

26

Ministry to Up-and-Outers

*Locked gates and security systems cannot keep out the
inevitable pain and confusion of life.*

—MARK MATHESON

I once participated in the funeral for a high-level corporate
executive and community leader. The service was held at another, larger church to accommodate the great number of
attenders. The pallbearers consisted of mayors, a former gov-
ernor, an astronaut, and other community leaders. The pro-
cession to the cemetery was led by twenty stretch limousines,
and several hundred cars followed.

I went to the bereaved family's home following the service
and found a catered reception. The large tent standing in the
backyard made the event seem more like a garden party than
a funeral reception.

Feeling awkward, I wondered for a while if I was needed.
Finally the caterer left and the tent came down; the friends
and relatives said their good-byes and departed. Yet, grief and
loss lingered, and I was glad I was present to help meet the
needs that remained.

This experience, however, has not been that unusual. My
congregation is full of professional athletes, politicians, high-
level corporate executives, and self-made businesspeople—
"up-and-outers"—who hold positions of great wealth, power,
and influence in the community and yet find themselves in
need of ministry.

Relating to this group has presented unique challenges. Theirs is a world of roomy, custom-built homes, late-model luxury cars, lavish parties, and elaborate weddings. These, not to mention second homes, Colorado ski vacations, and European trips, sometimes intimidate me. I live in a modest home, drive a well-used car, and for most vacations visit grandparents.

Yet while many up-and-outers may live in houses hedged behind high walls and secure gates, the locked gates and security systems cannot keep out the inevitable pain and confusion of life. Sometimes, the hurt is even more intense because up-and-outers are so isolated.

In addition, these people are often responsible for the livelihood of scores of employees. The fiscal and personnel responsibilities can bring enormous stress. And because they are frequently in the public eye, they also have the extra pressure of constant public scrutiny, controversy, and inevitable commentary.

So, up-and-outers, I've discovered, deserve special ministry attention, as do other definable groups such as singles, the elderly, and youth. Over the years, we've had some success in ministering to up-and-outers, and here are some keys we've found helpful.

Fine-tune ordinary ministry

Up-and-outers, in spite of their unique place in society, respond to ministries that are effective with other subgroups. With up-and-outers, though, I fine-tune the ministry.

For example, while many may not be attracted to church to hear a preacher, they will come to hear one of their peers. Successful Christian businessmen and businesswomen can share their stories and relate to the up-and-outer in a way that many preachers cannot. Restaurant dinners and breakfasts with a Christian businessperson as speaker are also excellent opportunities for ministry.

Any businessperson in Florida would recognize the name Jack Eckerd, founder of the Eckerd drug store chain. He spoke at a prayer breakfast, and the business community responded overwhelmingly. I'm sure many came hoping to get a tip on how to start a successful business, but they came away having heard how Jesus Christ had changed Eckerd's life.

Seminars on marriage and family living are also successful. The stress of being an up-and-outer naturally affects the family. The wealthy and powerful, too, want to be better husbands, wives, and parents, and this desire can bring them to special ministries of the church.

Family sickness, struggles, and the death of loved ones also provide opportunities for ministry. During crises, I have found up-and-outers to be uniquely vulnerable. For some it's the first time they realize that money and power cannot keep them immune from tragedy.

With up-and-outers, sometimes their hurts become known to the entire community, and that puts more pressure on these individuals.

One of our members is an executive of a large organization. I was watching the evening news when the lead story reported a near disaster at his company. The pressure on him was tremendous. He greatly appreciated my letter of encouragement and offer of prayer support.

Exert confident leadership

We must be secure in our calling and position if we are going to minister to the movers and shakers. Their leadership qualities, charismatic personalities, and material resources force me to rely on God's calling and guidance in these contexts. I regularly have to remind myself that true success and strength come not from position, personality, or prosperity, but through faithfulness to God's call.

I'm most effective with up-and-outers when my leadership

is based on this confidence. Although up-and-outers are accustomed to leading the parade, they will follow good, assured leadership. Leadership, of course, means making difficult decisions and hearing disagreements about important subjects.

One of our members was highly vocal that a full-time youth director should be our next staff addition. I, however, felt just as strongly that we first needed a minister of education. We discussed the matter over lunch. After healthy give-and-take, neither of us changed our positions. Our meeting concluded with his comment, "Pastor, I disagree with you, but I will support your leadership."

Up-and-outers might disagree strongly, but they respect confident leadership.

Challenge them to new heights

William Willimon, in his book *The Gospel for the Person Who Has Everything*, says, "Persons of strength do have needs, and one of their most pressing needs is a need to be challenged beyond the narrow confines of their own lives. . ." Consequently, I try to challenge gifted people to use their gifts for the work of the Lord.

One-on-one discussions during breakfast or lunch are excellent forums for challenging up-and-outers. I usually try to go to their turf and look at their businesses or job sites. I ask questions about their companies and their responsibilities. I also share dreams and goals for the church and follow up by asking for their responses.

I don't assume up-and-outers know the church's needs. Many simply do not have the time to focus on them. Also, I try to present needs and challenges in a way that elicits their ideas for solutions. I have come away from numerous meetings with the promise of help and involvement.

One of our leaders was the president of a large company and well-respected in the church. He was usually present at the church services but preferred to remain in the background. His quiet demeanor appeared to signal his lack of interest in the church.

Yet at a lunch meeting, we talked about our church's personnel policies. I asked him to look them over and make suggestions. Not only did he look them over, but he also became chairman of the personnel committee and employed the resources of his company in researching and updating the existing personnel policies.

On another occasion, I told him about our capital stewardship campaign and said I felt he was the man we needed to lead this important drive. He agreed to be the lay chairman. Up-and-outers are gifted people who are accustomed to challenges. We need not fear challenging them to become more involved in the church.

Capitalize on short-term assignments

Many up-and-outers, rightly or wrongly, don't have the time or the temperament to make long-term commitments to church responsibilities. Therefore, the challenge of short-term projects motivates them better.

One of our up-and-outers is a marketing strategist. He had been asked to serve on committees or teach Sunday school, but he always begged off because of his job responsibilities and travel schedule.

However, when the need for a first-class marketing and publicity campaign emerged out of a building program, I knew he was the man. We met and discussed the need and responsibilities of the position. He agreed to a twelve-week commitment. His efforts were marvelous, and the campaign was a huge success.

Furthermore, when up-and-outers have success at a short-term project, they become more likely to adjust their schedules to make longer-term commitments. But whether their commitment is short- or long-term, my goal is to help up-and-outers see that their contribution is vital to the church. "What do you give a strong person who seems to have everything?" asks Willimon. "One thing you can give is a new perspective on his or her strength. You give a challenge. You give an opportunity to see those strengths as gifts from God. You give the freedom to use those strengths for something greater than one's own selfish desires."

Don't get caught in attached strings

Unique temptations accompany wealth. People of affluence are used to controlling their lives and the lives of others. And individuals who control people and events outside the church at times fall prey to the temptation to control people and events within the church.

Several times I've been tempted to decide an issue solely because someone has threatened to withhold their giving if I don't. At such times, I remind myself that not everything has a price, especially not the pastor's integrity. Furthermore, I remember the Lord will provide for his work, even without a big check.

I must use wisdom and discernment when church members offer gifts and support. The vast majority offer them out of genuine love for me and my family, but once in awhile the offer comes with strings attached.

Discernment and discretion are key here. I make mental notes about attitudes during conversations and meetings. A person's attitude toward the use of money usually remains consistent, whether at home, work, or church. If an individual is outspoken about "my" money, "my" business, or "my" giving to the church, then it's likely he or she enjoys being in control. Consequently, I am reluctant to accept gifts or favors from such a person; such kindnesses may be given with strings attached. When one such individual offered me a membership to an exclusive golf and country club, I had to turn it down graciously.

On the other hand, some people have the true spirit of giving and offer their gifts with purer motives. One of our well-to-do families volunteered the use of a mountain home for our family vacations. We accepted the offer and have used it several times. Our gratitude to the owner is always met with the simple response, "We're glad you can use it."

Good news for the successful

A brief glance at the ministry of Jesus and the early church reveals that ministry to the up-and-outers is nothing new. Nicodemus, Zacchaeus, and Joseph of Arimathea occupied prominent positions in their society but had needs that could be met only by Jesus.

Barnabas, a highly successful real estate broker, was so transformed by the gospel that he divested himself of his many holdings, gave the profits to the church, and became a missionary. The apostle Paul mentions several up-and-outers in his letters, including Philemon, Chloe, Priscilla and Aquila, and the Christians in Caesar's household.

As I look at the prominence of people who seem to have it all, I sometimes wonder what I have to offer them. But then I remember that from the very beginning, the gospel has been good news to all people. Up-and-outers simply have special concerns that must be addressed. And the more effectively I address those needs, the more up-and-outers will become prominent in the kingdom of heaven.

27

Ministry to Multiple Generations

*It's easier to start an additional congregation, even with a
fully graded Sunday school, than it is to build a new facility.*

—JOSH HUNT

We never planned it this way. We had no strategic plan to
do seven church services each weekend. It just happened. But
now the multicongregational approach is an important part of
who we are. Along the way, we learned a few things, some the
hard way, about making it work.

Like many churches, we began to grow and ran out of
space. So we started a second service. We continued to grow,
and we ran out of space again. Instead of launching a construction project, we started yet another service.

On it went, until we reached seven weekend worship services: four on Sunday morning, one on Saturday night, and
two on Sunday evening.

Is this the end? We don't know. As our church continues to
grow, we may continue creating new congregations.

Many churches have more than one worship service. Except for the number, our approach wouldn't appear to be
unique, except that (1) we have designed some services to
appeal to some people but not others, and (2) in many ways
we consider each service a fully functioning congregation. We
follow the Willow Creek model of having two types of services—seeker services and believer services. The five Satur-

day night/Sunday morning meetings are for seekers, and the two services on Sunday night are for believers.

To put it another way, instead of worrying whether multiple services will divide an otherwise united congregation, we've begun to intentionally create multiple congregations. We don't expect all the staff or any one pastor to be at every service.

Recently, as I was reading the book of Acts, I wondered if this wasn't merely a variation of what the early church did. After the thousands had been added to their number at Pentecost, "every day they continued to meet together in the temple courts."

I had always thought, *What dedicated people these must have been to meet seven days a week.* We can hardly get people to come two or three times a week! But then I realized the text doesn't say that every believer attended every meeting. It says the church met every day—in temple courts, and they also "broke bread in their homes." Could it be that the average believer in Jerusalem in the first century attended one large "temple court" meeting and one or two small "breaking bread" meetings per week?

The church could meet every day, but each church member would not attend each meeting. Maybe they were, to some degree, multicongregational. Our seven services over two days each week looks pretty modest by comparison.

Even though our approach was unplanned and has evolved over the past few years, we're now convinced it works better for us than constructing a larger building to get everyone into one or two services or making Sunday morning the main event and other times auxiliary events.

We are not only willing to risk breaking our congregation into "cliques," we're encouraging it. In fact, we are beginning to call ourselves a "multicongregational church."

Money advantage

We moved in the direction of a multicongregational church by providence, but we've already seen the many advantages it affords.

First, we save a Mount McKinley of money. Dollars not spent on I-beams, cement, and bond interest can hire staff, raise funds for mission projects, and pay for aggressive outreach programs.

How much do land and buildings really cost? Land prices, of course, are fixed at the time of sale. But constructing buildings is another matter: Church consultant Lyle Schaller says, "Experience tells us [it] will turn out to be two or three or four times the original estimate." A pastor's worst nightmare.

As a Southern Baptist church, if you divide our total Sunday school attendance by the total property assets of our churches, we've spent $6,000 per attendee on land and buildings. That's a lot of overhead. Schaller points out that the result of all this investment may be "very attractive, but most of the time empty buildings."

Plus there are the ongoing expenses for maintenance and utilities. Walk into an empty auditorium and ask yourself this question: If McDonald's spent this much on little-used overhead, could they stay in business? (That causes me to reflect on the grace of God!)

Second, the multicongregation approach allows us to specialize. We use two styles of music in our services: in some services it's semitraditional, in others contemporary.

One of our members recently told me that he went to a different service each week, depending on how he needed to see God that week.

"I need to see both sides of God," he explained. "Sometimes he is reflective and serious. Sometimes he is exuberant and exciting."

I hope someday we can offer other music types, perhaps an even more traditional, high-church style, or a country-gospel service, or, in our area, a mariachi style.

Specialization is no small advantage. When we started our 9:45 Sunday morning service, the number of college visitors jumped dramatically. We gained the reputation of conducting "a service for students." Others have told me straight out that if we did not have the contemporary service, they would not attend our church. This variety can reach baby boomers while still ministering to our more traditional members.

On the other hand, if we ran only the contemporary service, I would not have my job. And we wouldn't be touching people needing the more traditional structure.

Diversity adhesive

A church trying this approach will need to deal with at least two issues. First, how do you keep a multicongregation church from becoming fragmented and isolated? Can such diversity be unified?

In a traditional church, one or more "whole-church events" still punctuate the week, whether on Sunday morning, Sunday night, or Wednesday night.

This contributes significantly to the unity of the church.

The multicongregation church has no such luxury. What sociological glue holds the multicongregation church together? Although we're still discovering the various adhesives, a major part of the answer lies in the staff.

A minister of music at a traditional church once told me, "If the staff is divided, the church is divided. It will not be long before the church begins taking up sides. A united staff is the only way to have a united church." If this is true in a traditional church, how much more so in a multicongregation church.

The multicongregation approach has worked well for us because staff members share the same vision for the church and are friends with a high level of trust. We are working on the same objectives and the same agenda. We are each comfortable with our role on the team.

An appreciation of diversity also bonds our church together. All of us do not like the same kind of music, but we
all believe that different styles of music should be provided.
We do not all find it convenient to worship at the same time,
but we all agree that choices should be provided. Our over-
arching philosophy of ministry helps keep us moving as one
body.

Another adhesive is the common identity of being a part of
Calvary Church. Suggest to a Saturday night attender that he
or she is not part of the real Calvary, and they would wrestle
you like a bear. This is true of people in every service. They
all share a common identity of being members in full standing, not second-rate members. There is no pecking order
among the various congregations.

New service launch

The second issue the multicongregation approach constantly raises is when to start a new service. Three factors
enter our thinking.

First, we consider the capacity of our meeting room. We
follow the theory that when a room is 80 percent full, it is
full. Any more people than that will thwart the growth of the
group.

I was serving as greeter one Sunday night when we had an
especially full house. Four college students arrived late. I explained, "There are no more seats, but we'll soon pause in the
service to greet each other. When we do, we'll get some chairs
out of the choir loft and bring them down." They complied,
but I haven't seen them since. Was the seating hassle part of
the reason? I suspect so.

Our auditorium holds about 280. This means that if any
one service averages more than 200 for a month or two, we
know that at our rate of growth (about 15 percent annually)
we will soon hit the 80 percent mark, so we know it's time to
start planning a new service.

Second, we consider the calendar. Because winter is the growing season for most churches, beginning a new service in early fall allows the longest growing season before the slower summer months. On the other hand, Easter can also be a good time because it attracts outsiders. We would never start a service, however, between Easter and Labor Day.

Third, we consider congregational stress. We only start a service when we feel the church is healthy. If we try to introduce such a change during an already volatile time in church life—right after the loss of a staff member or during a controversy concerning a church business decision—people will receive it poorly.

Slow start

We've found we can't just casually announce the beginning of a new service and then do it. Prayer and sensing God's direction is key. But in addition, before starting a new service, we do a number of things to give it a greater chance of success.

Give people plenty of time to think. I read somewhere that people do their best thinking after the meeting is over, usually in the car on the drive home. This was true as we prepared to go multicongregational. We formally voted to start our Saturday night congregation three months before our opening service. We held numerous meetings with committees, deacons, and Sunday school teachers. We let the idea sink in without hectoring for closure. We resisted the sales technique, "You must sign up now." Doing that to people you want to support a new congregation can spell multiple disasters.

The nice thing about the multicongregation approach is that you can take it gradually, a step at a time. We may have thirteen congregations eventually, but at any one time, we present the need for "one more."

We have found the word *experiment* to be very useful. We use it often.

Start one week before you start. When we birth a new service, we hold a dress rehearsal. This is especially true when we want to offer a new format or different type of music. Expectations for the practice service are different if attenders know it is a dress rehearsal, and that gives us elbow room for mistakes.

When we started our 12:15 Sunday service, only twenty people showed up, including the staff and musicians. But that was okay. No one was discouraged because it was "practice." The next week attendance started to climb.

Advertise. We punch a new service with as much advertising as we can afford. Then we double the amount.

We have used both telemarketing and direct mail. Both are successful, but telemarketing takes an enormous amount of work, and in some cases, even though it brings people in, it can also put people off. So we've begun to use direct mail exclusively, especially since it's just as effective with less trouble and fewer negative side effects. Yes, it costs more, but we've found that the money invested in advertising is generally repaid in six months.

We spend about fifteen cents per piece of mail, which includes postage, printing, and processing. Of those who receive the mailing, between half a percent and 3 percent have attended one of our services. In other words, if we send 10,000 pieces of mail, we may see one hundred visitors. They don't all come the same week, of course, and they don't all fill out cards indicating they received our mailing. But if a third eventually join, many end up giving twenty dollars a week, that would mean the advertising pays for itself in about half a year to a year, depending on how quickly people join the church.

We advertise to ensure a critical mass of new people at the new service (consultant Elmer Towns says that you need 125 for critical mass, but I think it also depends on the size of the building). Besides, new people make a new service exciting and provide an extra incentive for our people who attend the new service to invite their unchurched friends.

Move groups by moving leaders. Try as we will to get current attenders individually to change times, most will not. We've discovered two principles: (1) people go in groups, and (2) people follow leaders. Our 8:30 service succeeded because the choir moved to 8:30 en masse. Our Saturday night congregation took hold because many young marrieds and young singles migrated together. (The young marrieds didn't like getting their kids up on Sunday morning; the young singles liked staying out on Saturday night.)

When we started our 9:45 service, we encouraged those in the church college department to attend. To get a viable group started, we also target a handful of key players to join the team. Others will usually follow.

Give people a reason to move. We who preach can overestimate the preacher as the reason people attend any one service. The preacher is critical, but there are at least four other determining factors: the convenience of the time, the musical style, the peer group that attends, and the location.

My secretary, for example, told me she and her husband would attend at 8:30 no matter who preached, who attended, and what the musical style. For them, the key value is the convenience of the time. For others, the key value is their friends. They would attend at any time as long as their group went with them.

Very few people will change times simply out of a sense of duty. They will not inconvenience themselves, leave their friends, or endure a musical style they don't like simply because the church needs it. The new service must benefit them somehow.

Point newcomers to new services. When I call on visitors, I encourage them to attend one of the new, less populated congregations. "Many of our young marrieds attend on Saturday night," I will say. In the newer services, they are more likely to find people who are looking for friends. People in the established services may already have their networks

formed. That's not bad—people need close friends. But it
means that one of the advantages of a new congregation is
that people are still finding their way around, and newcomers
can fit in more naturally.

Share the preaching load. Our seven services occur
within a twenty-six hour span. We've found that it's not realistic to expect anyone to preach more than five times on a
weekend. So we try to share the preaching responsibilities
among the staff.

Still, it can be a problem. I once told our pastor, "Sam,
you're too good. Everyone wants to hear you and only you. If
you were not quite so good, others could preach some, and it
would be fine."

Expect lingering problems. Multicongregations mean
multiple problems, but then so does any path to ministry. For
us, for example, staffing a fully graded Sunday school can be
a hassle. Starting the 8:30 Sunday morning service was a
piece of cake. People could attend the 9:45 Sunday school
immediately afterward. When we started a Saturday night service with a complete children's program, it was a migraine—
not enough teachers or students. To run a fully graded Sunday school we had to increase our teaching staff by a third
overnight.

But I'm convinced that it's easier to start an additional congregation, even with a fully graded Sunday school, than it is
to build a new facility.

Unimpeded freedom

Conducting seven services each weekend is mind-boggling
trouble and work. And it hasn't completely eliminated our
need to expand our facilities.

Still, we're committed to this experiment. We often recall
the words of John R. W. Stott (in *The Spirit, the Church, and
the World*):

Change is painful to all of us, especially when it affects our cherished buildings and customs, and we should not seek change merely for the sake of change. Yet, true Christian radicalism is open to change. It knows that God has bound himself to his church (promising that he will never leave it) and to his Word (promising that it will never pass away).

But God's church means people not buildings, and God's Word means Scripture not tradition. So long as the essentials are preserved, the buildings and the traditions can go if necessary. We must not allow them to imprison the Living God or to impede his mission in the world.

The multicongregation church is working for us. Although it is neither easy nor a cure-all, we believe it is an effective way of doing church.

PART 7

Serve

28

Unlikely Allies

*The local church should look for windows of opportunity to
ally with both government agencies and business to stem
cultural decay.*

—RONALD J. FOWLER

The bar was called the Green Turtle, a sleazy basement li-
quor establishment in a weather-scarred apartment building.
Here, rumor had it, prostitutes picked up clients and then
used the upstairs apartments to ply their trade.

The Green Turtle was on a strip of Arlington Street known
to locals as "Satan's Headquarters." The infamous street was
lined with bars, infesting the community with drugs, alcohol,
prostitution, and gambling.

On Arlington Street was also a church. In the early 1970s, I
had become its new pastor, succeeding a long tenure by my
father. Shortly thereafter, the mayor contacted me, asking if
the church would consider, as part of a minority relocation
program, moving closer to the suburbs. The city would make
the land available to us at a discount and assist us in its
development.

His offer was tempting; a fresh start elsewhere would allow
us to escape the blight of Arlington Street. We declined, however. The area, we believed, needed a Christian witness.

City partners

Several years after refusing the mayor's offer, our church experienced significant growth, requiring us to build. But no vacant lots existed in our seedy pocket of Arlington Street to expand our facilities.

Reflecting on the mayor's prior willingness to assist our church, I called an assistant in the mayor's office who had contacted me several years earlier. The mayor would see me, she told me, and she arranged a fifteen-minute appointment.

When it arrived, I didn't want to waste my fifteen minutes, so I quickly made my point. "We have a need, and you have a need," I began. I relayed our church's history, explaining our need for expansion. And then I told him about his need.

"You have a major section of the city that cannot attract business development because of the crime," I said. "Nor can it attract new housing developments. The property values of the area are plummeting.

"If you would assist us in dealing with the social problems in our church's neighborhood, we would like to make a major investment by expanding our church facilities on Arlington Street. A new facility could raise area property values and increase your tax revenue base."

The mayor slowly straightened in his chair and riveted his gaze on me. He picked up the phone and asked the chief of police and health director to come to his office.

When they arrived, the mayor said, "Reverend Fowler, could you repeat your story to these two men?"

In short, the mayor agreed to link arms with us. As a part of a complex agreement, the city agreed to be more aggressive in cleaning up the crime on Arlington Street. (Their previous crime policy on Arlington Street was containment: They treated its crime with benign neglect as long as it didn't spread.)

They began rigidly enforcing the city's building codes on the local bars, causing most to shut their doors. Then the city beefed up their police patrol, making numerous drug and prostitution busts, eventually closing down the Green Turtle and other businesses that we believed contributed to the area's crime, rooting out Arlington Street's unwanted clientele.

The city also made a proposal to HUD to redevelop our street. Before the city could receive federal funding for Arlington Street's face-lift, officials needed to show investors were interested in the area. They needed our $850,000 expansion investment. For that to happen, however, we needed a place to expand, so the city purchased a block adjacent to our church, declaring eminent domain, and then sold it back to us at a reduced rate.

We finally were able to build.

From that experience I learned that the local church can work together with other institutions for redevelopment. We can look for windows of opportunity to ally with both government agencies and business to stem cultural decay.

Purposed institution

After reflecting on what transpired between Arlington Church of God and the city of Akron, I see at least two reasons why the local church is in a position to aid our nation in its war against crime, the endless cycle of poverty, and the other evils destroying our nation from the inside out.

The church is in the business of changing lives. That's the heart of the gospel. One Sunday each year, our church holds a camp meeting sixty miles from Akron. (We still hold a church service in Akron on that Sunday, though it's usually a bare-bones service for those not able to attend the day at the camp.)

This Sunday was no different. Most of our people had headed out of town for our meeting. I would preach at the early church service in Akron and then make the sixty-mile trek to the camp.

With the choir gone, our minister of music led the remnant

of approximately twenty-five parishioners in a few congregational hymns, and then I got up to preach. After my sermon, a person unfamiliar to me walked up to the pulpit to make a profession of Christian faith.

As we talked, I invited him to come to my office the next week.

"I'll be there, pastor," he replied.

I then drove to our camp meeting. Later that morning, sitting on the platform where I would be speaking, I leaned over to my associate and said, "Guess what? While all the saints were rejoicing here at the camp ground earlier this morning, back in Akron, a man made a decision to follow Christ."

"Great!" replied the associate. "What was his name?"

I told him.

"Pastor," he gasped, "do you know who he is?"

"No."

"That man is rumored to be a drug pusher," he said. "He lives just a few doors down from the church."

Later I learned that this man had stepped outside his door one morning several weeks prior to his conversion, looked up, saw our church steeple, and was moved to get his life squared away with God. He didn't respond immediately, however. A few days later, two of his cronies were found dead, a bullet through each of their heads in an execution-style gangland shooting. He had planned to accompany them that evening, but at the last moment decided against it.

Several weeks later, when he came through our church door, his life began to be transformed. He is now holding a legitimate job, and is growing in his faith, attending our church regularly.

His story illustrates the power of the gospel of Jesus Christ to change lives. His seeing our church steeple and subsequent coming to faith is a testimony to the lasting change only the local church can provide. When it's appropriate, then, maximizing our efforts by linking arms with city hall to bring about that lasting transformation makes good sense.

The church, by working within the system, can help shape the government's attitudes toward needy people. One of my church members went to apply for welfare, and I decided to tag along. I dressed deliberately in my grubbies—worn jeans and T-shirt—to see firsthand what she had to endure. I had been working in my yard earlier in the day.

We drove to the welfare office, waited for our turn, and when my parishioner's number was called, we walked to the window. "What are you here for?" the clerk asked, tersely.

"I want to apply for assistance," my friend Sonya said.

The clerk motioned for us to go to the back of the service area where she would be interviewed. The person who assisted us then started grilling Sonya mercilessly, shoving forms at her with seeming contempt. Even the clerk's tone of voice was negative and disrespectful.

"It's doubtful whether you'll qualify for the next month," the clerk said. "This process may take two or more months."

I bet they don't treat everyone like this, I thought.

Just then one of the department administrators walked by the cubicle where we were seated. I happened to look up.

"Reverend Fowler," this administrator oozed, "what are you doing down here?"

"I was working in my yard today," I replied, "and decided to run a few errands with a friend from my church."

"Do you know who this is?" the administrator said to the clerk. "This is Reverend Fowler who sits on the school board and is pastor of Arlington Church of God."

All of a sudden, we were told that my parishioner's check would be sent immediately. The entire tone of the interview moved 180 degrees.

Their treatment of my parishioner frustrated me. An institution designed to aid my parishioner was dehumanizing her. But that experience also reminded me that we need to work to change both individual lives and governmental structures. My parishioner needed the aid provided by the government. The governmental agency needed renewal too.

Because we serve the same constituency, why not link arms when meeting the physical needs of our shared community?

The church ought to be asking, "Who has the resources to help those needing food, clothing, shelter?" Some desperately needing faith in Christ also need the tools to move toward independence, breaking the cycle of poverty.

Marketplace ministry

After my experience partnering with city hall to build our new facility, opportunities arose for helping various community groups work with the disenfranchised of Akron. When I could, I did this in addition to my parish ministry.

My work with these various agencies took me into the power structures of the city, to people who would not normally enter a local church. It struck me one day that I was more than just the pastor of Arlington Church of God, that I also had a calling to be a priest in the marketplace. Making this a part of my calling has been one of the most satisfying aspects of ministry.

Not long ago, one of the city's business leaders said, "Reverend Fowler, you're the only pastor I know whose congregation is larger outside the church than inside."

Though she's not a member of my church, she still considers me her pastor. Through the years I've ministered to her family, once when one member endured a painful illness. She and her family are faithful to another church; I don't pressure them to attend mine. When I know I'll be speaking at someone's church at a later date, I often say, "I'm going to be preaching at your church, and I'd sure love to see you there. If you have time, let's go out for brunch after the service."

Like salt, the purpose of my ministry is to penetrate the secular areas of my city with the presence of Christ, deliberately carrying Christ's attitudes and concerns to the lonely, desperate men and women who are making monumental decisions affecting the lives of thousands in our community.

I've done that by sitting on the school board and the board of a local bank, and by initiating community projects in tandem with local business and governmental agencies. Through these opportunities, I've made a special point to develop friendships with no strings attached.

The president of a foundation that had given our church a grant for a community project asked me to come to his office to evaluate the success of the project. While we were sitting in his office, the telephone rang. The foundation president swiveled his chair around to the credenza, picking up the phone.

As he talked, with his back turned to me, his voice lowered, and his responses shortened: "Okay." "Yeah." And "All right." He hung up the phone.

When he turned, tears were streaming down his face. I gently said, "Can I pray with you about something?"

"Reverend Fowler," he sobbed, "what do you do when your heart has just been broken? That was my daughter. She's just been served divorce papers. She has two children. We always hoped this would never happen to our family."

We prayed there in his office. Moments such as those come along in marketplace ministry.

Marketplace addiction

Though my congregation has given me permission to minister outside the church walls, I've had to be on my guard. Here is a list of dangers endemic to a priestly ministry in the world of business and government.

An addiction to excitement.   Real growth, more often than not, is painstakingly slow. But in the marketplace, getting things done is the way business is conducted.

That can be intoxicating to pastors who battle to get parishioners to attend a monthly board meeting. There is a subtle pull, when working with outside agencies, powerful business-types, the movers and shakers of the community. We are tempted to lose interest at home, to sabotage our ministry through neglect.

Losing credibility at home.   Pastors who invest an inordinate amount of time away from their churches risk losing the trust of their people.

If our ministry is stumbling, needing more attention than we're willing to give it, our hard-earned credibility will slowly erode. We have no business being elsewhere when things are shaky on the home front.

Politicizing the pulpit.   Just because I sit on a school board doesn't mean I have the right to use Sunday morning to influence my listeners to vote yes on an upcoming mill levy.

I've often felt drawn to pound the pulpit about certain social ills plaguing our city. I've seen firsthand the broken lives and think I know what it will take to turn this evil trend around. But I resist that temptation. My people need to hear God's Word on Sunday morning.

Going in debt.   The first axiom of the marketplace is, "I'll scratch your back if you'll scratch mine."

I've consciously attempted not to play that game. As a priest in the marketplace, I'm carrying the presence of Christ, not networking and schmoozing with the powerful. In addition, I do not want to be indebted to politicians, business leaders, and government officials because these people will come to collect.

When I went to the mayor about redeveloping Arlington Street, I asked him to do it for the good of the community, not because I cared only for my parochial concerns. I never say, "I'll support you if you'll support me."

Losing your vision.   With all the social ills boxing me in, I have to be careful not to become so socially minded that I'm no spiritual good. For me, the hard question is, Am I helping people know God? Am I impacting their core belief system? Am I seeing lives changed?

My highest concern is to prepare people for eternal life. Any allies I make in the business world must not divert my commitment from what is eternal. I must balance my concern for the total person with a passion to see people draw near to God.

Trust payment

Not long ago, I received a call from a leader of a foundation that supports an educational training program for young people in our community. Our church is the headquarters and coordinator for the project.

"Reverend Fowler," he began, "we're at the end of our fiscal year. We're convinced you're serious about helping people. We have $2,500 left to distribute before our cycle ends. We'd rather not put it back in the pot, carrying it over to next year. Do you have any idea what you could do with $2,500?"

I choked back my first reaction to shout, "You bet we do!"

"May I have your fax number?" I said instead. "We do have a program we'd like to launch. I'll send you a proposal this week."

The check arrived three weeks later. His confidence in our ministry has been earned through years of our working with children, the youth, the poor, and single moms.

Many businesspeople view clergy as slick talkers but woefully ignorant of wise business principles. The only way I can link arms with business, government, and community leaders is if they trust me. I've found several factors that build credibility:

Stay put.   Some have told me that one reason they trust me is my long tenure as pastor of Arlington Church of God—twenty-five years.

Administer shared programs well.   The first time I went to see the leader of one of the largest foundations in Akron, I asked him if he would support a program to provide low-income, minority youth with job experience in areas of their vocational interest.

"Reverend Fowler, I want to help you for two reasons," he said. "First, I'm tired of building buildings. Our foundation has been financing hospital and university buildings for years. I want to help people.

"Second, it's hard to give away money intelligently. I must be able to trust those whom I'm financing."

His comment reinforced my obsession to carefully manage other people's money. The leaders of our church work hard to ensure that good bookkeeping practices and management procedures are in place so that funds are appropriately used.

In several instances, our church didn't expend all the financial resources given to us. So we called the foundations, asking if we could hold the funds over for the next year, and they granted us permission. Whatever funds we receive must be used exclusively as budgeted.

It's attention to these details that ensures fiduciary integrity, laying the groundwork for increased responsibility and trust by others.

Continue to identify needs that can realistically be met. The idea for one project hit me while visiting an elderly woman in one of our area's nursing homes. As a professor of English literature at a well-known Ohio college, she had devoted her entire life to young people. She was one of the founders of what is now a national youth convention to inspire young people to faith and to train them for the real world.

The day I visited her, the stench of the nursing home was so foul I could hardly stay the few minutes I did. It struck me that here was this woman, who had no family structure and few resources, stuck in this institution with no hope. She had invested her life in people, and her final days would be spent alone in a rotting institution.

As I left that day, I asked God to provide the means for people such as this woman to live out their days in dignity. Not long afterward, I ran into an old friend at a youth convention.

"What do you have cooking on your burner?" he asked.

"I'd like to develop a home for the elderly around the biblical concept of *koinonia*," I replied. "We would create a family atmosphere where they could live life fully until they die."

This man eventually donated $60,000 to the project. We built a home near Arlington Church of God. Because most of the residents receive only $400 a month in social security, we needed more than what the residents could pay to cover our debt service.

Eventually, several banks and major corporations also contributed financially to the Wilson House, the city sold us the land at a reduced rate to build the house, and our church provided the volunteers and coordination of the project. The Wilson House is now a separate entity from our church, with its own board of directors.

Today there are sixteen residents in the Wilson House. The other day I went to see one of the elderly women in the home. She was sleeping when I arrived.

"Mother," I said, "this is Pastor Fowler. How are you doing?"

"I'd recognize that voice anywhere," she said, turning over. I bent down and kissed her on the forehead. She smiled and said, "Do you know what it's like to be an old lady and receive a kiss?"

I silently praised God for providing the resources to create an environment where old ladies get kissed and can live out their years with joy. It shows what can happen when the church partners with business and government to meet the needs of "the least of these."

29

What It Takes to Stay Downtown

A dying downtown congregation can survive, even thrive, if it is willing to become a true inner-city church.

—Joel Hempel

Trying to function like a suburban congregation in downtown Cincinnati was not working for Prince of Peace Lutheran Church. We realized that unless we became a neighborhood church, the prognosis was certain death. We were attracting few new people. The membership was growing older, and the leadership was getting tired. We might have survived another five years at best.

To survive, we began to realize, we could not be a suburban congregation whose only identity with the inner city was that we happened to meet in a downtown building. Major changes had to be made.

By God's grace, Prince of Peace now is growing slowly into an inner-city church. The principles that guided our change were revealed through the processes of prayer, listening to the neighborhood, and what I call graced luck: accepting the fact that when we stumble onto something that works, it is because God's Spirit guides and nurtures our attempts.

Inclusive transition

The first principle directing our change was inclusiveness. In the inner city, diversity is the norm. We could not stay homogeneous. We knew eventually the white middle class would become in our congregation the minority. Two-parent families would become the exception.

Our transition to inclusiveness mainly just happened as we struggled to discover how best to serve our neighborhood. For example, Prince of Peace, through a staff member, became the representative payee for thirty people who cannot manage their own finances, many of whom are mentally, emotionally, or socially retarded. When these people started making themselves at home in our midst, we could either bar them or accept them. We chose the latter.

Later came the decision to try no longer to remake the inner-city people into traditional, middle-class Lutherans who dressed like us, worshiped like us, and enjoyed our music. Some of our leaders began dressing casually for worship, and we made the service more informal. We sought the advice of neighborhood attenders, and they were bold enough to point out changes that made us more inviting.

During our midweek fellowship, you'll now see people of all races, single-parent families, the mentally ill, low-income and rich folks alike. This weekly supper and worship service mixes the homeless and indigent with those who have solid, middle-class incomes. They wait in the same food line, sit at the same tables, and pray to the same God for his blessing on the meal they all receive free.

Family matters

Similarly, we have come to embrace the idea that we are family. Many people come to the church out of a broken or abusive home environment, so we seek to offer the healthy components of a biological family: support, nurture, education, confrontation, recreation, and freedom to be oneself.

This family atmosphere didn't happen until we in leadership decided to work on the little things: calling people by name when seeing them on the street, greeting people warmly (often with an embrace), giving people opportunities to help with some task or ministry, praising people and expressing appreciation at every occasion, carefully challenging people when they are doing something harmful, being generous with the church resources and personal resources, respecting people's culture and tradition by inviting their input for worship. These and similar expressions of interest let folks know we welcome their presence and value their participation.

We found that, at least initially, new members from our low-income neighborhood likely would bring to our family more needs than resources. For instance, many people wanted to be a part of our family but were not ready to commit themselves to membership. One woman became involved with us when her children enrolled in our nursery school and she began attending the weekly fellowship. When a crisis developed in her family, she sought counseling from our pastoral counseling service. When she needed food, we gave her emergency assistance.

After being a part of the family for years, she eventually decided to receive additional instruction in the Christian faith and become a member. Why? After experiencing the church's commitment to her, she finally was ready to return that commitment and give more of herself to others.

Our worship, where everyone comes together, is the "showing off" place for the cultures and races of our family. The worship committee strives to arrange that, over a month's time, all members of the family can feel at home in worship, singing their kind of songs, seeing their kind of folk in leadership, and participating in a mode of worship that reflects their tradition. Both members and nonmembers, children and adults, read Scripture and lead prayer.

With two white male pastors, it was decided that a black, and ideally female, pianist from the Baptist tradition was needed. We found her, and our worship hasn't been the same since.

As might be expected, we met some initial resistance as we changed from a rather formal and liturgical form of worship to a more open, spontaneous, and inclusive form. When the ideas for a more nontraditional service were first introduced to the congregation, we heard comments such as: "Why do we have to give up being who we are?" and "We need to teach these people how to worship."

This was painful. I thank God that he kept us moving slowly and respectfully, but we also decided not to be overwhelmed by people's natural reluctance and fears. Through our music, the variety of people up front, and the language we use, our worship now demonstrates our openness to different kinds of people.

Justice work

When people discover a church that will help them with physical and financial needs, they tend to be more open about their emotional and spiritual needs. Therefore, a third principle is assistance. We make food, clothing, transportation, and money available to people who need them.

This means we have to raise thousands of dollars every year and give it freely as a symbol of God's grace. A man's father dies in southeastern Kentucky; money is given for his travel expenses. A woman cashed in some food stamps at the beginning of the school year to buy clothing for her children and ran out of food by the middle of the month; food, money, and a referral to another helping agency were given.

Of course we sometimes have to say no when money runs short or wisdom tells us we are being conned. Many times our wisdom fails us, and we're conned anyway. But we'd rather err on the side of generosity.

Our low-income neighbors have been good models, helping us all to risk greater openness ourselves, and in so doing, we have received care, too. At moments when I feel hurt or upset about something, seldom is it long before someone from the community notices and says, "Pastor Joel, you look down." When I acknowledge it, the brief encounter often ends with my receiving an embrace.

Besides providing material assistance, our congregation has also raised a prophetic voice in our community to assist our lower-income neighbors. When a friend of the congregation was facing eviction from her apartment because the landlord wanted to destroy her building to create parking space, we felt compelled to confront the process. Our friend and her neighbors, who had been responsible tenants for years, would have been forced into less-adequate housing. A city ordinance requires a public hearing and city council decision before any structurally sound building can be razed, so various church members spoke out at the council hearing. This time the tenants' rights were respected.

We become involved because we've seen that when people are kicked out of their homes, or treated unjustly in other ways, their self-image is knocked a little lower, confirming their feelings of not being valued. And it is exceedingly difficult for people with low self-image to believe God loves them just as they are.

So at times, members of the congregation and staff have argued concerns before city council. Some have joined task forces and committees. At other times, we have even marched to demonstrate our concern. Though clear victories are seldom won, some headway is made in slowing the forces of injustice. In addition, just standing together for a cause contributes to healthy pride and Christian bonding.

Money appeal

Every inner-city church must learn to beg, borrow, and appeal. After all, personnel are limited. The facilities are in desperate need of repair. Materials and machinery for running programs are not readily available. There is little money, and the new members from the low-income neighborhood need their meager incomes to get by. We entertain no choice but to ask for help.

Our methods are many. We sell crafts. We make requests to be included in the budgets of sister congregations. We stuff contribution envelopes into a quarterly newsletter. We seek sponsors for nursery school children. We stock our thrift shop with clothing retrieved from rummage sale leftovers. Government surplus food is purchased. We recruit groups from other congregations to prepare and serve meals at the Wednesday fellowship. Any grants from foundations and service organizations we can wrangle are gratefully received. Also, the Lutheran Church–Missouri Synod has been approached repeatedly, and it has responded generously.

One anxiety-producing (and faith-stimulating) aspect of inner-city fund-raising for me is my responsibility for finding my own income. It drains the creative energy I would rather invest in people and ministry development. But there just isn't enough money in our church to pay all the staff members. So we raise our own support.

Frankly, I am better at asking for financial assistance for others than for myself. At first, I had to work through feelings. Am I not worthy of a salary? And in asking for money, I was afraid of rejection. With time and practice, though, I developed more self-confidence by necessity.

What remains, however, is the tension of asking for income for myself, knowing the poor are always with us—and in greater need. I'm not foolish; I know my family and I cannot be without an adequate income. Yet my proximity to the vast suffering around me accentuates the disparity. Most helpful has been the assistance that caring people, generally lay professionals and businesspeople, have provided by working to raise support for me.

If it's difficult for an individual to ask for help, it also is for our church. The fact that other churches and businesses sometimes get tired of seeing us with our hand out does not make it any easier. But this is a humbling and necessary aspect of inner-city ministry.

Deck hands

We try to involve everyone in the Prince of Peace family in ministry. This is a challenge, but because the opportunities for ministry are so plentiful, it's necessary.

When people come through our membership instruction classes, we emphasize stewardship of time and energy. We consider involvement in ministry not only a response to ministry needs; it also provides an occasion to give and not just receive. People's self-image builds when their contributions are appreciated.

At the Wednesday fellowship, for example, teams of people prepare and serve meals. Others assist in leading worship. Still others create art pieces to decorate our worship area. Then there are those who volunteer to help in our second-hand store, answer the phone, stuff envelopes, clean the church, or serve as officers and elders.

We are undecided about paying workers to do various jobs. Volunteer work is a way of paying back the church and even strengthens sagging self-image. On the other hand, a few dollars can mean a lot to some of our people. Our informal policy is to pay a small amount—sometimes no more than lunch—for short-term jobs, but keep on a volunteer basis ongoing ministries such as Sunday school and our thrift shop. And we offer our workers major portions of appreciation.

Besides the regular appreciation (which cannot be overdone), the staff officially recognizes workers through an annual Congregation Appreciation Day. Following a special worship service, the staff serves a meal and offers a personal thank you to each member of the congregation. In addition, every fourth Sunday we highlight one of our ministries in our worship service, giving the workers and their ministry deserved recognition.

The majority of our workers and leaders are always women. That's because, in our setting, the preponderance of families are headed by women. This was one more area where we had to wrestle with how to translate our theology and practice into our context. We concluded that for our neighborhood, it is not only pragmatic but pleasing to God for women to serve as officers and in key staff positions.

Fun needs

The longer we minister in the city, the clearer it becomes that if we expect people to participate in worship, meetings, and learning experiences, fun and entertainment must be part of them. The stress and pain in people's lives are lightened with laughter, play, food, and fellowship. And we have found that people from different economic classes and educational backgrounds meet more equally when at play or in less formal settings. Our Saints and Sinners co-rec softball team and our monthly summer picnics are examples of coming together for play. But we try to interject fun into other, typically more serious, church activities.

Awhile back we noticed most of the low-income members were not staying for the voters' meetings on Sundays after church. The church business proved too boring for some. Others felt overwhelmed by financial reports and official proceedings. Still others felt excluded from the decision-making process. So we created an advisory council to supplement the quarterly voters' assemblies, as a way to relax the setting and mood for doing church business. This advisory council is composed of neighborhood representatives, elected officers, and staff. They meet quarterly in a retreat format. We provide supervision of children, a meal, and snacks. Together we worship, carry on light conversation—and conduct a business meeting. The turnout has been excellent. People feel included and able to express themselves more openly. No Robert's Rules dictate the process.

Not that the idea is new. Scripture indicates the early Christian congregations generally mixed business and plea- sure: "Day by day, attending the temple together and breaking bread in their homes, they partook of food with glad and generous hearts, praising God and having favor with all the people" (Acts 2:46-47).

Stage fright

Mixing new people from the neighborhood with our faith- ful stalwarts created a tension: How do we meet everybody's needs? Our people newer to Christianity required more of "the milk of the Word," nurture in their basic Christian faith. We met their needs with most of our resources until we came to the painful awakening that we were not attending to those more mature Christians who needed "the meat of the Word." Our old regulars were starving.

When these folks, our leadership, began showing signs of burnout, we decided experiences and classes were needed to care for them as well.

So we began a "spiritual companioning group" that brought people together for structured spiritual discussion and prayer. In these groups, the ability to be introspective and reflective of life experiences was required. Few low-income members come to these groups. For many, the pressures of survival distract from time for introspection. Perhaps spiritual devel- opment that requires an ability to go on the "inner journey" is a luxury of those who are more privileged.

But we have learned to accept that because people are in different stages of spiritual development, not everyone will be interested in the same learning experience. Likes and needs lead people to exclude themselves from some activities. Being family does not mean we all have to be together all of the time.

Our church, as with all churches seeking to be God's people, is not consistently faithful to these principles. Workers get tired. Promises are broken. Plans falter. Sometimes people are inconsiderate or too critical of the very ones we seek to include, and people get hurt. Still others fail to follow through with commitments. When needed ministries never get off the ground for lack of money and personnel, we sometimes begin to wonder if God is still in charge.

Yet our experience has shown us that a dying downtown congregation can survive, even thrive, if it is willing to become a true inner-city church. The necessary changes, like surgery, take time and cause pain, but on the other side lies a prognosis of many more years of life and vigorous service.

30

Pastor to the Community

I decided that serving the community was one of my core values.

—DAVID GALLOWAY

Strangely, I felt that there was hope for healing the divisions in my city when I saw what didn't happen after Annie Ray Dixon was killed in the summer of 1992.

Mrs. Dixon was an eighty-four-year-old grandmother, a double amputee, and African-American. A botched drug raid went to the wrong house, and a white deputy busted through Annie's bedroom door. Tragically, his gun went off and killed Mrs. Dixon as she lay in bed. The African-American community in Tyler, Texas, was outraged; the incident had the potential of blowing up the city.

I was about two hundred miles away in Houston when Mrs. Dixon was killed. Some fellow members of a citizens' action group, Tyler Together, phoned me and asked if I could intervene and keep the peace.

Our first stop was the sheriff's office; he was considering limiting the investigation to his internal affairs department. But we convinced him that such a limited approach would only increase the outrage and fuel the rumors of cover-up. He wisely decided to forgo an internal investigation and called in federal investigators instead. Adding to the frustration of the black community, though, the deputy was not indicted for misconduct, and he returned to the streets on active duty.

Then the NAACP called for a march and rally in Tyler to dramatize the racial situation there. Responding, the Ku Klux Klan announced a simultaneous counterdemonstration and filed for a parade permit around the courthouse square. Fans of writer John Grisham will see remarkable similarities in *A Time to Kill,* which chronicled a fictitious confrontation between the NAACP and the KKK in a Southern town.

But this wasn't fiction. My fear of racial violence was heightened by the anger I heard as I visited both sides. The national news media descended on Tyler, with satellite trucks ready to broadcast any violence that might ensue. City fathers were up in arms about the image being projected of Tyler, a town known as the "rose capital of the world." That August weekend was so tense it felt as if the city would explode.

Miraculously, the city kept its composure; both demonstrations took place peacefully. Through the whole affair, there was not one incident of violence.

Part of the reason, I believe, was the prayer of committed Christians. Another was the work done before the crisis erupted. Several leaders in the community had worked together to address the racial tension, which allowed a space for negotiation in the squeeze of confrontation.

My role in this crisis comes out of my philosophy of ministry. In the Episcopal tradition, the community is an extension of my parish. It's not enough to have a happy church if it's insulated from the community. Part of my pastoral role, I've determined, is leading our church to serve our community. Helping to heal the surrounding community is what I call "city therapy." It's a challenging vocation but ultimately rewarding. Here are five principles I have learned about making a difference where you live.

Loving the community

The first and most important principle in pastoring your community is to love it. When I came to Tyler in 1990, I wasn't sure I even liked the town. East Texas is the antithesis of everything in my hometown of Atlanta. I grew up in a family with a long history of civil rights involvement in a city where race was constantly on the public agenda. Tyler, by contrast, was virtually in denial about the issue of racism.

A colleague, Ray Bakke, author of *The Urban Christian*, put my call to Tyler in perspective. The most important element in changing a community, he told me, is to love it. I began to pray every morning that God would give me a heart for Tyler. "I don't think you can make me like it," I told God, "but maybe you can help me love it."

In time, God gave me a passionate love for Tyler. That inexplicable love helped me to decide that really serving the community—to help change it, to help heal it—would be one of my high priorities. To put it in terms Stephen Covey used in *Seven Habits of Highly Effective People*, I decided that serving the community was one of my core values.

Understanding the history

The second key to pastoring your community is to understand it. I began thinking of Tyler in the therapeutic terms I had learned in marriage and family therapy. I had studied systems theory (for example, how individuals operate within a family) in graduate school and decided to apply it to the church and city to assist me in diagnosing and treating the problems.

In individual therapy, you compile a history of the factors that formed the person into who he or she is. The same is true with a city. I began to study the history of our community.

In the 1930s, when the rest of the nation was fighting the Great Depression, Tyler was thriving from the east Texas oil boom. There's a monument to that prosperity: a park donated by Sears & Roebuck, given to the city because Tyler was the only place the store chain turned a profit during the Depression.

The townspeople grew accustomed to living well. Most of the townspeople, that is. Like many communities, Tyler exists in two parts. Mostly African-American Baptists live in north Tyler; white, upper-middle-class Protestants live in the south. For most of its history after the Civil War, Tyler lived by an unspoken code: the African-Americans would continue to depend on the whites for their jobs and opportunities, and, in return, keep quiet. It was a modified plantation mentality, but with so much money to go around, everyone benefited to some degree.

My diagnosis grew out of a conviction that every city has its peculiar sin; Tyler's is comfort. The oil bust of the 1980s changed much of that, however. The white community had trouble adjusting to the economic problems, and the African-Americans began to realize that if they were to make any economic and political gains, they would have to change their approach to life in the city.

Refocusing the church

Once you love and understand the community, it's essential to help the church look outward. How can your church open itself to the community?

Our church wasn't known for that. Christ Episcopal Church was a good parish but had a reputation as a country-club church. I joked that worshipers came for spiritual hors d'oeuvres before having lunch at the club.

I decided to find out what Tyler thought of the church. Within a week of moving to Tyler, I went downtown and to the mall, without my clerical collar. I interviewed the first twenty-five people I met in each place. "Tell me what you know about Christ Episcopal Church," I said. Half the people didn't even know there was a Christ Episcopal Church; the other half said it was a church of rich people.

"Would you feel comfortable there?" I asked.

No one said he or she would.

I reported my findings to the vestry [church board]. "How does it make you feel," I asked, "that people either don't know you're here or think you're a bunch of country-club people who are not welcoming?"

Such an image disturbed them, but we were not sure how to transform that perception within the community. "In what ways could we reach out to the community," I asked, "that would reflect who we are as Christ Church?"

We divided the vestry into groups of three to brainstorm for an hour. The first ideas were pretty unimaginative and completely out of character for the church—knocking on doors, for example.

We broke into triads again for another hour.

When we came back together, one of the oldest and least-likely candidates for trying fresh approaches said, "Why don't we reach out to people through television?" The idea was intriguing, but still we faced the tough issue of how.

Two days later I got a phone call from a church member who works for the local NBC affiliate in Tyler.

"We're about to do this thing called 'Discover America,'" she said, "a yearlong promotion tied to the Olympics and the five-hundredth anniversary of Christopher Columbus's voyage to America." The station wanted four blue-chip sponsors. It already had signed Southwestern Bell and McDonald's.

"We have one opening," the member told me. "And I was thinking you might want it."

After talking with the staff and looking at the budget, we decided to be a sponsor. The logos appeared almost every hour for a year—McDonald's, Southwestern Bell, and the Chi-Rho from Christ Episcopal Church. We also began "Episcopal Minutes," thirty-second spots during the ten o'clock news on Sunday and Wednesday nights. I would simply talk to people on the air, introducing them to Christ Church in a nonthreatening way.

"Are you looking for a church," I might say, "where you

don't have to check your mind at the door? At Christ Church
we not only tolerate questions—we enjoy them. Come join us
in your search for your faith."

Our church got more mileage out of that opportunity than
anything else we did. It created openness within the church
to people in the community. The short spots also established
a positive image of the church crucial for us to proceed with
our task of making a difference in the community.

Taking action

Ultimately, it came time to take action, to lead the church
to serve the community in some tangible way. In our situation, that began in the fall of 1991, when I helped launch
Tyler Together, a group of concerned citizens with a common
goal: making Tyler a better place to live. Eventually we concentrated on five issues: health care, regional identity, education, recreation, and—the hottest of the bunch—race.

The issues of race were hot because they hadn't been publicly discussed before. So Tyler Together sponsored a yearlong
series of public forums where Tyler's citizens could talk about
their experiences of discrimination and racism.

A wide variety of people attended the forums. We intentionally held them in various parts of the city—at the predominantly African-American high school on the north side,
at a predominantly white high school in the south. We held a
forum at a large white Baptist church and another at Christ
Church. We also sponsored one forum at Texas College, an
African-American teacher college.

In addition, we worked hard to involve city officials. We
wanted them to listen to the pain of the community, a pain
many denied was present. One city official, in a telling interview with a major newspaper said, "Tyler does not have a
racial problem."

In twelve-step language, many in the city had to stand up
and say, "Hi, I'm Tyler, Texas, and I have a racial problem." As

they say, this is the first step to recovery. The forums, at least the first few, were a hot media item, complete with remote broadcasts from the town meeting sites. The coverage provided a lot of exposure to the racial problems African-Americans felt, resulting in some positive feeling in the black community that access to influence was finally beginning to be opened to them. However, many people in the white community wondered whether Tyler Together was stirring up problems.

Meanwhile, many people in the African-American community were skeptical that anything positive would result. But the value of the forums was proven the next spring, when the Rodney King verdicts came down and Los Angeles erupted. Suddenly, race was the big national issue. We were already doing something about it: Tyler Together had been proactive.

Then Annie Ray Dixon was shot. Her death became the focal point for a lot of the rage seething in the African-American community. But because we had organized those town meetings, we were able to defuse, in a positive way, much of the anger. Later, in fact, a biracial coalition prompted the city's educational board to move to single-member districts that promoted racial representation on the school board.

There was resistance, of course. We were involved in the politics of race, after all. Some resistance came from white families who no longer held as much economic or political clout and who feared a loss of control. But the big surprise to me was the reaction that came from some people in the African-American community, who could not see that each sector of the community would need to be responsible for its future.

Developing leaders

Whatever action you take to pastor your community must include developing strong, capable leaders.

About two years ago I started Leadership Foundation to train minorities in leadership skills; financing came from an agency called the Communities Foundation of Texas. The classes meet at the Christ Church building, with about thirty people in each yearlong program. I lead some of the training, but my main job is to interest other people in committing themselves to one Saturday per month for a year. We bring in top trainers from around the country, people who consult for IBM, Texas Instruments, and other companies.

We start by describing the personality of a community leader. We also run the Myers-Briggs type indicator, to show trainees what they bring to the task of leadership. We teach communication skills. Then we move to a practical session, "Running an Effective Meeting." Many people come with passion about community issues but don't possess the skills to run a meeting. We also help people with conflict resolution, change management, and organizational skills. However, the greatest value of the training is that we awaken people to their power to influence their community.

Waking up

It's easy for us in pastoral leadership to limit our focus to the pressing problems inside our parish. But our communities need us, and we can make a difference in them.

When the NAACP scheduled its rally after Annie Ray Dixon's death, I was the only white person asked to speak. While I knew that my speaking would anger some in the city, even my parishioners, I knew that it was an opportunity for a prophetic word to our community to imagine a city respectful of all of God's children.

In crafting my words, I felt prompted to borrow a metaphor from the last sermon Martin Luther King, Jr., preached—at the National Cathedral in Washington, D.C. Dr. King used the image of ringing alarm clocks to talk about the nation's need to wake up. In my speech, I talked about alarm clocks, too, and added something new: snooze alarms.

"You set the clock," I said, "and the clock tells you when to get up. But when the alarm goes off, it's cold, and you don't want to get up. You want to slap that alarm and shut it off. Tyler has been doing that in various ways throughout its history. The alarm clock's going off, saying, 'Wake up, Tyler.' And we've slapped it and said, 'Just a few more decades.'

"But now the time has come for Tyler to wake up. The alarm has sounded, and it is time for us to get up, to take action, to enter a new day together."

That rally was a tense reminder of how much reconciliation remains to be accomplished in Tyler. But the black and white community joining for the common good in Tyler Together served as a sign that healing had begun.